BACHARACH

MAESTRO! THE LIFE OF A POP GENIUS

MICHAEL BROCKEN

BACHARACH
Maestro: The Life Of A Pop Genius
by Michael Brocken

A CHROME DREAMS PUBLICATION

FIRST EDITION 2003

Published by

CHROME DREAMS
PO BOX 230
NEW MALDEN
SURREY
KT3 6YY
UK

WWW.CHROMEDREAMS.CO.UK

ISBN 1 84240 219 6

COPYRIGHT © 2003 Michael Brocken

EDITOR   Rob Johnstone
DESIGN   Sylvia Grzeszczuk

Printed and binded by
Toruńskie Zakłady Graficzne „Zapolex" Sp. z o.o.
ul. Gen. Sowińskiego 2/4, 87-100 Toruń
POLAND
www.zapolex.pl

BACHARACH

MAESTRO! THE LIFE OF A POP GENIUS

"I cannot understand the description of Burt Bacharach's music being 'easy listening' ....It is very dramatic and has such strength."   *- Elvis Costello*

Chapters

Chapter 1

What's It All About? – An Introduction

They sweep around Las Vegas as if on some kind of monorail. Mike Myers – or 'Austin Powers' as he is named in this particular farce – drools and dribbles over his quarry and pops the champagne cork. He's the icon of an era: a man of mystery with taste and an ear for a melody as well as an eye for the girl. His eyes light up in anticipation of the perfect shagadelic soundtrack. In a classic example of postmodern irony Myers/Powers turns directly to the camera and announces 'Ladies and Gentlemen, Mr Burt Bacharach'. Burt is seated at the Steinway at the rear of Powers' transport for the evening: an open-topped London Bus (of course). The captivating, lilting opening bars of 'What the World Needs Now' begin to drift over the scene. All is well with the world.

As I write, Burt Bacharach remains popular and influential with listeners and musicians alike, but this is not the chronicle of a typical popular music songwriter! He is as magical a legend as is Shangri-La, that *Lost Horizon* he set to music with lyricist Hal David. Brian Wilson cites Burt as his favourite songwriter. Frank Zappa praised him for his compositional sophistication. NRBQ's Tom Ardolino worships him, as do Donald Fagen and Walter Becker of Steely Dan fame. Tributes from perhaps unexpected areas have also been paid to Bacharach. Jazz great McCoy Tyner recently recorded an album of Bacharach compositions entitled *What The World Needs Now* with a trio and symphony orchestra.

From even further afield avant-garde musician John Zorn released an appreciation of Bacharach in his *Great Jewish Music* series. This probably revealed more about Zorn's religious essentialism than Bacharach's faith – Burt has never flaunted his Jewish background (see on). But Zorn's zeal is not restricted to ethnic elitism. He actually went as far as insulting a prominent jazz critic who took umbrage at his performing a Bacharach song!

Furthermore, younger musicians such as Oasis' Noel Gallagher – who, at least in word if not musical deed, repudiates the burden of 'rock-ism' that has for so long wreaked havoc on his rock predecessors - frequently cites

Bacharach as a major influence ("if I could write a song half as good as 'This Guy's In Love With You' or 'Anyone Who Had A Heart', I'd die a happy man"). For an appearance at London's Festival Hall in June 1996, Gallagher actually joined (it must be said) a somewhat baffled Burt on stage to sing 'This Guy's In Love With You'!

Other contemporary artistes such as Sheryl Crow, Luther Vandross, Diana Krall, Dr. Dre, Stereolab, Japanese artistes Shonen Knife and Pizzicato Five, Eric Matthews, Elvis Costello, REM, Grenadine, Combustible Edison, and Will Young (the list is almost unending) have all paid homage in interviews or through recordings and live appearances (Young, for example, as a last-minute addition to Burt's Liverpool's Albert Dock gig during the summer of 2001).

Burt's output actually rivals that of Mozart in quantity at least. He has had more than 500 compositions published; been recorded by almost 1200 artists, enjoyed 66 US top 40 hits, won five Grammys and three Oscars – not bad for someone who only began playing piano to keep his mum happy. Tony Parsons (1995) suggests that within the industry, estimates of Burt's combined royalties from all sources, including the supermarkets and elevators of the world (!), could amount to as much as $40 million.

Few composers are able to stand up to such varied praise and interpretations, and this appears to be part of what has always separated Burt Bacharach from the rest of the songwriting horde (and consequently, attracted performers of all genres to his songs). The material remains undeniably difficult to perform yet myriad artists engage in his compositions as a kind of rite of passage through which they attempt to express themselves, validate their own existence, and also massage their inflated egos! Burt Bacharach's music, then, is regarded as a popular music performance high watermark, provided the respective vocalist can overcome (or not, as the case may be) its complications.

Yet, almost correspondingly for others, Bacharach's name has become synonymous with terms such as 'elevator music', 'muzak' and 'easy listening'. Rock fundamentalist Nik Cohn typified this mind-set thus:

> [Bacharach's] stuff didn't vary much. Always it was tasteful, attractive, a bit gutless. Seemingly he could turn out hit songs

almost at will, complex melody lines and cute backings, full of cellos and French horns and so forth and, taken one at a time, they were very pretty music but, when you heard them at length, they sounded limp [...] Between them, [Dionne Warwick] and Bacharach brought muzak to its highest point ever. (Cohn, 1970: 196-197)

Readings such as this rather po-faced early 'rock-ist' text are delivered from a reception, rather than a performance, point of view. Cohn's text captures the essence of the 1970s R&B vinyl junkie scratching his balls in the second-hand record shop. Since the early 1990s, however, such evaluations have varied, becoming signs not only of criticism, but also postmodern commendation. As those Count Five albums became practically impossible to find, and the car boot sales continued to throw up mint copies of *Reach Out* a generation of record collectors came out of the musical closet and owned-up to loving 'The Look Of Love'.

Therefore, while the music of Burt Bacharach was regarded by some as representing a kind of 'bland' invasion of private space ('man') via the background music of the supermarket or hotel elevator; by the mid-1990s both he and his music were also ironized so that one could 'like' Burt's music in a similar way to 'liking' (say) 'Singalong Sound Of Music'. These negative and ironic interpretations are due to a number of significant reasons: all actually dissociated from the man and his music.

For instance, to some over the past forty years or so Burt's music has been directly associated with the apparent featureless superficiality of the post-WWII American bourgeoisie and their obsession with products of leisure, opulence and exotica. Certainly, such artists as Burt Bacharach - who graced his 1960s and 1970s album sleeves sporting 'casual wear' and/or a deep tan - seldom ever received anything other than a caning from the 'alternative' *Rolling Stone* 'school' of rock journalism at the time (when he was actually reviewed at all, which wasn't often: try obtaining information about Bacharach from the *Rolling Stone* website!).

Also, while the sometimes rather silly but ever-fascinating postmodern loungecore scene of the mid-1990s succeeded in removing the shackles of the above-mentioned rock discourse, it did so by ironization. Loungecore celebrated the previously 'unmentionable' in music - from anonymous cover versions to exotica - and as a consequence set free a number of hidden histories in popular music (for which we must be truly grateful). This fad, however, also stereotyped Burt Bacharach as some kind of "Lounge Wizard" (*NME*, 1996), "A Gentleman [who] Prefers Diminished Sevenths" (*Mojo*, 1998) who was "imprisoned in music's metaphorical lift for years" (*Q*, 1996).

Moreover, the reputation garnered by Bacharach in the first instance was at least in part structured at the Brill Building - that site of constant struggle between artefact, artifice and art with which many popular music writers are seldom ever able to feel completely at ease. Issues of inauthenticity, non-organic methods, the music industry as a malevolent spectre, publishing as a quasi-criminal activity, are pitched unfavourably against all of the usual underground paradigms (of whatever era) and cited as invalid. These topics all have to be taken into account when considering why there has never been (up until now, that is) a serious study on Burt Bacharach.

Reconstruction/authentication

Burt has actually witnessed his music being (in turn and simultaneously!) fashionable and then unfashionable; cool then uncool and then cool again; not worthy of study and worthy of study; trendy then 'cheesy' and now more or less both. All of these inversions have taken place not simply as an upshot of the varying status of the music **as** music (which also obviously occurs through time), but also as a consequence of its [non] relationship with the rock 'canon'. Rock discourse, together with the [un] fashionablity of the 1960s, and its recontextualisation via mid-'90s postmodern irony (*a la* Mike Myers) has condemned Bacharach and his music to a profile way beyond his control.

So, the idea that any music can directly express some kind of fixed identity remains specious. Like all great music, perhaps, Burt's music has faced considerable social reconstruction and yet it also remains 'the same'! As any closer examination reveals, his meticulously crafted and technically brilliant compositions are anything but 'easy listening', polo neck pullover-attired cheese or examples of Brill Building standardisation.

The great British singer-songwriter Elvis Costello, once described by a UK popular music journalist as 'Dionne Warwick with fangs', collaborated with Burt Bacharach on 'God Give Me Strength' from the *Grace Of My Heart* soundtrack and then the highly rated *Painted From Memory* album. He informed popular music writer and broadcaster Spencer Leigh that he "cannot understand the description of Burt Bacharach's music as 'easy listening'". He went on: "it may be rhythmically gentle in its expression but it is very dramatic and has such strength". (Costello to Leigh, 2000: 213)

Costello makes a valid point. All music is notoriously difficult to categorise and loaded descriptive language such as 'sophistication', 'easy listening' 'mainstream' and 'middle-of-the-road' are misleading (to say the least). They are in fact pejorative expressions that inform us as much about those uttering the jargon as the music being depicted. They are also frequently diametrically associated with 'uncommercial' and 'hip' genres perceived uncorrupted by commerce and the mass media such as folk, rock, blues and dance. These dichotomies are obviously false but the mythologies prevail.

As we shall come to discover, African American rhythm and blues – that paradigm of authenticity so valuable to the host of popular music 'wiggas' of the past forty years (i.e. those white middle-class music lovers who inflict 'Blackness' upon African Americans: Calcutt, 1998:190-206) - was never far away from the early 1960s Bacharach recipe, despite those confusing categories. Indeed, Spencer Leigh further stated to Elvis Costello in the above interview that "the [R&B-influenced Merseybeat] groups did quite a few Burt Bacharach and Hal David songs like the Merseybeats with 'It's Love That Really Counts'". Costello concurred:

> Yes, and people living in England have an advantage over other countries in that some of those [Bacharach and David] songs were hits twice. They were hits for the local artists [...] and then you would hear the originals by Dionne Warwick or Jackie DeShannon, and some of those would be hits as well. We had the benefit of getting steeped in those songs. That's why I thought it was extraordinary that people were surprised that I should like Burt Bacharach. That must be in the minds of people who only know his music from the Carpenters. In the '60s his music was very intertwined with beat music and a lot of beat groups played his songs even though they struggled to play them correctly because they didn't have the same orchestration. (Costello to Leigh, 2000:213)

10

But we must be careful not to authenticate Burt's music via that pathway of 'righteous' rhythm & blues that has so beset popular music essentialism of the past 40 years or so. African American music is cited as a kind of spontaneous, organic root that provides the 'yellow brick road' to authenticity (Gregory, 1998). It seems that the Blacker one is, the bluesier one can be. This, of course is fundamentalist dogma (indeed inverted-racism) of the worst kind: something that has afflicted much popular music writing on both sides of the Atlantic for some considerable time.

'Easy' - or difficult?

In fact, we also need to be aware that the claim for a kind of 'sophistication' in Burt's music could also be harmful. Look at the facts: we can detect from the Costello interviews quoted above that an inference lurks behind ideas about such sophistication. The language surrounding this word ('orchestration', 'structural', 'difficult', 'disciplined') is alone sufficient to close down further debate for many popular music writers and scholars, for it prevents interrogation of a topic that would inevitably have to move into the area of crotchets and quavers – horror of horrors! Popular music discursive practices are not, on the whole, comfortable with such formal areas of musical rituals.

Perhaps some of the comments (unsympathetic or otherwise) that for at least twenty years metaphorically and actually condemned Bacharach's music to 'beautiful' radio have to do with the tension alluded to by Elvis Costello (i.e. "struggled to play them correctly"): between a product being hypothetically easy to sing or play – coming as it did from that apparent source of musical standardisation, the Brill Building – and the paradoxical evidence that confronts us the moment the karaoke microphone is switched on. It has always been a considerable challenge to learn, cover and/or rearticulate a Bacharach composition – indeed, rather too difficult for some. To paraphrase diva Dionne Warwick, one practically needs a music degree to articulate this stuff! In addition to discussing the limitations of the 1960s Merseybeat groups, Elvis Costello also vouched for the structural impenetrability of Bacharach's music:

> […] there would always be a crucial structural change made by one examining the other's composition. Sometimes we would write bar by bar and note by note, sitting at a piano together. That

was very difficult, but we managed it. (Costello to Leigh, 2000: 213)

Burt's musical complexities are difficult to map out and re-arrange and his chord structures and time signatures can appear incredibly complex to a generation of musicians who have grown up with little or no formal musical training. Costello discussed this further in an interview with *Mojo*:

> It was an amazing disciplining experience to write in response [to Bacharach]. Sometimes the character of the music would immediately imply a story or some sort of notion. And then I would take back a rough sketch and sometimes Burt would say 'well, you've misread this'. I do pick things up aurally faster than [written notation]. Sometimes I would write a word that fit my conception of the phrase, and Burt would point out that it actually added a note. Or that there was a pick-up note where there shouldn't be, or some little detail like that, which would require me to find different words to say […] but that wasn't a bad thing, because overall I got more disciplined. (Costello to DiMartino, *Mojo*, 1998)

In the same interview Costello also described dealing with Bacharach's music as "nerve-wracking"! (ibid)

It is certainly an education for a rock artist (in fact a guitarist such as myself!) to attempt to work with such stylistic complexities. Despite Bacharach's great successes in the US and UK Pop charts, he still finds rock music (as he sees it) a struggle, affirming: "I wouldn't know how to function in that language" (ibid). This is an interesting confession and via an analysis of historical context and motivations for Burt's popular music incursions of the mid-1950s, something that this work intends to further illustrate. There is indeed a musical-cum-social gap between the man and his many admirers from the rock field. This is undoubtedly based upon, among other things, (a lack of) formal musical training (and, importantly, can also account for Bacharach being defined by his detractors as 'cheesy').

One example illustrates this well. It has been said by Noel Gallagher (BBC TV documentary 'Burt Bacharach', 1996) that he was so delighted to have physically worked-out the chord progression to one Bacharach composition on his guitar ('This Guy's In Love With You') that he reversed it, moved it up two keys and turned it into a song of his own ('Half The World Away'). It took Gallagher two years to (somewhat bravely) learn by rote the works of a man who probably doesn't even consider the word 'extempore' to exist as a musical expression. Very flattering, to be sure, but one can only wonder about Burt's bewilderment at such 'off the cuff' behaviour!

Composition

> It's a question of what you hear. What's going to fit, in the rhythm section, on the second and fourth beat [...] not how can you show everybody what great orchestrations you can write. It's a goddam crossword puzzle and what I keep is what I think will help the song and free the singer [...] if the song isn't there, you're not going to disguise it with beautiful strings. (Bacharach to Saal, *Newsweek,* 1970)

Burt Bacharach, in tandem with principal lyricist Hal David, not only played a major role in the mainstream pop music of the 1960s, but he (practically single-handedly) revolutionised popular music composition. Historically, the conventions considered to be intrinsic to popular music composition include AABA and verse-chorus-verse patterns, middle eight structures, major chord descending bass lines, etc., all linked to (usually) 4/4 time signatures.

Bacharach utilised all of these devices (and more) but by the mid-1960s he began to draw our collective attention away from the standard patterns that effectively 'enclosed' his music, moving towards counterbalanced musical units for mood design and enhancement. Tonality and rhythm were both of seminal importance to Burt, as too, was atmosphere – his approach was almost mathematical: like a musical version of engineering. Bacharach was constructing a musical reality from assimilated textures and genres.

This should not come as a surprise, for few (if any) compositions emerge from a kind of musical bell jar. Those of Bacharach's were highly contextual and belonged to an age when mood was everything. As we shall see, the easy listening landscapes of American supermarkets and department stores built in the 1950s called for arrangements with recurring patterns and ghost tunes. He incorporated these devices into his songs (taking note of jingles and adverts along the way). His music was 'knowing' and these units of mood counterbalance were used to expand the possibilities of the standard conventions of the popular song.

 For example, Bacharach's juxtaposition of minor 7ths with major 7ths on many of his best compositions creates a deliberate mood of indistinctness and disclosure. In practical terms, this combination is a reasonably simple three-fingered exercise on the piano, and (whether we play or not) most of us are so practiced in listening to popular music of all kinds that we now regard the familiarity of these progressions as almost 'natural'. But although Burt beguiles us with such 'naturalised' extended major/minor repetitive expressive units these approaches were not replicated by his Brill Building contemporaries – they were part of his unique approach to popular music songwriting. Such a simple musical device, then, is not really 'sophisticated' at all. But it **is** clever for over time it has become a natural resource in our everyday listening practices.

 Bacharach is very much a 'chord' man. He extends each chord as far as is emotionally possible without resorting to cliché, creating on the one hand fine, melodic commercial popular music and on the other a complex melange of mood. Sheer joy is followed by deep sorrow (take a listen to the inquiring tone colours of 'Alfie', for example, or those in 'The Last One To Be Loved'). Burt is also able to take (usually Hal David's amazing) lyrics and place them together with a melody line that works note-for-word over these units of changing mood and dominant melody. This means that most of his melodies (especially those post-'61) were very complex and difficult to sing. They required precise arrangements for them to work – something at which Burt Bacharach was also highly skilled.

 As a case in point, if we consider (say) the arrangement of Jerry Butler's reading of 'Make It Easy On Yourself' we are given two different points of identification – the ultimate counterpoint, if you will. The song begins with the chorus as a minor key pronouncement – very moody and sombre. An almost spoken narrative then follows, where every syllable has a note attached ('[…] If you really love him […]'). Behind this we are invited to involve ourselves with the scored arrangement and another pattern, that of tempo, which gives the song a pulse and makes it almost (but not quite) 'danceable'. In this one song, Bacharach gives us different sets of musical proposals to consider.

While an industrial site of popular music composition was indeed a starting point for him, it was not by any means a kind of totality (unlike, say, [with respect] the music of Neil Sedaka or Paul Evans). In Burt's songs every particular formation has its own lyrical and extra-lyrical meaning. Even over the course of a song that might only last between 2-3 minutes, he has the listener subconsciously considering each unit in both general and specific terms. Fittingly, Bacharach has often described these songs in interviews as "three-and-a-half-minute movies" or "mini-movies":

> [...] I've tried to make these mini-movies [...] they have some big moments, they have some quiet moments. That's built into the song. If it's not, you're not going to do it, orchestrally. Very often when I'm writing I'm hearing when things all come in and go out. They kind of go hand-in-hand. It's the advantage of being able to orchestrate as a composer, see. (Bacharach to Rowland, *Musician*, 1996)

In music such as this, the reception of these elements becomes significant. The songs develop, in their response, profundity after every additional hearing and, in doing so achieve both cult and archetypal appeal. For example songs such as 'Odds and Ends', 'Here I Am', and the latter-day 'God Give Me Strength' have enormous appeal based on both the melody and the gravitas of performance. These are songs that people can hum, fall in love to, but also admire for their craft and depth of feeling; songs like this are few and far between. Hence it is little wonder that covers of Bacharach's material continue to proliferate as each new generation of musicians (having first been liberated from the apartheid of the counter culture!) discover the beauty of his methods and approaches. As I write (2003) the neo-garage White Stripes have covered 'Always Something There To Remind Me' on their lo-fi masterpiece *Elephant*.

Appealing – to whom?

There is now both a cult and mainstream interest in the music of Burt Bacharach; his work is truly loved for a variety of complex reasons. Famed Beatles and Byrds publicist Derek Taylor's superb liner notes to perhaps Burt's most successful album, sales-wise, *Reach Out* (A&M, 1967) suggested that Bacharach's artistry lay in bestriding both musical fundamentalism and fame:

Put down by no one, whether peers or followers, put on by nothing, whether fame or wealth; put off by neither pressure nor competitor, Bacharach is a very special man. He bestrides like Gulliver, the warring worlds of the Establishments' Academy Award system – from whom he has wrought two Oscar nominations for 'Alfie' & 'What's New, Pussycat' – and the contemporary Top Forty scene where the buying power lies in the hands of the very young. It is effortless to praise him because he has done so much, so widely and so well. (Taylor, 1967)

Wonderful words from disaffected Scouser Derek Taylor, who understood popular music with a meticulous constancy. But, on its own, this broad appeal conferred upon Bacharach's music by the erudite Taylor is still not quite enough. Bacharach and David have supplied a world where receivers can quote lyrics, musical phrases, concerts, episodes in the two mens' lives as if they were part of the private world of the fan – along with, of course, all of the organic failures and imperfections. This appreciation runs greater than merely love of the music. It reflects relevance, what this writer would describe as achieving the 'historical'.

Therefore, instead of popular music appearing to confine itself to the immediate present as a kind of refuge or prison, it offers us, via Bacharach's melodies, a sense of ourselves as active agents in its reception. This response is then also a creation – we create Bacharach's music just as much as the man himself – it is ours. This music requires neither a permanent passive adolescence, nor a pervasive sense of defeat. It is positive, uplifting and never tries to run from the world. Certainly not 'trendy' *a la* Coldplay or Radiohead, but very, **very** 'historical'!

Some might suggest there is also a spiritual dimension to his work. Few would consider works such as 'Reach Out For Me', 'The Look of Love', 'A House is Not a Home' as spiritual, as such; the idea that such music can change the physical space of a concert hall or living room simply by its presence is no longer popular. This is a pity, for the counterculture radicalism of the 1960s and 1970s (which, in a way, led to popular music being taken more seriously) made room for a consideration of the spiritual in certain kinds of music.

But more often than not this private hippie world tended to scoff at the kind of adult positivity one finds in a Bacharach and David composition and, instead, champion a kind of reverse-egomania, a childishness (even today's undergraduates still flock to the 'ego-freeing' sufferings of Nick Drake and/or the new-age depression of Tim and/or Jeff Buckley) - an erosion of adulthood. Former rock musician Andrew Calcutt comments on this vacant spirituality:

> In their eagerness to free the ego from the constraints of rationality and history, the counter culturalists [...] wanted to dispense with purposive behaviour also. For them 'enlightenment' was the suspension of instrumentality and rational calculation [...] the sort of thing which one might expect to see in a flashback sequence in the television comedy series *Absolutely Fabulous*. (Calcutt, 1998:70)

One feels that few of those in search of this kind of self-indulgent spirituality found it in the upbeat affirmity inherent in a Bacharach song! Perhaps it is hardly surprising that Burt's muse left him in the mid-1970s. By this time an audience of pretentious progressive rockers and maudlin folkie self-indulgencies had surrounded him like Comanche around a wagon train.

I shall not dwell on this aspect of Bacharach's appeal. Safe to say, however, that in this writer's opinion, a composer or singer/songwriter dependent upon subjective factors has to face the possibility that musical utterances reduced to subjectivity usually end-up employing a tonal vocabulary that few understand (or care to understand). They are closed to rearticulation. Unlike that of Burt Bacharach, their music becomes, on the whole, unimportant and (eventually) 'unpopular'. Bacharach's compositions, on the other hand, are open-ended and thus enduring. They are hidebound neither by disappearance nor self-indulgence. We are allowed to interpret his songs via a wide variety of different pathways without ever reducing ourselves to the surrender of the individual inherent in the music of the singer/songwriter.

Determinacy

Popular music writer and academic Keith Negus submits that in order to understand in what condition popular music exists "The issue of determination – the way that 'external' forces shape human behaviour [...] (that production determines consumption) [...] (Negus, 1996:53) is highly significant. But we must not get carried away with this rather redundant neo-Marxist concept of production constantly determining consumption. The processes through which Bacharach's most successful works passed were more akin to collaboration than outright 'production', and were based upon judgemental values rather than 'racing certainties'.

Working at the Brill Building, Bacharach certainly experienced the reality of determinacy, admittedly often the context (but not necessarily the defining criterion) for much popular music activity. However, equally, Bacharach's best works have a high degree of scope that strikingly differentiates his work from other popular songs that can be somewhat determinate in comparison.

Perhaps it is within this contradictory environment of constraint versus creativity that we can find more clues to Burt's great skills. Burt Bacharach was working in the US popular music industry at a crucial synchronic moment in entertainment history – the post WWII era that determined and codified so many sounds via corporate control. Burt was forced to improvise, making creative **and** industrial use of his formal musical skills. This late '50s, early '60s era epitomized the classic environment for the music industry to appear as villain:

> A ruthless corporate 'machine' that continually attempts to control creativity, compromise aesthetic practices and offers audiences little real choice. (ibid: 36)

As we shall discover, Bacharach, too, repudiated this system. Yet he also paradoxically blossomed in this industrial environment; he honed his skills as a composer within the deterministic Tin Pan Alley system.

Perhaps not unlike Paul McCartney writing (say) 'I Saw Her Standing There' in between gigs in the back of an old van, Bacharach comprehended the realities of popular music pressure in the working environment of New

York's Tin Pan Alley publishing houses. Pressure can actually be viewed historically as an apposite force for Burt Bacharach.

So, although we shall come to see that Burt Bacharach worked within a popular music business system (e.g. Famous-Paramount Music, Atlantic and Scepter Records, the Brill Building *et al*) that, as Bernard Gendron states, rationalized music "to maximize the power of management" (Gendron, 1986:28), I would suggest that one cannot look to the techniques of mass production or the economics of market concentration **alone** for anything like a full explanation of the Bacharach songs that radiated from the Brill Building.

These standardisation procedures certainly expressed a rigidity that frustrated the hell out of Burt, but they also issued forth great creativity from this man. The composer, under these pressures, might experiment without making that experimentation too damn obvious. By mixing a little of everything with the knowledge that everything chosen has come from a repertoire that has stood the test of time, one can please the men in suits and oneself. When only a few of these formulae are used, the results can be disappointing – 'cheesy', in fact. But when the repertoire of formulae is used wholesale, with creative invention and abandon, then the result is musical architecture like nothing before.

By succeeding in rising above the system, Bacharach also answered one of the great questions in music i.e. whether this place that we inhabit is one of pleasure where people entertain one another in an enjoyable manner – with music as our example - or whether it is actually some kind of a school where only 'good' music can be 'serious'. Bacharach shows us it is both. If we can indeed learn from one another then we can also entertain while educating. His way of adapting melody to speech – the ordinary non-elevated language of Hal David – not only develops new possibilities musically (e.g. for pitch and dynamics) but also allows us to escape the incarceration of self-limitation. As Bacharach archivist Robin Platts suggests:

> [...] those simple emotions were conveyed in music and lyrics
> that were very artfully constructed – songs that were actually
> much more complex than they sounded. Bacharach and David
> made it sound easy, but it wasn't. They took the American song

19

writing tradition to an exciting new place, with groundbreaking words, rhythms and melodies. (Platts, 2003:6)

Music such as that of Bacharach is, therefore, the locus of all combined values – it is commercial, melodic, entertaining sound existing in a much higher state than popular music is usually expected to exist. That is why I describe Burt's appeal as 'historical'- his place in history is assured.

Rock-ism

If this introduction might have sounded more than a little anti-rock journalism, then congratulations, dear reader, you are quite correct - it **is**. Allow me to explain.

It is quite clear via the remarks of Elvis Costello and the work of writers such as the above-quoted Robin Platts that differing perspectives have now outgrown many of rock's theories about musical authenticity. Joseph Lanza (1995) even suggests that the mavericks and heretics of the past fifty years or so have not actually been immersed in the rock canon much – if at all. Lanza cites such musical genres as bossa nova, exotica and Muzak as places of tension, struggle and influence on a par with any apparently progressive 'noodlings' of the likes of Pink Floyd and Genesis.

Both Lanza (1995) and David Toop (1996) go on to suggest that it is composers of a kind of ambient narrative of the 20th century that have challenged 'ideal' or 'high art' culture as expressed through music. They have exposed the paradox between what people should do according to certain norms and values and what people actually do in every day interaction. It is this collection of musicians (rather than the more trendy rock performers of the same era) that has actually discovered a meaningful modern equivalent for old musical currencies. One might even suggest that rock-orientation has merely superimposed its own canons over those of the classical.

Certainly, rock value judgements between the authentic and inauthentic have created a measure of unreality in a great deal of popular music writing over the past thirty years or so. The study of rock music and its associated subcultures was very significant, but the primacy of this kind of analysis (e.g. that of Hall, Hebdige, Willis, etc) is now questionable and its discourses are long outmoded.

My own experiences at the Institute of Popular Music, University of Liverpool, between 1992 and 2001 bear testimony to this replication of outmoded thought. Many postgraduate students merely duplicated and mythologized this strain of thought via their own subcultural studies. Thus their evaluations were exclusive rather than inclusive and, as a consequence, the works of the likes of Burt Bacharach, Percy Faith, Ray Conniff, Francis Lai and Annunzio Paolo Mantovani remained systematically ignored because these artists did not fit the students' own rock mythologies. We have surely gone beyond such limited discourse. Genre analysis, alone, is far too complex for petitions to such homespun authenticities.

Moreover, those who continue to play a key role in generic definitions - including a host of pop and rock gatekeepers such as critics, reviewers, taste and opinion makers – persist in having their ideas disseminated throughout the rock press and have come to be more widely experienced than the music to which they apparently cling. The egomania of a great deal of the rock press knows few boundaries: they expect people to like what they like, to denounce what they denounce, and to live a lifestyle commensurate with their own. We really ought to lay to rest the misguided perception that rock music journalism is all encompassing – it is, in fact, anything but.

So, in the opinion of this writer, both the rock-based academia and the rock press have by and large not served popular culture well. They have borrowed both the rhetoric and the concerns about excellence from 'high' culture and have systematically debarred as much as they have apparently integrated. The rock press, in particular, have removed the individual from interpretive strategies and in doing so have prevented any possibility for direct analysis of a performer or composer. Indeed the very word 'classic' exemplifies this process: we have concrete totalities ruled by generic associations. These are attractive because they are simple rather than complex and emotional rather than intellectual.

Thus, from Satie to Bacharach, Debussy to Randy Newman, Vaughan Williams to George Martin, certain styles and techniques have been bound together in a kind of web of secondary outsider-ship. I have already suggested that their music has been disapprovingly branded as 'sophisticated' – an all-encapsulating word, which, on the one hand, submits itself to a refusal to analyse and, on the other suggests a lack of spontaneity (and hence 'cool'). I would like to add further that suggestions that all compositions should be written 'on the hoof', in a kind of folk mythology of organic unity, are also the vainglories of elevating rock discourse.

Rock is now used insidiously as a definition to valorise songwriters (however disparate). It is used to hail trends, however discordant. We need to realise, therefore, that rock is not only a descriptive category, but also an evaluative one – such a pity when it actually belongs to a category of contested concepts, and enchants via confusions and ambiguities. It took years for rock to be taken seriously. It will now equally take years for thoughtful, crafted composition to achieve the status of rock!

Balance

This work, then, exists by its very presence to at least attempt to redress this balance. Changing musical, economic and social circumstances brought about the advent of rock 'n' roll and altered music perception, but this arrival did not 'do away' with other soundtracks. In fact the music that Joseph Lanza describes as "the moodiest years on record" (Lanza,1995: 67) witnessed both the advent and decline of rock as a musical force! This book will argue, too, that Burt Bacharach's outsider status has meant that, despite influencing countless rock musicians, his lack of direct links with the counter-cultural aspect of the rock aesthetic has relegated his work to that of a 'hidden history' in popular music.

The narrative within will concentrate upon the man and his music and present both as a kind of journey. Burt came to work within the popular music charts of the 1950s with a set of differing aesthetics and an intuition for the insertion of differing generic influences – the aforementioned bossa nova, for example. Burt's insight for a variety sounds led his musical fantasy into areas that were more specialised, more idiosyncratic – maybe even more hermetic – than any other composer of his day, including Lennon and McCartney. This specialisation was, as we shall see, created via a combination of assimilation and (metaphorically) hitting his head against a brick wall – his genius is contextual.

For example, Burt actually studied under avant-garde composer Darius Milhaud. This gives us further clues to his muse. Bacharach's music seldom (if ever) sounds like that of his mentor but, as we shall see, Milhaud was also fascinated by polyrhythmic structures, asymmetrical phrases and good old-fashioned melody! It is therefore no surprise to learn that among those sat at the feet of Milhaud was Dave Brubeck, who worked, like Burt, with time signature experiments in a highly melodic and atmospheric framework (e.g. 'Take Five', 'It's A Raggy Waltz', etc.).

This exposition of the life and work of Burt Bacharach seeks not only to catalogue and embody the work of a great composer, but also to highlight his work at a very important synchronic moment in 20th century popular music. One could argue that if we put Bacharach at the hub of a combination of the melody, harmony and dynamic range of the LP together with the timing, timbre and beat of the 45, we see a radical development in the history of popular music composition.

Historians might describe the era in which Bacharach came to compose his wonderful music as 'synchronic'. This idea suggests that very specific moments in time are of great significance. This kind of history is interesting but incomplete unless we show how it becomes so, how other events, paradoxically, 'create' its uniqueness. To do this we must use a level of diachronic methods; in other words we must draw different conjunctures together in order to help us understand how and why composers such as Burt Bacharach came to write in the way they did. As we shall see, some of these reasons are musicological, but equally, many of them are cultural and sociological. Let us begin, therefore, with a little context.

Chapter 2

A House Is [Definitely] A Home! – A Little Context

The history of Western music has witnessed many encounters between pre-existing traditions and change, but there is little doubt that the post-WWII era in popular culture was one of significant musical change and creativity. Despite various attempts by historians to belittle the efforts of artists from that period (let us say 1945-1985: the latter referring to the first year of mass produced digital technology and composition), some of the most enduring music ever to be recorded (such as the Bacharach and David catalogue) came to be in that very short space of time.

I use the word 'recorded' deliberately here for the record, from at least the commercial advent of the magnetic tape recorder, the vinyl long player in 1948, and the 45 rpm vinyl single a little later, was of such seminal importance that every other preceding medium paled into insignificance. But these formats represented different facets of music use, different ideas about domestic space and different concepts concerning the use of music.

Magnetic recording technology advanced rapidly during WWII. German Magnetophons were captured by the allies and used as a basis for further research (Millard 1995) in both the US (Ampex) and the UK (Ferrograph). By 1948 not only was the microgroove long player and the application of vinyl developed, but the Ampex Company placed its '200' professional tape recorder into the market. This latter device was snapped-up by the industry and immediately used for masters in recording studios and as a transcription tool in radio stations. Pre-eminent in the financing of magnetic recording was Bing Crosby who, weary of interminable live broadcastings, was keen to use the new technology.

Neither the 45rpm single nor the 331/3 long-player was simply a material object, as many (e.g. Auslander, 2001) would have us believe. In fact audiophiles - that group of hi fidelity experts of usually above average income with an interest in classical music - were already intrinsic with the technology. Andre Millard states:

One sample [in 1948] found that 38 percent of the purchasers [of microgroove LPs] already had a collection of more than 500 records. Most buyers made special trips to their dealers for special demonstrations [...] here was a group of people who were devoted to collecting and listening to records and who were willing to pay any price for improved sound reproduction. (Millard, 1995:208)

Tom Dowd, for example, who engineered so many great recordings for Atlantic Records (and then duplicated them for the majors' white market), was one such electronics expert - described by Jerry Wexler as a 'wunderkind'.

The LP was a window into other worlds: those of hi-fidelity, exotica, and a state of auditory grace on the sofa. The new records sounded so much better than the old 78rpm recordings and expectations were raised by the advent of the LP. One could truly experience sound in a pure sense, one could elevate one's sensory perceptions to previously unheard of proportions. Although resisted by some, the LP was coveted for its revered place in society – thanks be to the LP for extending to us, via technology, the possibility of travelling to hitherto unimagined musical and spectacular geographical places!

The vinyl 45 on the other hand, offered equally exciting, but different, possibilities. It was apparently disposable, yet as was immediately obvious via its size, beautiful proportions and badge engineering, highly collectable. The 45 brought about crucial change in both the economy of music production and consumption. Like the LP, it accelerated the shift in listening to music inducing [...] "the replacement of an audio visual event with a primary audio one, sound without vision" (Laing, 1991:7-8).

The 45 also brought about the possibilities of unfettered listening, of listening practically anywhere, of listening on the move. The advent of the 45rpm record (and with it rock 'n' roll music) was one of the most important social and cultural events of its day. Richard Peterson states:

It is arguable that rock, its aesthetic and its associated culture did more to shape the political and social events of the times than vice-versa. (Peterson, 1990:97)

But, of course, rock was not universally welcomed by any means, and the systems that were in place for lounge enhancement, were not there because of rock. Far from it in fact, for most of the LP market was made up of 'twenty and thirty-somethings' with a lounge to enhance.

Romance and homebuilding played key roles in both the US and UK of the 1950s. Technology, housework, and the domestic space were often seen as challenging enterprises. Hi-fi was, in fact, but one area where romance and practical concepts conjoined, and gender relationships were re-fixed after that previous period (WWII-late 1940s) when women were forced into the jobs market. The 1950s symbolised a time when they were forced back towards the kitchen sink. Different kinds of white goods, family aspirations, ideals of family life ("a chair is still a chair, even when ..."), transistor radios, hi-fi sets, long playing records, television were all integral to the democratic and domestic 'settlement' of the mid-1950s.

It is, therefore, important that we appreciate that although Burt Bacharach as an individual may have tied himself to one form of popular music entertainment by 1957 – the Brill Building, the single and the charts - he was, if not a veteran, then certainly a trouper within these pre-existing systems that put both him and his cabaret cohorts into place in the immediate post-WWII era. This was not a system geared towards the rock 'n' roll single at all, but rather in the direction of the formally trained, technologically developed mainstream (also existing around live performances in clubs and concert halls). The growing symbiotic relationship between small radio stations and independent record companies such as the aforementioned Atlantic Records – an activity centrally important to the advent of rock in the mid-1950s - had largely by-passed Bacharach (in practical terms he was in the army for the first two years of the 1950s).

Radio and records

Prior to WWII very few records were played on the radio. Even by 1948, when the American radio industry basically consisted of four major networks competing with each other for what Richard Peterson describes as "slice strategy" (Peterson, 1990:103), the hits of the day were played by a variety of studio orchestras together with the popular vocalists. There were also comedy and variety programmes with personalities such as Jack Benny and Bob Hope enjoying millions of listeners per week. Just as Burt

Bacharach was deciding to launch some kind of career in popular music (this writer remains unconvinced of any Bacharach inclinations towards the classical concert halls), the hit songs at the time were written, arranged and performed by professionals to fit the musical conventions of the day.

It was a relatively simple task for studio bands to authentically replicate the sound of the record: most songs had a kind of easy swing arrangement or, in the case of Mitch Miller productions, a kind of 'Gang Show'-cum-military band style of scoring. It was what one might describe as a homogenous market: the fewer the competitors, the more homogenous the product.

There were no 'disc jockeys', as such, but presenters who would act as master of ceremonies in the 'correct' tone of voice. There was even a programme in the US entitled *Your Hit Parade* that featured the best selling records of the day as performed by a live band with a guest vocalist. Frank Sinatra made his name on *Your Hit Parade* in two important phases of his career: firstly between 1943 and 1944 and again from 1947 until the programme's co-option into TV in 1950.

Your Hit Parade began its life in 1935. It was sponsored by Lucky Strike cigarettes and was broadcast on the radio each and every Saturday night by NBC until July 1950 when, like many other successful radio shows, it was transferred to television. However, *Your Hit Parade* was a generic programme suited only to radio, not TV. It did not really succeed as a regular television programme and was broadcast only intermittently until its demise in 1959. In any case, pre-recorded originals rather than live covers became increasingly important musical objet d'art following the dawn of rock 'n' roll!

By the time Sinatra was in his second spell with NBC, the record industry was, like radio, geared towards a homogenous concept and was also organised largely via four firms – RCA, Columbia, Decca and Capitol. The industry was vertically integrated and woe-betide an interloper! Music industry authority Richard Peterson further illustrates this with his discussion of a 1948 cover version:

> The practice of producing cover records provides an excellent case in point. When one of the companies had a significant hit

on a song, the other oligopolists would immediately 'cover' it by putting out a recording of the same song by one of their own singers or orchestras. The practice of covering hits also helped to keep independent companies from successfully competing in the market. When in 1947 Bullet records of Nashville released 'Near You' by the Francis Craig Orchestra it gained considerable record sales in the region because the Craig Orchestra was a regular performer on WSM, a powerful radio station broadcasting live from Nashville. Within weeks of the success of the Bullet recording, each of the four major record companies released their own version, and all of these reached hit status in the weeks that followed, completely eclipsing the original version by the independent record company. (Whitburn, 1973) (Peterson, 1990: 112)

But, from 1949 onwards – the first truly successful year for US TV - radio programming gradually moved over to record shows as a means of disseminating music. Record shows were cheaper – especially in the States where one did not essentially collect revenue from recorded music airing - and with the advent of 45rpm records and transistors these sponsored 'jukebox formatted' shows were easy to broadcast and very popular particularly among younger audiences.

Furthermore, the development of cheap record players in the 1950s completed the equation – turning commodities into sites of resistance – confirming the image, but engaging other senses. Music continued to be commodified during the 1950s but these new consumers did not surrender to the commodity in perhaps the same ways that their older brothers and sisters had done. Independent radio stations, independent record companies, and portable technologies all contributed to the advent of new tastemakers. The independence of smaller companies reflected the markets they served. The market for music was no longer homogenised, but consisted of myriad small firms each competing with one other for niche markets.

Commodities

If a commodity such as a popular music format presents different ways of listening, if it radically alters the perceptions of those willing to invest, then it also modifies the very construction of the sound that it carries. It is not simply the material supports for the music that are altered, but the very creation of music for those formats. Technology not only helps to create a kind of spectacular consumption, fetishising objects – it also carries the potential to illuminate all kinds of creativity: compositional, technological, generic even demographic (i.e. creatively targeting a specific age or income group).

Peterson argues that the commercial culture industry in which Burt Bacharach began to take an interest, circa 1948, was still "deaf" (Peterson, 1990:113) to the desires of young people. Its structure, habits, marketing and integration was geared towards the cabaret, variety and domestic utopian end of the market. But before long it received the shake-up it so richly deserved from technology, independent record companies, and radio stations.

Texture

The industry was already fully aware of its markets among the older demographic, however. Full orchestras with large dynamic ranges came to dominate the LP market throughout the 1950s. Bandleaders and arrangers such as George Melachrino, Esquivel, Martin Denny, Jackie Gleason, and Ray Conniff discovered the possibilities open to them as arrangers. The specular possibilities that were attracting Bacharach, the production values, the technological highs, were coming from within the sector of the music industry less concerned with youth and more about hegemony. It was less to do with resistance and more about excellence, less to do with spontaneity and more about careful arranging.

Ray Conniff, for example, used the LP to experiment with arranging the human voice on vinyl; Mexican bandleader, Esquivel even included the sounds of radio waves and compressors. These arrangers created complexity hitherto unavailable on record and were assisted in this by specialised departments within the integrated recording industry. As we have seen, a great deal of sound production at the advent of Bacharach's career was integrated: this cannot be over-exaggerated. All stages in production, promotion and distribution were handled in-house.

Thus texture became an important watermark for those vinyl albums aimed at the matrimonial plot. Not only was the record itself a tactile object, but it also expressed a texture, via sound, that created a feeling of well-being. Not only could we buy and cherish a material object, we could have access to, via a particular sound quotient, certain textures that soothed the body and soul.

By the early 1950s, Conniff had already experimented with a chorus singing throughout a recording session and had come to realise that a formula of instruments and vocals created an interesting mood. By the time his first LP was released in America in 1956 (*S'Wonderful* – US Columbia) he had developed a sound around an echo-based 'chorus invisible' of four women and four men working with eighteen musicians. It was a pulsating but comforting style entirely suitable to the domestic environment of 1950s suburbia. Joseph Lanza maintains:

> The style was so vibrant, yet so relaxing; so haunting, yet so comforting – a formula so singular and precious that no one else to this day has been able to copy it. This pure alchemy was achieved by combining the base metals of brass with the Conniff choir's golden throats. (Lanza, 1995:106)

It was this sound that became something of a precursor to that of Burt Bacharach. The arrangement of female voices and muted brass stabs was certainly not lost on Burt. One listen to, for example, Conniff's arrangement of 'It Might As Well Be Spring' (1959) gives the game away. Apart from being full of the usual do-doos and ba-baas, this arrangement contains many elements that are familiar as Bacharach motifs. Consider the thoughtful intro with that touch of velvety brass, subtle females voices and lack of 'bottom end'. Listen to the laid-back underscore performing a second melodic function, the subdued build-up and then that brass, that constant, melodic brass. It's all in there – just a different prescription, that's all.

But the evergreens Conniff used as vehicles were often less interesting than the very sound textures. For example, if he was ambitious in his scoring, he was decidedly unambitious in his selection of material. Sure, he had a captive market who knew and loved such standards as 'You Do Something To Me', 'The Way You Look Tonight', 'Begin the Beguine', and 'Moonlight Serenade'. But Conniff was never going to attract a younger demographic with these tunes. There was absolutely no way that a younger audience of the 1950s was going to buy records that effectively reflected the repertoires of their parents or older siblings. Sure, the sounds were enticing, but the material? Do me a favour!

In fact, listening now after all of these years, one gets the distinct impression that Conniff had little or no interest in the material per se. He was later to admit that:

> Instead of playing trombone solos that other musicians liked, I made an about-face and wrote my arrangements with a view to making the masses understand and buy records. (Conniff in Lanza, 1995:107)

One can perhaps detect the machinations of a cynic, here. These evergreens were appealing, but already grossly overworked by the late 1950s.

Composition

Ray Conniff's superb arrangements were one thing, but composition along these lines was an altogether greater challenge. By the end of the 1950s, a composer was needed who could present dynamic range, tone colour, warmth and all of the textural devices used by the great LP makers of the 1950s. But this composer also had to embrace the qualities inherent in the 45 – standardisation as art, interchangeability as an advantage and mass production as a creative sphere.

Burt Bacharach was, like Conniff, trained within the canon of Western classical music but via accompanying a variety of artists after his demob in 1952 (see on), had also worked extensively within the above realms of timbre and connotation. By adding a range of melody and harmony to the popular song and by, conversely, adding texture and timbre to the European music tradition, he was a budding composer in a position to take advantage of these socio-cultural and musicological consequences. Working from within apparent restrictions of time and place (space, even) offers the opportunity to create music that is at once mainstream and subversive, simple and complex, wearisome and exhilarating.

So, in the rapidly changing popular music environment of the 1950s, Burt Bacharach acted as a kind of linkman – both with the legendary composers of the past (particularly the Impressionists such as Debussy and Satie), the standardised and rather adult structure of the pre-rock 'n' roll music industry, and with the technologically driven popular music formats (and accordingly **desires**) of his own era.

Between the moments he joined the US Forces in 1950, and then rented his office in the Brill Building on 1619 Broadway in 1955, Burt witnessed the music industry change beyond recognition. In fact, Richard Peterson states that:

> In a matter of two dozen months between late 1954 and early 1957 rock was forged in this cauldron of entrepreneurial creativity. (Peterson, 1990:114)

Bacharach undeniably saw his opportunity and made the conscious decision to try his hand at song writing. He figured, according to Robin Platts, that "hearing the mediocre material being pitched to [the acts that he accompanied such as Paula Stewart and Georgia Gibbs] by song pluggers" … [he] … "could do at least as well as the stuff these other songwriters were turning out" (Platts, 2003:pp10-11).

This actually sounds more than a little premeditated, which is a fascinating hypothesis when one considers his subsequent influence on all of western popular music for the next 50 years! Frustration, ambition and expediency may have led to some of the greatest popular music of the 20th century.

Burt was also able to create lineage between other acknowledged greats of the 20th century such as, on the one hand, Jerome Kern, George & Ira Gershwin, Cole Porter, Harold Arlen and on the other Alban Berg, Webern and Schoenberg. Even though his music does not resemble that of either Gershwin or Webern, the complexity of his work, aided in no small terms by the equally 'grown up' lyrics of Hal David (about whom more later), continues what many see as a tradition of 'clever' popular music that pre-dates the advent of rock music. But perhaps his greatest contribution was to create music that reflected a harmony between these dramatically changing patterns of production and consumption in this synchronic era of post WWII popular music.

Standardisation

Many critics of popular culture such as T. W. Adorno see this link of production to consumption as a negative. They see connections between functional artefacts such as mass produced records and textual artefacts such as the music on those records as being ideological. Adorno (*On Popular Music,* 1941) attempts to expose the destructive ways in which the capitalist mode of production affects all forms of popular music:

> Music for entertainment [...] seems to complement the reduction of people to silence, the dying out of speech as expression, the inability to communicate at all. It inhabits the pockets of silence that develop between people moulded by anxiety, work and undemanding docility [...] it is perceived purely as background. If nobody can any longer speak, then certainly nobody can any longer listen [...] Today [the] power of the banal extends over the whole of society. (Adorno, 1978:271-4)

A powerful and scathing polemic against all popular music, but particularly against the genres I have attempted to illustrate above – those attempting to create mood, texture and accompany function. Adorno's writing has many strengths – he certainly understood that the Tin Pan Alley hit repertoires of the 1930s-1950s revealed a level of sameness that was, according to Richard Middleton:

> [...] stultifying. This is backed up by the accounts we have of the many aspects of the economic structure of the music business then: the drive for profit, the trend towards monopoly and conglomeration, the conservative appeal to the predictable and universally understood. (Middleton, 1990:37)

But Adorno fails to see the crucial differences between these functional and textual artefacts. These differences lie in an understanding that the progress made in the 1950s and 1960s in technology – the very technology that gave us the LP and the 45 - did not constrain music composition, but enhanced the possibilities for it. If anything, the possibilities for variation were greatly expanded by mass production. From the 1950s-onwards, the music industry was surrounded by new technologies that were certainly able to maximise profit. Yet in order to do this the industry had to allow a certain amount of "free space" (ibid,62) for relatively unplanned texts and procedures to develop. Their approach had to be by necessity pluralistic. Adorno's criticisms are merely Marxist/purist incantations of the practised recluse. A Burt Bacharach composition is (and always will be) a material asset.

Bacharach's move into the rock 'n' roll sphere by 1955/6 appears to have been caused out of a variation on this 'Adornian frustration', fuelled as it was by the apparent 'low quality' of contemporary popular music. Burt wanted to attack the songwriting process by becoming part of it. As previously stated, he was certainly miffed at the poor quality of songs aimed at those he accompanied such as Polly Bergen, his first wife Paula Stewart, and the Ames Brothers. Like Adorno, he seems to have been primarily concerned with two important traits that emerged in the Tin Pan Alley era.

Firstly, part-interchangeability; by the statements credited to Burt in Platts (2003), Bacharach appears to be of the opinion that too many songs were sounding like other songs. Interchangeable parts to songs were qualitatively indistinguishable. As we have seen, this was undoubtedly linked with an issue of homogeneity in some areas of US popular music. Donald Clarke (ed.) discussed this in his review of the period immediately prior to the advent of rock 'n' roll:

> [...] the quality of new songs seemed to slump badly as the golden age of Broadway and American popular song faded [...] vocalist [were] singing songs which in many cases were no more than jingles [...] Good albums were being made which are still selling today, but the rise of the radio 'play list' was the worst thing ever to happen to popular music, and is still a curse decades later; some people stopped listening to the radio when 'How Much Is That Doggie In The Window' was no. 1 for 8 weeks in '53. (Clarke [ed.], 1990:994)

Secondly, the issue of pseudo-individualization appears to have been another Bacharach hobbyhorse. As Gendron states, pseudo-individualization is the "indispensable capitalist complement to part interchangeability" (Gendron, 1986:21). We are seduced into thinking that differences in packaging reflect differences in essence. Pseudo-individualization glamorises style over content. One can certainly understand this in a mid-1950s context when cover versions were de rigeur. Not only was music glamorised in this way, so too were all kinds of mass-produced goods in the post-war 'Great Society'.

For example, the year that Bacharach got down to some 'serious' (actually that could be a matter of opinion!) writing at the Brill Building – 1956 – the 'Eldorado' became the first Cadillac to sport the famous tail fin. The public appeared ready, willing and able to pay primarily for differences in style rather than mechanical quality. The public seemed to be as equally compliant in their willingness to shell-out for Georgia Gibbs' (of whom more later) bleached-out 'Dance With Me Henry' rather than Hank Ballard's meatier 'Roll With Me Henry' (issued the previous year, 1955). The song, in itself, was part interchangeable: one was evidently suitable for one marketplace, the other for a distinctive 'other' (i.e. 'licentious Black people'!).

Despite his success at the Brill Building over a period of about seven years, Bacharach continued to express his distaste for a system that constrained music as a form of assembly line production. The rock 'n' roll revolution that attracted Burt did put Tin Pan Alley out of its compositional misery, somewhat, but did not bring to an end the industrial standardisation of music (and Burt is on record stating as much – see on). However, what Bacharach perhaps did not appreciate in such statements was that although emanating from within the system, his music was an example of quite the reverse trends! This suggests that the industrial presence in music is often greatly exaggerated.

Creativity v constraint

Bacharach's works (and not simply Bacharach, but the compositions of Gerry Goffin and Carole King, Barry Mann and Cynthia Weil, Jerry Leiber and Mike Stoller, Jeff Barry and Ellie Greenwich, Neil Sedaka, Neil Diamond, Doc Pomus and Mort Shuman (the list is almost endless) were created in an industrial-like environment such as existed at the Brill, but the factors that account for the standardisation of music texts do not fully explain either their creation or reception.

35

The listener to a Bacharach composition such as (say) 'Make It Easy On Yourself' was both stretched and entertained, not repressed. Bacharach's music also changed almost beyond recognition from 'Magic Moments' to 'Walk On By', so some level of apparent liberalism, pluralism and musical dissent was allowed to flourish! One might argue that these changes were only stylistic (hence merely surface alterations), but nothing challenges the songwriter quite as much as a consumer wanting change - as Burt, himself, later discovered when *Lost Horizon* appeared in the public sphere!

Rather than supplanting the dance and big band arrangements of the pre-LP era, Bacharach was able to combine their rich variety of timbres and compositional techniques with the audibility of the single. Unlike other unconventional pop composers and bandleaders of the 1950s such as Esquivel and Martin Denny, Bacharach used the 45rpm record and was able to impact on US culture at a much greater level. He was able to use the constraints of a 45 rpm record to hone his compositions into 2 and 3-minute opuses (one might say that this was a particularly unusual gift, but actually, as we shall see, his musical background contributed greatly to this understanding of musical miniatures).

Despite being influenced by the sounds of the great 1950s LP makers such as (e.g.) Conniff, Denny, Melachrino and Les Baxter, his work in rhythm alone far exceeds the feel, the groove (and perhaps the limitations?) of jazz-orientated music. Very few of his songs 'swing' through 12/8 and 4/4, as such, and one could argue that, compositionally, the Impressionist school of music with which the young Bacharach was familiar is not without significance. To draw this section to a close I quote Erik Satie, writing in a note to Jean Cocteau:

> Furniture music for law offices, banks, etc […] No marriage ceremony without furniture music […] don't enter a house which does not have furniture music. (Lanza, 1995:18)

Satie could have been describing Bacharach's musical touch, here. Explorations in mood and movie soundtracks were also Bacharach's stock-in-trade. Certainly the long playing mood song of Ray Conniff was of vital importance to display what could be done with sound and technology, but, perhaps from the moment he heard the Impressionists, the post-war serialists such as Webern and Berg, and a blast or two from Dizzy

Gillespie, Burt Bacharach had some kind of post-industrial music art form already in his head.

 Bacharach self-consciously shaped his songs to fit specific images created by specific singers. He also pushed the boundaries of creativity in the popular song to undreamed of levels. But he was also clearly intent on doing whatever it took to entertain an audience – including not expecting too much of their time and concentration. He needed to keep everybody's attention. Thus the twin polarities of creativity and constraint were undoubtedly bedfellows in the Bacharach process.

Chapter 3

Early Burt

There are five Bs [...] Beethoven, Brahms, Berlin, Bach, and Bacharach: Ira Gershwin. (in Djordje Nikolic, *Arcade*, 1998)

Burt Bacharach was born into an Austro-German/Jewish household on 12th May 1929 in Kansas City, Missouri, USA. By all accounts, his upbringing was very loving. Burt's mother Irma was a portrait painter of some renown and his father, Bert Bacharach, worked in Woolf Bros department store. Bert (the elder) was to later recall to the *Saturday Evening Post:*

> in a moment of fatherly pride, I decided the Bacharach family was ready for a Big Bert and a Little Bert [...] [but Bertram] [...] might be considered a nice name in classy circles, but it was comparable to Algernon, Percy or Reginald in Atlantic City, where I went to Grammar School. (Platts, 2003:7)

A 'u' was inserted where the 'e' had been and thus Burt was fashioned. When Burt was still a child of 8 years his father became a columnist for King Features, who syndicated his articles to most men's fashion magazines of the day. Bert senior became nationally renowned and continued writing articles and appearing in Universal International newsreels for the next twenty years. He also authored two best-selling books in the 1950s; *Bert Bacharach's Book For Men* and *Right Dress*. The younger Burt undoubtedly loved both of his parents deeply and probably inherited his father's flair for that trademark casual fashion! Burt was to state in typically honest fashion to Lillian Ross of *The New Yorker* in 1968 that:

> I've got a great dad. Bert Bacharach, the columnist. And I've got a great mom – she has grey hair too, which she keeps grey. Lovely hair. And she's a lovely lady. (Bacharach to Ross, *New Yorker*, 1968)

This upwardly mobile young family had already moved to Kew Gardens in Queens, New York, by the time of Burt's second birthday. By his eighth birthday Irma had organised piano lessons for her diminutive son, even going to the pecuniary measure of purchasing a Steinway. Bert Bacharach the elder brought to mind that "Burt threw himself into his instruction and absorbed absolutely everything offered to him".

Loyalty to his son may well have been clouding his memories a little, however, for it has also been variously recorded that Bacharach's teacher regarded Burt only as an adequate student – certainly without the indicators of compositional brilliance that were later to come to the fore. Burt is also on record (*Biography Channel*, 2003) as stating (with a passion for someone as understated as he) that he hated (with equal passion, one presumes) his music lessons.

Burt actually aspired to other things. He was a very sporty child and his burning ambition was to become a professional ('gridiron') US footballer (these days he has more interest in soccer). Irma was very supportive of the young lad (perhaps at times overly-so) but both she and her son realised that his sporting ambitions were unrealistic. In a mid-60s *Newsweek* interview, Burt was to later recall:

> What a drag for a kid […] practicing piano […] but what else did I have to do?

Lamenting on his lack of physical stature and his apparently diametrically opposed penchant for sports and girls he admitted somewhat curtly that he "was too short for either" (ibid).

Despite his growing interest in all things musical, Burt continued to harbour desires for the football field. Irma, however, recurrently insisted that Burt devote substantial 'free' time to his music studies – including cello ("I couldn't keep time to the radio. I was also a cellist. It was a rented cello. They even gave me a bow: the whole outfit" [Bacharach to Saal, *Newsweek*, 1970]), drums, and piano from the age of 12 years – and her word as a Jewish mother was legislature.

Burt later admitted to *New Musical Express* that this period was a difficult one that has continued to affect him throughout his life. He is quoted as stating that he had " 'terrible difficulty in making contact' with anyone in a high school where he was the shortest of 3,000 kids. Including girls. As the man rolls back the years he insists 'even as a celebrated composer, you still carry some of this stuff with you'" (Williams, *NME*, 1996).

He is further quoted by Tony Parsons reiterating this insecurity about his stature. It appears that a complex about his Jewish background compounded this lack of confidence:

> I pretended not to be Jewish, which is a terrible thing to do, but I liked the Catholic kids I grew up with and they always spoke disparagingly about Jews. When we played football against a Jewish team we would be in a huddle and my team would say, 'Lets go and kick shit out of these Jews'. So I never let them know. I was also very short – there was not a girl in a school of three thousand kids smaller than me – so I had enough to get on with without admitting to being Jewish. (Parsons, 1995:113)

In fact, by the time that Burt reached his formative years as a teenager, Irma and Bert had sat the insecure lad down for a family conference. Sports were out, apparently. Platts reports that Bert the elder was later to recall to the *Saturday Evening Post*:

> His mother and I told him we thought he had a good future in music, but that only he could determine what he wanted to do. (Platts, 2003:6)

Perhaps to please his mother, the 13 year old informed his parents that he too wished to continue with his music studies ("he was their shining star" – Joel Grey). This was despite a young Burt apparently half-expecting to follow his father into the men's clothing business:

> I thought I'd probably wind up in the men's clothing business. That's where my dad had affiliations […] I thought it was the easiest, most accessible job that my dad might introduce me. (Bacharach, *Sunday Morning On CBS*, 2002)

Irma attempted to educate her young son in 'high art' music from an earlier age but it did not initially prove successful; Robin Platts:

> In the long Sunday car rides back to New York after visiting relatives in Philadelphia, Irma would tune-in to the New York Philharmonic, but Burt wasn't impressed. He found most of the Philharmonic's repertoire – heavy on the Beethoven and Strauss – too serious and sad, even depressing. (Platts, 2003:8)

According to Burt the music seemed to blend in with the dark night sky on these wearisome journeys, particularly in the fall or winter, generating in him a dismal feeling all the way home. Burt was to further elucidate to both *Us* magazine in 1996 and *The Times* in 2002 that memories of these childhood days were not altogether joyful. Firstly to *Us*:

> I used to hate the rides from Philadelphia with my parents in the car. Sundays, listening to the New York Philharmonic because my mother had it on the radio. The music was serious; it was sad, it was depressing. Those were not great moments for me [but] I heard some music that cut through the drudgery: Debussy, Ravel's 'Daphnes Et Chloe: Suite no. 2'. That was an opening for me. (Bacharach to Hunter, *Us*, 1996)

Bacharach is on record as stating that he was simply the kid who "hated to practice the piano" until he discovered the exposed quality of Ravel's unabashed sense of melody (one can hear traces of 'Daphnes Et Chloe' in Burt's 'Looking With My Eyes'). This was further enhanced by the uplifting sounds of the French Impressionists. Burt informed *The Times*:

> My mother made me take piano lessons as a child and I hated it. She forced me to practice every night, when all I wanted was to be outside playing. But then two things changed my mind. The first was hearing Ravel for the first time. I thought that I hated classical music, but when I heard the French Impressionists I realised that I was wrong. The second was discovering jazz and big bands. (Bacharach to Cowan, *The Times*, 2002)

Most groups, even small family units, have their leaders. Irma was such a leader. But good leadership within a family involves an understanding of how this perception of others affects the family processes. Both Burt and Bert understood that Irma wished something very specific from her son. In that domestic sphere, they were compliant and Irma usually got what she wanted.

However, Irma was no tastemaker and she could do little about her son's aesthetic rejection of German Romanticism. It was the challenging but melodic sounds from the French Impressionists rather than the somewhat "depressing" sounds of the New York Phil's Germanic repertoire that first began to suggest to the young Burt that music could be an agreeable experience. Let us, then, briefly explore this influential music: Impressionism, the Impressionists, and 'Les Six'.

Impressionism

Already, by the end of the 19th century, there were the first rumblings of a musical revolution. In Europe Dvorak, Debussy, Ravel, and others in England, such as Vaughan Williams, were challenging the "Germanic grasp on composition" (Vaughan Williams). These composers were producing music that was considered distinctly peculiar by some. The days of Romanticism in music were drawing to a close and the voices of a new breed of composers were being heard: those who loved melody but were unhappy with the cloying sentimentality of the Romantics.

In particular, there were those French artists who later proved to be an influence on the young Bacharach during his formative car rides and (even later) his musical training. They were, not unlike their 1940s bebop counterparts, trying to shake-off the pattern laid down by the previous (in this case) 'Teutonic' musical orthodoxy – especially that of Wagner (although, as we shall see, our hero Burt did not ignore Wagner's *leitmotiv* when it came to film scoring). They have been described as 'Impressionists'. Like so many terms in music, 'Impressionism' has been borrowed from the visual arts – in this case painting – and Debussy, in particular, developed a style in which atmosphere and mood took the place of strong emotion or narrative – it was kind of 'ambient', one supposes.

For example, Debussy used new chord combinations and exotic rhythms and scales (he was very taken with Indonesian Gamelan music – later a feature of the movie *Lost Horizon*, incidentally) and in place of the usual harmonic progressions he developed a style in which chords were valued themselves, as little units, and remain unresolved. Actually, Wagner had done something similar with his own interest in chordal non-resolution – but we shall let that one pass! Certainly, for any one not taken with the works of Mahler, Brahms and Richard Wagner, such as the young Burt Bacharach, Impressionism was an interesting and melodic alternative. Donald Fagen of Steely Dan informed *Melody Maker* in 1993:

Poulenc and Debussy were [Burt's] models and, when applied to soul and gospel, it had this very ethereal effect, especially with Dionne Warwick's voice. I love this combination of classicism and soul. Walter Becker and I were both huge fans of Burt Bacharach records and they were definitely an influence. (Fagen to *Melody Maker*, 1993)

Erik Satie

Of particular interest to us here is the work of Erik Satie. Satie's musical education was, like Bacharach's, somewhat unsatisfactory and he was also regarded as a composer of weird little ditties. Like Burt, many of Erik Satie's works were miniatures for the piano. Satie was always well acquainted with the music of other composers and like Bacharach did not care for the larger scale material of the likes of Wagner, Richard Strauss or Beethoven. Satie also understood popular idioms well: he played piano and accordion and wrote popular songs in cafes and bars in Montmartre.

Famous Satie compositions include 'Trois Gymnopedes 1, 2 and 3'. These are little three-minute variations that not only tear at one's heartstrings, but also sound unusual, spacious and experimental. But, amusingly, these days they also crop up – like Bacharach's music - in the 'cheesiest' of contexts (television 'trails', advertising features, film sequences, etc.) that appear to attempt to create an overemotional atmosphere. Bacharach remains philosophical:

> A song is a very compact form – probably the most compact form. It's supposed to create an emotional response from a listener in two to three minutes time, an emotional response that people can identify with. My idea was always to search for a new way, a fresh way of portraying the emotion. I've always thought of myself more as someone who writes from an emotional point of view rather than a cerebral one. (Bacharach, see *Library of Congress*)

This remains an interesting comment, coming as it does from a composer who is divergently regarded as being both 'sophisticated' and 'cheesy' at one and the same time. Perhaps these two worlds have collided, intersected, in any case. Perhaps, like Satie, Bacharach does not worry about this musical appropriation. As he admits above, he certainly does not feel the

43

need to be considered cerebral. It is, after all, a term inherent with high art/ low art dichotomies: something that was anathema to both composers.

Obviously, both Satie's and Bacharach's music are multifaceted. On the one hand outwardly quite simple and straightforward in terms of harmony and in using structures with turnarounds and engaging in little apparent musical development (at times even perhaps a little repetitive). But Satie also used unusual scales such as the old forms of modes and behind the apparent simplicity lay something very different and thought provoking (likewise Bacharach according to music academic Robin Hartwell "Art concealing art").

The music of both Satie and Bacharach has attitude, certain sadness, and often displays ambivalence. This makes it very difficult to fathom (and, as we have seen above, allows for different interpretations by the listener!). It is this ambivalence and ambiguity that is particularly important when we look more closely at the work of Burt Bacharach. In an interview with BBC Radio 2 disc jockey Steve Wright, Burt was asked about the complexity of his songs to which he replied:

> I always try to make them like little movies or little stories, emotional – ups, downs. I don't think you can stay at one peak, those are the kind of records that you play for two weeks and you don't want to hear again. I like songs like '24 Hours From Tulsa' that tell a story, which get emotional. (Bacharach to Wright, *BBC Radio 2*, 2000)

Rather than merely considering Bacharach as a seldom examined connection with French Impressionists such as Erik Satie, perhaps we also should be considering both men as members of some kind of school of musical thought, stretching from pre-WWI Paris via 1920s Dada-ism to the Brill Building in New York – what Joseph Lanza describes succinctly as "The 'Canned' Avant-Garde" (Lanza,1994:14). Music academic (and Bacharach aficionado) Robin Hartwell suggested as much to this writer:

> Bacharach told the press at the 2003 Polar Music Prize that he had intended to be a composer of 'serious' music (and that he had hung out with Darius Milhaud, John Cage and others), but because of the pressure to earn money he ended up being

a 'commercial' musician, [...] for me, the musical language of Bacharach suggests this sophisticated mindset not just sophisticated music. This is already better than, say, Sondheim, because it proposes all kinds of possibilities. (Robin Hartwell, personal interview, 2003)

Shortly after the death of Erik Satie in 1925, devotee Darius Milhaud stated that the great man had prophesised the major developments in music over the forthcoming 50 years (that is, to the year 1975) within his own body of work. This has been described as 'Erik Satie's Crystal Ball' (Caitlin Crowley among others). As we shall discover, it was Milhaud who taught Bacharach a great deal about such developments and complexity.

 It has been suggested that the young Bacharach had ulterior motives for his interest in 'serious' music. Burt, according to these sources (e.g. Platts, 2003:8), apparently wished to "improve his social standing" and felt that a hefty dose of symphonies might do the trick. An appreciation of 19th century Romanticism might have done just that in pretentious mid-20th century Queen's society. However this does not really square with Burt's ever-present melancholy at the mention of listening to the New York Phil's radio broadcasts of the Romantics ("too heavy, too heavy"). And an interest in Impressionism probably disguised a real interest in composition.

Burt and jazz

Burt graduated from Forest Hills School with all of the above – and more – swimming around in his head. First and foremost, he decided that he should continue his musical studies. But another important piece of the musical jigsaw puzzle fell into place when Bacharach reached the age of 15. Like many of his contemporaries, he enjoyed the music of Harry James (he of 'One O' Clock Jump' and 'Two O' Clock Jump' fame):

I'd listen to the bands in clubs when I'd have dinner with my mom and dad. We'd listen to stuff like Harry James and the Dorsey Brothers, and it was OK, it was really nice. (Bacharach to Cumming, 2001)

In fact it has also been reported that, on one particular occasion, travelling to a piano lesson on a Manhattan bus, Leonard Bernstein – then a fellow student - overheard Burt whistling 'Two O' Clock Jump'. They got talking and, according to Bernstein's recollection, Bacharach informed the young Leonard that he had never heard of him; evocatively, however, as the bus reached Bacharach's stop, Burt suggested that he would (to paraphrase the retiring aside) 'see him at the top'.

Yet, terms such as "really nice" and "OK" hardly imply earth-shattering adoration from our ambitious budding musician. As agreeable as the work of Harry James and the Dorsey Brothers might have been while eating a porterhouse steak with his parents, it was music for an older generation. Burt needed something dangerous, exciting and musically uncertain:

> [...] one day I peeled back a whole barrier, and suddenly there was Charlie Parker, and Bud Powell, Thelonius Monk. They were jumping 25 years ahead of everybody. It was very exciting to hear this music. (ibid)

He eventually sneaked into the famous Spotlight Club in Manhattan and witnessed a mind-blowing set from none other than the Dizzy Gillespie Big Band.

The music of Gillespie had not previously adulterated the taste buds of the young Bacharach, but from that moment onward it appears that Burt understood the power of music to deeply affect one's sensibilities ("It certainly made me like music" [ibid]). Indeed, Robin Platts (2003) argues with some force that this was the moment when the music grabbed Burt rather than the reverse. Platts suggests that Burt previously used music as a way to improve his chances with girls or to strengthen alliances with his parents (and as a vehicle to 'the top', perhaps). But for the first time in his life, music had actually fashioned an emotional response from him.

This is certainly an interesting theory. But, from at least a musicological perspective, there does not appear to be a great deal of musical evidence within his compositions for Burt's absorption and re-articulation of the music of Gillespie and Parker. Obviously we must not get too quantitative about this – there are myriad ways in which a young musician can receive sustenance from different musical genres and not all of them manifest themselves in future compositions!

However, whereas Skip Heller (1995) claims that Burt's "dose of bebop helps explain the complex chords that mark his style" and it is also true that Burt himself has often informed those interested that he "would go to the clubs on 52nd Street with my phoney I.D and just listen" to the music of Charlie Parker and Dizzy Gillespie (ibid), bebop's way-out atonality, strange harmonies and melodies do not, on the surface, appear to have been a major contributor to Bacharach's various compositional eras, styles or techniques.

In interview, the man himself never really gives us any real clues as to the direct musical influences of bebop on his work. One is left proposing, then, that perhaps bebop's influence was as much to do with associated autonomy of lifestyle as autonomy of musical practice. In an interview in 2002, Bacharach confirmed that, as an impressionable 15 year-old:

> Thelonious Monk, Dizzy Gillespie, Charlie Parker; all those guys changed my life. They got me interested in bebop and kept me interested. (Bacharach to Cowan, *The Times*, 2002)

It is perhaps bebop's prodigious energy as much as anything that attracted white middle class youth such as Burt Bacharach to its adoring ranks. Not only was the music edgy, cool and unsafe, it was also cultured, urbane and sophisticated – perfect fodder, in fact, for the pretensions of white middle class teenagers from Queens. The immediate visual and aural impact of bop and the 'cool' of stars such as Gillespie and Parker empowered middle class white youth (not unlike rap, today). Perhaps we should contextualise bebop a little at this stage.

Bebop

Bebop did not arrive on the jazz scene trailing any kind of glory behind it. Bebop, or Bop as it is also called, was more evolutionary than revolutionary and many of jazz's audience were simply not ready for the sound. Some musicians such as Cab Calloway and Tommy Dorsey reacted violently towards it. Calloway is said to have described it as "Chinese Music". Yet, these responses were somewhat reactionary, for bop was something of a natural progression for many of its participants and, as suggested, the genre had been incubating within the jazz movement for some time.

The pioneers of bop were personalities who could not be imitated or appropriated and they had deliberately placed themselves well outside of the mainstream of popular music of the 1940s. They were also political. The point was quite simple: if US society refused to recognise Black artistic achievement and continued to apparently disinfect and yet assimilate Black music rather than give it its own voice, then, the question was asked, why should Black musicians persist in working in a kind of jazz middle-of-the-road?

Marshall Bowden suggests that Lester Young was an important precursor of the bebop aesthetic:

> Young became adept at gliding forward with lengthy phrases that took no notice of the natural division of the bar line, which had been a problem for some earlier jazz soloists. (Bowden, *'Jazzitude'* website: www.jazzitude.com/histbop.htm, 2001:2)

Young was certainly highly influential upon Charlie Parker. Parker respected Young's waywardness in not playing tenor sax within the prevailing idiom of the day – that of Coleman Hawkins. But there were none more auspicious in the early-mid 1940s than Earl 'Fatha' Hines. Hines was a pioneering jazz pianist (he had developed stride piano playing years previously) and continued to thrust forward in attempting to develop jazz as a musical language in its own right.

In 1943, Hines' band included vocalists Billy Eckstine and Sarah Vaughan, horn players Charlie Parker and Dizzie Gillespie and tenor man Wardell Gray. This group was groundbreaking but, sadly, never recorded owing to a strike by the American Federation of Musicians. By the time the strike had ended over a year later, Parker and Gillespie had moved on and it was as bandleaders in their own right that Bacharach witnessed these two revolutionary players.

By the immediate post-war era the men that were to fascinate the teenage Bacharach - Gillespie and Parker - were in the vanguard of African American musicians working in NYC who had developed not only a new musical, but also a new social language. Bebop, hard bop, (call it what you will) had become a way of life. It exuded very different morals, lifestyles and musical sounds from the previous experiences of jazz in the 1930s. It was especially self-conscious in its musical and chemical explorations!

Thus, at least from this vantage point it is not difficult to see how Bacharach was influenced by the language, image and stance of bebop. To suggest that an entire set of social-cultural signifiers can emerge from a piece of musical spontaneity was certainly revolutionary. This would have undoubtedly held appeal to a young man such as Burt –intermittently restricted by the kind of formal musical education experienced by many.

Gillespie and Parker actually suggested to the likes of the young Bacharach that everything in life could indeed be musical. Bebop advocates vibrations, acoustics, intuition and, perhaps, above all, a high degree of contextuality and, conversely, autonomy. Although bebop appeared to be 'new' it was (of course) forged within the context of extending musical methodologies. One might even suggest that, as a result of the enormous social impact that this music had on the post war popular and non-popular musical world, its musical influences are possibly even somewhat exaggerated because of (conversely) its immense social impact in the United States.

University

By the time Burt was 15 (1943) he had already joined a band while attending Forest Hills High School. Studies were one thing, but there were also social gatherings and local hops to play:

> When I was 15, some of the guys at school and I formed a band: ten pieces, with myself on piano. We played at parties and local dances. (Bacharach to Ross, *New Yorker*, 1968)

And:

> [...] being in a dance band was my way to meet other kids. I even got to meet a couple of girls. And they looked at me a bit differently because I was now sort of important. (Parsons, 1995: 113)

Burt was obviously still insecure, without friends of the opposite sex, and lacking in self-confidence.

During the first summer after the end of WWII, Bacharach, still at school, elected to go on a tour of US Army hospitals. Despite his bebop influences, he played mainly boogie-woogie piano for the wounded GIs. It was a seminal experience, as Bacharach rather dispassionately recalled in 1970:

> The first place was Martinsburg West Virginia, a special hospital for plastic surgery [...] for guys with their faces shot off. It was my first time away from home and my mother let me take off my braces for the tour. When I came back I wouldn't put them back on. (Bacharach to Saal, *Newsweek*, 1970)

The following summer he formed a quintet with, among others, Eddie Shaughnessy, the famous jazz and cabaret drummer who spent many years in the 'Tonight' TV show band. The quintet played at a hotel in the Catskills. The Catskill resort was where thousands of New Yorkers spent those steaming hot East Coast summers in hotels and holiday camps: and there was money to be earned! Sleeping in a converted chicken shack across the road from the hotel, the band were engaged to perform the popular hits of the day to residents and non-residents alike each evening until the last one fell over or went to bed!

Shaughnessy took care of the finances and, to begin with, the band received $200 each week. Business was bad, however, and the hotel management reduced their salaries to only $40 per week. Shaughnessy was looking after his infirm mother at the time and received most of the money. The band, therefore, was broke. According to Saal (ibid), Bacharach stated that they came to feel "like prisoners", but fortunately relief was on its way. The band woke up one morning to the sound of fire engines – the hotel had burned down and they were free. "We cheered", stated Burt (ibid).

Following his graduation from High School, Burt enrolled at McGill University in Montreal – at that time struggling against a rather 'second division' tag. Thus McGill was not his first choice of college. He was unable, in fact, to enrol at any US music college worthy of its name and so he determined to head to Canada to further his musical education. McGill, on Bacharach's own confession, was "one of the few schools that I could get into at that time [...] my high school grades were that bad. So [McGill] was not my first choice. I would rather have gone to Oberlin or Eastman, but I wasn't accepted" (in Platts, 2003:9).

According to Robin Platts, Burt "wowed the Dean with a Debussy piece on the piano" (ibid:8) thus securing the only available place left on the course. This is interesting for, apparently, Burt's audition was stopped about half way through due to the insistence of the Dean. He had heard enough - either satisfied that the young student was accomplished enough to join the University for the next three years, or disinclined to listen to any more. One cannot help but speculate at the Dean's abruptness and whether it was (diametrically or otherwise) in proportion to the young Bacharach's abilities at the piano.

Burt describes his time at McGill somewhat diplomatically (he was awarded an Honorary Degree in Music by the university in 1972) as both a "good and bad" experience. As previously suggested, the University's conservatory was considered to be rather second-rate after WWII, but the opportunity to witness a few expert practitioners in Montreal itself was not lost on the young Bacharach:

> I didn't know what I was doing there. First it was one of the few schools where I could get accepted. It wasn't a great music school at the time, it really wasn't. I felt a little bit lost there. But there was good stuff going on musically – what's that street called, St. Catherine? At Rockhead's [a night club] you had Maynard Ferguson and you had Oscar Peterson. So you had good people. The music was exciting [...] being in Montreal was very different from being in the States. It felt a little more European. (Bacharach to Ward, *Ottawa Citizen*, 2001)

Certainly Burt confirms that, for him, while the three years were not exactly wasted, they were not the most memorable of his life, either!

> I don't remember developing [...] kind of just marching through the three years that I was there [...] I didn't study composition [...] I studied piano. It was not a great music school at the time. I know it's evolved into a much better music school now than when I was there. (ibid)

If Burt is a little coy about his rite of passage while at McGill, there is little doubt that he developed into an accomplished pianist by the time of his graduation. In fact, during his first year at the University he won the top award in the Canadian Scholastic Piano Competition – a nationwide contest. During the summer he would go out to Tanglewood to study composition as an extra curricula activity. But he was not developing as a concert pianist per se, either. Listening to the likes of Maynard Ferguson and Oscar Peterson at Rockhead's and having already gained considerable experience as a popular music pianist meant that Burt was somewhat 'out of kilter' with the formalities of a Canadian music education.

The presence of these particular two 'jazz' personalities are of further significance to the musical development of the embryonic muse of Burt Bacharach. The music of Canadian 'jazzer' Maynard Ferguson was strident, to say the least! He performed with Boyd Raeburn on reeds and then became a high note specialist with Stan Kenton between 1950 and 1953 before forming his own big band in 1957. He was certainly respected by his peers for his technique and versatility but remained (perhaps like Burt himself) more popular with the public than with critics.

On the other hand, fellow Canadian Oscar Peterson performed music that was quiet. Peterson also revelled in a phenomenal technique and was (like Bacharach) rooted in classical music. But, as with Ferguson, to this very day critics are divided about Peterson as a jazz musician. Some do not regard him as an innovator at all. Yet his technical skills appealed to many punters. For example, by the time that Bacharach was listening to Peterson, the latter had long been regarded as a 'popular' (rather than 'jazz') artist in Canada (he was recorded by RCA Canada 1945-9).

This musical apartheid is hardly surprising in jazz circles where opinion and rhetoric often rule the day. But, once again we can see not only a communication divide between the production and the reception of music, but also a more fundamental distinction between critical theory and popular praxis existing around expressions of 'the popular'.

The young Bacharach actually wrote a song while at McGill that was published. It was co-written with a roommate by the name of Don Smith and was entitled 'The Night Plane To Heaven' – which sounds pretty awful. This writer could not trace it and Burt was later to admit that he couldn't even remember how the song actually went, confessing its apparent mediocrity:

> I wrote a song there called 'The Night Plane To Heaven', which was published and then died before it had lived. (Bacharach to Ross, *New Yorker*, 1968)

From this historical distance it is probably worth speculating that Bacharach may well have been bored out of his brains studying at McGill. It is quite evident that any musician of ability who encounters popular music and culture at an early age cannot help but wonder at the excitement of the scene surrounding it (as with bebop). Moreover, this excitement is also inflated when juxtaposed with the often arid environment of a formal music education. It is probably all the more to Burt's credit that he stuck it out. He no doubt realised that a compulsion to follow a career in the music industry of the immediate post-war era necessitated formal musical knowledge.

Burt was eventually to occupy a fascinating, if sometimes precarious, position between several musical worlds and he remained concerned, artistically, with attempting to build musical bridges between these all too often musically discrete spheres. When one considers how very different his music actually was from those others working in the Brill Building (and how African American artists were almost queuing up to sing his songs by 1963), one is tempted to suggest that this formal musical training gave him an advantage of sorts over his peers.

Despite his well-publicised irritation with the entire Brill Building set-up, his formal knowledge of scoring chord extensions must have been of some benefit when dealing with the rigours of the competition and the structures of 8, 12, and 16 bar blues and I, VIm, IV, V turnaround progressions.

This formal musical training certainly helped Burt, in a particularly practical regard. Unlike many of his fellow popular music composers, he remained able to get his musical ideas down on paper in the most inconvenient of places, without recourse to a keyboard or (later) a tape machine. He told John Williamson of the *Glasgow Herald* in 2002:

> It's like the situation if I were hearing something in my head and I couldn't get to a keyboard to check it out I could take a scrap of paper in a hotel or a restaurant and write it out. You learn the rules so that you can kind of break the rules. (Bacharach to Williamson, *Glasgow Herald,* 2002)

But he also admitted that his time spent in the various venues in and around Montreal further weakened his allegiance to classical piano music:

When you're sitting at the piano, you tend to go to what's familiar and you can get trapped by pretty chords. If you get away from the piano and hear the melodic contour as well as the harmonisation in your head [...] you're hearing a long vertical line. (Bacharach to DiMartino, *Mojo,* 1998)

Aside from his degree from McGill, Burt studied at various times at the Mannes School of Music in New York City, the Berkshire Music Centre and the New School for Social Research. He met and studied under composers such as Bohuslav Martinu, Henry Cowell and Darius Milhaud on his academic travels. At Mannes his keyboard talents were recognised and he won a scholarship to the prestigious Music Academy of the West in Santa Barbara. In the long run, Burt still considers his time at these specialised colleges to have been well spent:

I think all the technical study, the solfeggio [sic] and learning how to read music and write it down – it's all helpful. (Bacharach to Williamson, *Glasgow Herald,* 2002)

Quite obviously, to this very day, Burt retains the belief that a formal music education remains of assistance to the popular music songwriter: he has a point. He is hardly the first to realise the potential in bridging some kind of musicological gap for this has been a recurring debate throughout the recent history of popular music (much of it surrounding the likes of Bacharach!). The fact remains that the formally trained Burt Bacharach, not only identified the significance of popular music genres in social and musical terms, he also saw popular music activity as a site where the apparent universal values and associations of European tonal rhetoric could be both utilised and challenged.

However we must be cautious here. Bacharach was not in the business of deconstructing the whole European tradition - far from it, in fact. Let's face it his music does not sound like that of Erik Satie! Instead, he simply refused to fall back on European bourgeoisie art stock generalities and (eventually) offered his music and his training as an example of communicating **through** this divide between popular and classical/avant-garde music theory and practice.

This was not in order to throw the whole thing into a kind of homogenised musical mass, but rather to search for routes of passage between the various points where popular and classic coincide and, conversely, diverge. Written notation, therefore, was a provision to Bacharach, because he saw it as a way for all music to self-reflexively update itself. It was, in a way, a method for unfixing musical relationships, rather than (as is usually the case) cementing them – a kind of anti-structure, if you will. In this respect, his sometime tutor Darius Milhaud was of significant influence; a brief discussion of this French composer is essential, here, to further contextualise the work of Burt Bacharach.

Darius Milhaud

Darius Milhaud was born into a Jewish family in 1892 in the southern French city of Aix-en-Provence. He was trained at the Paris Conservatoire as a violinist and then a composer. After two years in Brazil as secretary to diplomat/poet Paul Claudel he returned to Paris in 1918 and was for a time in the circle of Jean Cocteau and a member of the diverse group of French composers known as 'Les Six' – which included Arthur Honegger (1892-1955), and Francis Poulenc (1899-1963). The lesser known Tailleferre, Durey, and George Auric completed 'Les Six'. Importantly, Milhaud was also a friend and devotee of Erik Satie.

The music of 'Les Six' was very challenging and carried such titles as 'Perpetual Motion', 'The Ox On The Roof', and 'The Bores' and, like Vaughan Williams, Butterworth and Grainger in Britain, they declared war on Wagner and all of his works. Milhaud was extremely prolific as a composer in many different genres and went on to more 'serious' things with his ambitious modernistic opera 'Christophe Colomb' (and Honegger became famous for his tone poem 'Pacific 231', which set out to convey the effect of an American locomotive). Milhaud also wrote music for theatre, opera, ballet and 'incidental' music, in addition to film and radio scores.

Although Bernard Brett and Nicholas Ingman (1972) have argued that works like Debussy's 'Golliwog's Cakewalk' and Stravinsky's 'Piano Rag-Music' and 'Ragtime' suggest that "**academic training got in the way** [my emphasis] and their attempts [at popular music] were never anything but a poor imitation of the real thing" (1972:103), such pieces (in the opinion of this writer) are high quality examples of enduring popular music. Milhaud,

55

too, wrote first-rate popular music. Of particular note is the jazz ballet 'La Creation du Monde', for example.

Darius Milhaud spent the Second World War and the period just after in the USA and it was here that he taught at the New School for Social Research, eventually encountering the young Burt Bacharach. It has been stated that Bacharach's style owes a great deal to Milhaud's eclecticism. When Burt discusses his time with Milhaud he suggests that his risk-taking reflects his mentor:

> I liked Berg and I liked Webern […] I hung out in New York watching Cage and Lou Harrison. I was aware of the angular side of music but I liked tunes too. There were five of us in Milhaud's class and for an exam we had to write a piece and I wrote a sonatina for oboe, violin and piano which had one particular movement that was highly melodic and quite different from what everybody was writing. And I felt ashamed, or should I say self-conscious at having written something that wore its heart on its sleeve so obviously. (Bacharach to Maconie, *Q,* 1996)

Conversely, in the interview above Burt also suggested that his own predilection for melody and commerciality was directly related to Milhaud's influence:

> The important thing I learnt from him [Milhaud] was not being concerned about letting melody shine through. He [Milhaud] told me 'don't ever be worried about something that people can remember, whistle or sing' (Heller, *Pulse*, 1995) […] I learned that and how to eat Mexican food from him. He was a very decent man. (ibid)

If, as I have previously suggested, we might be discussing a school of musical thought (something that may well emerge as an American tradition, despite its roots in Europe), then Burt's time with Darius Milhaud does appear to have been of seminal importance. Milhaud contributed widely to the repertoire of (especially French) song and his work is particularly impressive on the piano. His compositions were often both lively (e.g. the incidental music for Moliere's 'Le Medecin Volant') and attractive (e.g. the 'Pastorale' of 1935 for oboe and bassoon).

In fact, like Bacharach's music, these pieces continue to have a commercial appeal that is difficult to ignore. Milhaud supplied Burt with a musical vocabulary, of that there is little doubt. Whereas Gillespie and Parker's influences were perhaps of the more socio-cultural variety, Darius Milhaud presented Bacharach with a sense of musical possibilities. Burt stated to Stuart Maconie:

> I do voice things in a certain, recognisable way. It may be that I have [...] a more extensive musical vocabulary than some. I just wouldn't be able to write a song in three chords, simple vanilla G majors and that stuff. What, no suspension on the fifth? No seventh? I couldn't do it. (Bacharach to Maconie, *Q*, 1996)

And:

> I mean to get the emotion it has to be generated by somebody. I'm not trying to prove anything as a conductor, or as a pianist. Technically, I'm probably rotten at both. But it's heartfelt [and] it's honest. It's my music. I've got a feeling, you know, I'm not just beating time. I'm free and I don't care what I look like. (Bacharach to Saal, *Newsweek*, 1970)

One could quite imagine Darius Milhaud himself uttering these two observations. Milhaud died in 1974 but his influence and connections between the unusual but melodic work of Satie and the commercial but unusual work of Bacharach is vital in our understanding of the process by which songs such as 'A House Is Not A Home' and 'Alfie' came to be. Dave Brubeck, a fellow student of Bacharach's, commented on Milhaud:

> [Milhaud] didn't impose his style on his students ... he never imposed polytonality or polyrhythms, which is what he was most noted for. But you picked it up being around him and hearing his compositions. (in Heller, *Pulse,* 1995)

Significantly, Milhaud died only a year before Satie's Crystal Ball theory elapsed. Interestingly, Bacharach was also struggling to rediscover his muse at the same time, following the critical failure of *Lost Horizon*. But, before leaving this key authority, let us not confuse style similarities between Darius Milhaud and Burt Bacharach. Robin Hartwell, again:

Bacharach does not sound like Milhaud, of course – and this is significant. So, we must not suggest that influence is so direct (superficial, if you like). Instead, Milhaud is probably a kind of mentor; somebody who was able to give Bacharach encouragement to be himself. (Robin Hartwell, personal interview, 2003)

A composer needs his own language. Having established this language, he can then develop the freedom to be himself. Milhaud helped provide Bacharach with such a language of freedom.

Chapter 4

Army And Beyond

There appears to be some degree of uncertainty about how Burt regarded his own abilities at this early stage. Despite his comments at the above-mentioned Polar Prize 2003, he did not seem to regard himself as a budding avant-garde or concert performer (and his self-confidence seems in some doubt). Yet, in 1950, he was drafted into the army where he served as recital pianist for two years. His assignments included stints as the Governor Island Officer's Club pianist, as a concert recitalist at Fort Dix, and a dance band arranger, prior to his posting to West Germany.

> I was drafted into the army and toured the First Army area billed as a concert pianist, which I was not. (Cumming, 2001:4)

If Burt did harbour ambitions to be a serious concert pianist and/or composer, they certainly wavered during his two years in the army. Despite his 'billing', it seems that Burt was mostly asked to play pop medleys of the day and at other times, merely improvise. In his excellent sleeve notes to the Warner Brothers' *Burt Bacharach Collection*, Alec Cumming even describes this period as one of "playing cocktail piano for Army officers" (ibid).

It all sounds terrible, but one could argue that this constant reworking of material into an ambient stream of semi-consciousness was to later stand him in good stead. By being able to create atmospheric segues out of the most mundane Tin Pan Alley tunes of the day, Burt discovered just how important texture, mood, and feel were to an audience largely disinterested in the actual presence of a musician. Repetition, rotation, layering, and imitation: he was, to all intents and purposes, creating 'live' Muzak.

Furthermore (and perhaps ironically), Bacharach was actually playing what Satie had hinted-at in his 'Musique d'ameublement' from 1920 (and in his many letters and predictions). The kind of environment prevalent in an officer's club called upon musicians to work sympathetically, staying subtle enough not to over do it – effectively creating musical wallpaper.

These days, this appears to some a ghastly prospect (I'm not sure why – personally, I've always loved hotel music). But for Bacharach in Germany one might argue, "it was no longer the musical instrument that mattered so much as the conduits transmitting the tones" (Lanza, 1995:29). For Erik Satie thirty years earlier, this was tantamount to a serious musicological attempt to facilitate the minimal, the ambient:

> You know, there's a need to create furniture music, that is to say, music that would be part of the surrounding noises and that would take them into account. I see it as melodious, as masking the clatter of knives and forks without drowning it completely, without imposing itself. It would fill up awkward silences that occasionally descend on guests. It would spare them the usual banalities. Moreover, it would neutralize the street noises that indiscreetly force themselves into the picture. (Gilmour, 1988: 232)

Burt also latterly worked with a few bands while stationed in West Germany, but, conversely, was regarded by the military as a touring classical musician!

So, perhaps something of a confusing time for Burt but one that led, inadvertently, to his research into the ambient (if any reader doubts this, listen to his later extended orchestral version of 'Wives and Lovers'). Before moving on, a couple of points of clarification about the advantages of 'the lounge' are necessary here.

Firstly, twenty-or-so minutes are a long duration for something new but may not be a long time for a piece of pre-existing music. Secondly: 'sitting down in a concert situation' is a metaphor taken from traditional European art music practice. It usually has little or nothing to do with the process of producing ambient, cocktail bar music, which bypasses the idea of precision composition and practice for the sake of atmosphere. When one also adds his interest in bossa nova (see on), we have surely completed another part of the Bacharach musical equation.

It doesn't sound like Burt was much of a soldier, but he appears to have been a popular figure among his peers. In fact it is from this period in his life that the nickname 'maestro' seems to have emerged. However, Platts records that Bacharach was, for some, a figure of fun:

> [...] often seen conducting an imaginary orchestra in the barracks and, when in a new town, sought out the local concert hall while the other soldiers headed for the bars. Bacharach was eventually recruited to tour army bases and army hospitals across the US, doing a programme he called 'Bach to Bacharach'. (Platts, 2003: 10)

This is an interesting postulation and suggests, as do a few of his childhood reminisces, that Burt was not altogether happy (and perhaps even somewhat atomised). Like all budding musicians, Burt experienced criticism and ridicule for being 'into' something. Music is seldom ever appreciated as a method for negotiating one's cultural identity – at least until it is too late. The adolescent Bacharach went from being a 'swot' to being a 'maestro'. Were these terms of affection? Well, possibly, but more likely conditions of seclusion. It's all a bit 'Freudian', actually. There is nothing like an incongruent super-ego taking music (or, indeed, anything of substance) seriously, for alienating ones comrades.

Post-war Germany was in a state of economic and social reconstruction when Bacharach arrived. The Cold War (and indeed the conflict in Korea – for which Burt was actually enlisted) was also well under way and the entire country was occupied by armed forces from the USA, France, Britain and the Soviet Union in their respective enclaves.

The Americans were heavily dispersed in Southern Germany and it was in Garmisch, near Munich, that the young G.I. Bacharach found himself in charge of entertainments. There was a US Army recreation centre in Garmisch that contained a nightclub exclusively for the forces – the Casa Carioca. In fact, the entire headquarters in Garmisch was constructed along vast proportions, enclosing its own ice rink housed beneath a portable dance floor. The building even had a convertible roof that slid away to reveal the stars during an evening's entertainment – a classy joint, to be sure!

While on duty in West Germany Burt enjoyed a couple of notable experiences. First, he found himself to be stationed close to the village of Bacharach in Bavaria. This moniker was not simply coincidental, for Burt's migrant Jewish grandparents were from that actual village in southern Germany. Secondly (and more importantly) he met a singing soldier with the dog tags: 'Vito Rocco Farnola'; this was singer Vic Damone (b. 12 June 1928).

Damone had already enjoyed considerable success before his stint in the US forces. Milton Berle helped him into cabaret and prior to his National Service he had his own network radio show with CBS in 1948 just as television was beginning to take off across the United States. He recorded for the independent Mercury label from Chicago and enjoyed massive sales with big ballads such as 'I Have But One Heart', 'Again', and a number one record 'You're Breaking My Heart', all in 1949.

By the time of his spell in the army Damone was also appearing in films. He starred with Jane Powell in *Rich, Young and Pretty* in 1951 and appeared in the musical melodrama *The Strip* with Mickey Rooney and Louis Armstrong the same year. By the mid-'50s Damone had signed a lucrative recording deal with Columbia that eventually led to perhaps his most interesting spell of hit recording. Damone received great praise for his fine rendition of Lerner and Loewe's 'On the Street Where You Live' in 1956 – his third gold disc. Frank Sinatra once described Vic as having "the best set of pipes in the business" (ed. Clarke 1990:313). Burt and Damone got along famously and made plans when demobilization loomed.

Once Burt was demobbed in 1952 at the age of 24, he returned to New York City. He and Damone then toured the US cabaret circuit extensively over the next twelve months, with Burt conducting Damone's orchestra and (re)arranging his material. Burt received plaudits for these arrangements. Damone's material was ever popular, of course, but the songs being offered by song pluggers were often weak. Bacharach took it upon himself to strengthen bridges/middle eights and tighten up arrangements by scoring every band part – he was not (and never would be) an improviser by choice.

Bacharach did not work exclusively with Damone. He also played solo restaurant and club gigs and, after leaving Damone, tinkled the ivories and scored for the Ames Brothers, Georgia Gibbs, Polly Bergen, Imogene Coca and Paula Stewart, the latter of whom became his wife in 1953. He enjoyed the experience of touring and playing live. In fact, some years later he even toured US army bases in North Africa (in 1957) as a half-time act for the Harlem Globetrotters basketball team:

> I brought my sneakers because I hoped that Abe Saperstein, the owner, would let me into at least one game. Saperstein used to say to me 'Bacharach, I may have you suit up tonight' and I'd say 'Just one jump shot, Abe, please'. It never happened. (Bacharach to Saal, *Newsweek*, 1970)

His obvious talents as a top-rate arranger and accompanist attracted the attention of a hierarchy of classy solo singers. Georgia Gibbs, for example, had worked in radio and with dance bands led by the likes of Frankie Trambauer and Artie Shaw since the late 1930s and was a consummate trouper. Dubbed 'Her Nibs' by Garry Moore on the Jimmy Durante/Garry Moore radio show, she was renowned for her attention to detail and her exacting standards. These attributes brought her 15 Top 40 hits during the 1950s.

Gibbs fundamentally goes down in history as the vocalist who tapped-into the Black R&B market at a most important synchronic moment in time, covering LaVern Baker and Hank Ballard material and carefully watering down the lyrics in the process. But, in truth, she was much more than this. Bacharach, called upon as a pianist and arranger for her live work, helped her achieve her own self-imposed rigorous standards – no mean feat, it must be said.

The Ames Brothers were a vocal quartet of great renown who enjoyed 23 top 40 hits between 1949 and 1960. They had a distinctive style with precise close harmonies and great skill was required to arrange band parts to accompany their almost telepathic vocal dexterities. While Bacharach was working with the Ames Brothers they were riding on the popularity of hits such as 'Undecided', 'You You You', 'The Man With The Banjo' and 'The Naughty Lady of Shady Lane' (the latter was their only UK chart entry), and the quartet was rewarded with its own TV show in 1955.

By the time Burt Bacharach was working with Polly Bergen, she had just walked out on a very lucrative film studio contract. She headed for New York and appeared in the Broadway revue 'John Murray Anderson's Almanac'. Bacharach was working with her for only a short time on her one-woman cabaret show for she sadly strained her voice and was forced to undergo a painful throat operation. Polly continued with her acting however and became a household name in the USA via innumerable TV and film performances and through her successful business ventures such as Polly Bergen Cosmetics.

Burt confessed some years later to having the 'hots' for Ms Bergen. They worked together on a cruise ship that plied its trade nightly between Washington and Baltimore and Bacharach admitted to Hubert Saal in the same interview (ibid) that he "had a terrific crush on her". Evidently the confessions of a shy and perhaps somewhat retiring man, for the same writer quoted Bergen as stating: "What an accompanist. He knew when I was going to breath before I did" (ibid) – close, Burt, but not quite close enough!

Actress and singer Paula Stewart became the first Mrs Bacharach in 1953 (the couple were divorced in 1959). She was also of a theatrical and cabaret background and starred in numerous Broadway shows with Lucille Ball, Ed Asner, Steve Lawrence, Jerry Orbach and Donald O'Connor. It seems that the pair fulfilled most of the requirements of married life, apart from one important area – that of actually being together for longer than the proverbial 'five minutes'. Both Paula and Burt were motivated characters with careers more important to them than domesticity and children. It was not a marriage to last and they split amicably enough (although one feels that Burt felt a sense of failure). Predictably, there were no children from the nuptials although Paula went on to have a son with Jack Carter. Burt later intimated in a BBC documentary that he was tempted into a career in songwriting as a strategy to save his marriage:

> I thought, […] I'll come home, try to live a married life […]
> write songs! (Bacharach to *BBC: This Is Now*, 1996)

One suspects an element of hesitancy and hovering here.

When most people discuss Imogene Coca they usually mention the name of Sid Caesar in the same breath. From 1949 until 1954 almost everybody who owned a television in the US reserved Saturday nights for the comedic routines of Sid and Imogene. Coca is perhaps most famous for the sketch where she and Caesar mimicked the '1812 Overture', apeing the percussion section of an orchestra performing the Tchaikovsky epic. Woody Allen was to later declare:

> I saw Sid and Imogene at Michael's Pub, a place where I used to play the jazz clarinet, and they were doing a show. [...] They were both dazzling, really hilarious. (www.sidvid.com /imogene)

Imogene traversed the worlds of Broadway and cabaret for many years and Bacharach became her arranger for a short period of time in the mid-1950s.

The point of these brief pen pictures is two-fold. Firstly it is evident that Bacharach was mostly involved in performance of the 'old school' – cabaret clubs, music lounges, holiday resorts, etc and, secondly, he was part of neither the African American inspired rock 'n' roll nor the bebop revolution that swept the United States in the mid-fifties. In fact, one might argue that he missed this revolutionary bus entirely via working constantly as a touring arranger and pianist.

Burt was obviously not working in some kind of cultural/musical 'bell jar' but the material performed by (for example) the Ames Brothers, did not come within even 100 yards of a 'blue note', never mind a twelve bar blues. And, even though Georgia Gibbs did use 12 and 8 bar blues formats, it must be said that her rather anodyne variants were more renowned for replacing minor 7ths with 'vanilla' major chords (and her vocal technique was most certainly not noted for field hollers or flattened sixths!).

It is not without significance, however, that Burt at least began changing tack by 1955/6 – recognising perhaps that the cabaret scene within which he moved was under challenge from new/old genres of Black music. After all, he claimed that bebop was highly influential on him and the worlds of blues, jump blues, and R&B were but a short step away.

Yet Bacharach did not appear overly impressed with the white variants on this music. Like his low opinion of the Tin Pan Alley song pluggers that pestered his cabaret employers, he appears to have had a contempt of rock 'n' roll composition. Perhaps he thought that this apparent mediocrity could be bettered by his own involvement. Perhaps, too, he could also see that cabaret was becoming somewhat marginalized by recorded and published music. Why remain in the 'boondocks' when one can write one's way 'to the top' and into financial security? Hubert Saal:

> It was seeing the songs offered to the Ames Brothers that turned Bacharach to writing his own. [Bacharach:] 'I figured that they were so simple I could turn out four a day. I got an office in the Brill Building in New York and my songs sounded as if I turned out ten a day. It's not so easy to write a simple song. I worked there every day for ten months and never got a song published.' (Saal, *Newsweek*, 1970)

Marlene Dietrich (b. 27/12/01 or 27/12/04)

Although we shall discover that the Brill Building was beginning to loom large in his legend, Burt did not completely 'throw out the baby with the bathwater'. His reputation as an arranger was steadily growing after his time 'on the road' and he sustained this live facet of his career. Most weekends found him working as an accompanist and/or conductor with the likes of Joel Grey, Steve Lawrence or Georgia Gibbs. Movie scoring also interested him; he had certainly developed what one might describe as an awareness of contemporary forms and so a trip out west to make contacts with film studios in Los Angeles was organised. However, the trip did not go exactly according to plan after friend Peter Matz introduced him to the great Marlene Dietrich:

> I was on my way to California to try to learn something about film scoring and maybe get a chance to score a movie. And I got a call from Peter Matz, a friend who conducted for both Dietrich and Noel Coward. Matz was in a bind and asked whether I would consider, like, working with her. I said, shoot, yes, that would be great! I went to see her the next day at the Beverly Hills hotel in one of the villas. She was intimidating [...]. (Bacharach to Hunter, *Us,* 1996)

Initially intimidating, perhaps, but Burt found Dietrich an ideal outlet for his creativity (and for recuperating his ego and emotions following the imminent demise of his first marriage). The two got to know each other well and from 1958 to 1962 Bacharach concentrated a great deal of his energies on the career of the ageing German diva.

As expected, Burt's marriage to Paula Stewart had come to an end that same year – they were simply both careerists with little time for each other - and for the next two years he was at Marlene's side during the Indian summer of her cabaret and concert career. Indeed he was with her when she made a somewhat courageous return to Germany in 1960. He conducted the orchestra for her when she performed at the Titania Palast in Berlin. This was her first stage appearance in the country of her birth since 1929!

Dietrich continued to have an ambiguous, ambivalent (in fact downright confusing), relationship with her homeland. She had emigrated to the United States in 1930 after her triumph in *Der Blaue Engle* (The Blue Angel). She became an American citizen in 1934, resisting all attempts by Hitler's Germany to 'persuade' her to return to the Fatherland. She later stated, no doubt without any sense of false modesty, how much this had distressed her:

> I sometimes wonder if I might have been the one person in the world who could have prevented the war and saved millions of lives [...] it troubles me a lot, and I'll never stop worrying about it. (Dietrich in Hildreth, 1970:140)

Certainly the angst of war encircled her in a very personal way. She stated during the latter stages of WWII:

> Can anyone imagine the conflict one feels when ones own mother is hourly threatened by American bombers, and still one has to hope the Germans will not win this war? (ibid)

Following the end of the conflict, Dietrich was awarded the Medal of Freedom by the US State Department for her contribution to the US war effort, but she continued to be deeply troubled by her schizophrenic nationality. She later reported "while one department of the government was giving me medals, another was suing me for back taxes" (ibid).

By the mid 1950s Dietrich was also in something of a transitional stage. True, she personified many male fantasies of sultry sex appeal but by the time she met Bacharach she had turned 50 and her long film career that began in 1924 with *The Great Baritone* was drawing to a close (indeed she made only a handful of films following her signing of a three-year TV contract with Revlon for $2,000,000 in 1959). She remained popular in Las Vegas cabaret, however, but, by her own admission, her show was well past its sell-by date.

Bacharach was a key influence upon Dietrich, both musically and (apparently) emotionally. They certainly enjoyed a very close relationship. Burt was dedicated to Dietrich and helped to develop her into an extraordinary cabaret talent over the next few years by his own personal encouragement and sensitive and thoughtful arrangements. Dietrich was to later state:

> He used to tell me, just relax and sit back and let the notes come. When you know he is looking after you, you can sit back [...] I can't love him any more than I love him now. He's my teacher, he's my critic, he's my accompanist, he's my arranger, he's my conductor, and I wish I could say he is my composer, but that isn't true. He's everybody's composer. (see *BBC: This Is Now*, 1996)

Marlene was an interesting chanteuse but did not have a great singing voice, as such. However she was able to affect the sensibilities of her audiences with moving deliveries of songs such as 'Time On My Hands', 'Mean To Me', 'Miss Otis Regrets' and 'Das Lied Ist Aus'. Such songs were made even more conspicuous by Burt Bacharach's intentionally subtle scoring. Dietrich loved the arrangements so much that she continued to use Burt's scores well into her dotage. She was later to write:

> [It] was the luckiest break in my professional life, I had dropped into a world about which I knew nothing, and I had suddenly found a teacher. With the force of a volcano erupting, Bacharach reshaped my songs and changed my act into a real show. Later it was to become a first class 'one-woman show'. (Sporto, *Dietrich*, 1988:262)

Burt also conducted for Dietrich whenever she played concerts in England, France, Belgium, Canada and the US. In fact, he continued to work on and off for her for several years, arranging her recordings of 'Where Have All The Flowers Gone?' and her German rendition of 'Kentucky Bluebird'. UK popular music historian Spencer Leigh has stated to this writer that some consider this German version to be the earliest. Certainly, Bacharach adherents Mick Patrick and Malcolm Baumgart, in their liner notes for the Westside Records reissue of Pye's *The Sound Of Bacharach*, also suggest as much by describing Dietrich's 'Kentucky Bluebird' as "her German language original" (Patrick & Baumgart *www.spectropop.com*).

Sex and bisexuality

On matters of relationships with artists such as Dietrich (and Warwick), Bacharach stated in 1996 to *Vanity Fair* with a revealing degree of equanimity that he "never mix [es] the two" (i.e. work and pleasure – at least after his salutary experiences with Paula Stewart). That Marlene loved the young, affable musician remained something of an 'open secret' for years, however. Clues have regularly cropped-up that this was indeed the case. For example, Lillian Ross noted in 1968 on a visit to Bacharach's then apartment on East 61st Street in Manhattan that:

> We looked at framed things on the walls of the apartment. A three-foot square blow-up of a photograph of Dionne Warwick. Three different photographs, signed with varying expressions of affection and esteem, of Marlene Dietrich. (Ross, *New Yorker*, 1968)

However, whether Bacharach returned love in anything other than a platonic manner is of considerable doubt. He has stated many times "she loved me; I loved her" but Marlene was not the kind of person one could or should involve oneself with on an intimate level.

Dietrich was an extremely promiscuous bisexual with a particularly voracious appetite for female lovers. Her sexual exploits remain legendary and one incident illustrates this well. In 1930 Dietrich was returning to Hollywood (and to her mentor Josef von Sternberg, in particular) from Europe on board the S.S. Bremen and was befriended by a young and elegant American couple Jimmy and Bianca Brooks. Bianca fully expected the German star to attempt to seduce her husband. Instead Dietrich made advances to Bianca herself, sending her flowers and lesbian literature. She apparently informed her "In Europe it doesn't matter if you're a man or a woman. We make love with anybody we find attractive." (Sporto, *Dietrich*, 1988:58)

According to Malene Sheppard Skaerved (2003), this behaviour was absolutely typical of Dietrich throughout her long career and speaks volumes about the way she led her life. However, this decadent, 'Weimar'-inspired behaviour frightened rather than attracted the self-absorbed Bacharach.

For Burt, working with Dietrich was the great professional opportunity, to be sure, but it was also a way of overcoming his failed relationship with Paula Stewart (and the age difference between Marlene – 56 - and Burt – 30 - was already considerable). But he does remember his time with Dietrich tenderly and, importantly, with a deep sense of history:

> I think the most amazing time was doing the concert in Israel with her. It was the early '60s, and it was just after the German tour. It was the first time she had gone back to Germany after the war. And we went to Israel after that. She sang in German, which was discouraged. No one was allowed to speak German onstage, no German films. And Marlene sang nine songs in German onstage in Tel Aviv. And it was one of the most emotional experiences ever. The dam broke. Everybody was crying. It was an emotional roller coaster. (Bacharach to Wayne, *Vanity Fair,* 1996)

The reshaped Dietrich show actually opened in Europe on 31 November 1959 at Theatre de L'Etoile in Paris, introduced by another former lover (!) Maurice Chevalier. It was a great success and her new refined style a real hit with Parisians. By the time the tour had reached Germany she had taken 18 curtain calls in Berlin and more in Munich - although she no longer felt that she belonged, stating "The Germans and I do not speak the same language any more" (Sheppard Skaerved, 2003:149).

Giving away a few clues to Dietrich's powerful personality Bacharach also ironically stated to Lillian Ross in 1968 that he travelled "all over with her: Poland, Germany, Italy, Russia. When you went into a country with her, you went in as a conquering army" (Bacharach to Ross, *New Yorker*, 1968).

He also described how Dietrich assuaged her emotional turmoil with affectations for the astrological!

> Any time we flew anywhere, she had the dates checked out. I remember what convinced me [about the validity of astrology] was once we were in Brazil and she wanted to come back earlier, so she called the astrologer in California, and he told her not to take the earlier flight. Later we found out that flight had a crash landing in the Caribbean. That convinced me. (Bacharach to Wayne, *Vanity Fair,* 1996)

Bacharach also conceded to Hubert Saal in 1970 that Marlene was:

> [...] the most generous woman I know. If I had a cold she'd swamp me with Vitamin C. She once pulverised six steaks for their juice to give me energy. She used to wash my shirts. On the first day I met her, I played a song of mine called 'Warm and Tender' and she went to the phone and called Frank Sinatra, who wasn't too interested. 'You'll be sorry' she told him. 'You'll ask him to write for you one day'. (Bacharach to Saal, *Newsweek*, 1970)

And:

> When I arrived in Poland to meet Marlene, she was waiting for me, in a snowstorm, at the airport with this [twelve feet long] scarf, so I'd be warm. I can't wear bizarre clothes. I'd never be able to put on a Nehru jacket. But anything Marlene gave me always felt sensible and right. (Bacharach to Ross, *New Yorker*, 1968)

Dietrich, in turn, penned these liner notes to Burt's first album:

> My respect and my love for the musician Burt Bacharach is matched by my love and respect for the man. No matter how many curtains open and close between me and the audience – his approval is what I am seeking. What happiness to sing to his melodies and orchestrations, which carry me like a magic carpet to the theatres of the world. (Dietrich, 1965)

She was certainly very proud of her young protégé. While he helped, coached and encouraged her, she lived to satisfy him and trusted in him totally. Burt even admits, "She was very possessive of me. She used to say, 'nobody marry you Burt, over my dead body'" (Bacharach to '*Sunday Morning On CBS*', 2002).

This encouragement was not restricted to Bacharach, either. After a salutary experience on the chitlin' circuit in 1963, Dionne Warwick made her first European appearance with Marlene in Paris. Dionne remembers her with great affection and respect:

> She was a fascinating woman. She and Lena Horne are the only two ladies my mother allowed me to refer to as 'momma'. She really treated me like one of her children. She taught me an awful lot and was very instrumental in shaping whatever Dionne Warwick is today. (Warwick to staff writer, *This Is London*, 2002)

Marlene Dietrich lived a very long and extremely active life and passed away on 6 May 1992 in Paris. She not only understood Burt's immense musical talent, but also loved the man dearly, and most certainly foretold of his future success. Burt was to later admit "she probably believed in me more as a writer at the time than I believed in myself" (Bacharach to *Biography Channel*, 2003).

And, sure enough, Frank Sinatra eventually **did** make that telephone call. In fact, Bacharach was to testify to Stan Britt in 1972:

> He'd come to me with the idea of doing an album together [...] I would produce, conduct and do the orchestrations. I've got to say, in retrospect [...] that I really wish we had done it [...] Sinatra has done a couple of our songs and, sadly, I've been let down by what I heard [...] They [Sinatra and the Count Basie Orchestra] did it ['Wives And Lovers'] in four, the explanation being that the Basie band can't play in ¾ time. I can't believe that. Surely they can play a jazz waltz? [...] That song doesn't belong in that tempo and never will. (Bacharach to Britt, *Record Collector*, 1972)

Chapter 5

At The 'Casino Royale'? Brill Building, Hal David

I've got a lot of friends there still, but I can't go into that building. Never [...]. (Bacharach to Saal, *Newsweek*, 1970)

[...] It was like being in the army and dealing with any second lieutenant. Nobody was taking any chances. (Bacharach, see *Library of Congress*)

Tin Pan Alley

According to Spencer Leigh (2000:39), the expression 'Tin Pan Alley' was first used by the songwriter Monroe Rosenfeld in an article in 1899. Rosenfeld was referring to the phenomenon of new music publishers specialising in American popular, rather than 'Old World' Art, music. The founders of Tin Pan Alley publishing such as the Witmark Brothers, Edward B. Marks and Joseph Stern, Maurice Shapiro, Leo Feist, and others were young men who had discovered there was money in the popular song.

This discovery led to an application of entrepreneurial sales techniques, merchandising songs as products as well as aesthetic artefacts, and generally bringing the American music business into line with the spirit of go-getting that abounded at the turn of the century. The Tin Pan Alley men employed song pluggers, whose job it was to inculcate the public with the music. Constant repetition, or 'song plugging' became de rigueur.

Tin Pan Alley's hit making apparatus was fully operational by the beginning of the 20th century and its patterns only really changed as technology dictated. To begin with, its function was to stimulate sheet music sales via live performances. But its machinery soon embraced both mechanical and electrical reproduction i.e. recorded sound and (later) radio, with equal vigour and determination to make a profit. As more publishers went into business and more song pluggers were involved, the production of new material increased, but the shelf life of songs grew shorter. According to Russell Sanjek (1983:11), this life expectancy had been between two to three years in the 1890s, but by WWI that had fallen to less than twelve months.

After a revision of the Copyright Act (1909) copyright protection naturally became an important feature of publishing. By the 1920s the big money was going to performers and music publishers rather than songwriters – unless they happened to own the firm that printed their music (as did Irving Berlin). Societies such as the American Society of Composers, Authors and Publishers (hereafter ASCAP) (1914) and the Music Publishers Protective Association (1917) entered the fray to protect members and collect revenue. In 1923 ASCAP took the commercial radio stations to court over non-payment of royalties for broadcasting. The outcome was decisive for ASCAP – all broadcasters had to pay performance royalties to copyright holders.

By the advent of 'talkies' ASCAP's membership comprised the very best commercial writers in the US. It had become a cartel: enormously profitable and self-perpetuating, effectively controlling all popular music performance and publication the length and breadth of the United States.

The reduced life expectancy of popular music by the 1930s was being 'officially' charted and published on a weekly basis, thus increasing competition for new material in the industry to a fever pitch. Russell Sanjek:

> In two of these, appearing in *Variety* and *Billboard*, the hits were tabulated in alphabetical order. The third – the most widely recognised one, known as 'the sheet' – was printed in Sunday editions of the Enquirer, a New York newspaper and racing form. In it, listed in numerical order of performances obtained, each week's songs were cited in a column garlanded with colourful racetrack jargon, detailing 'the action' on three network owned local stations (WABC, WEAF, and WJZ) from 5:00pm to 1: 00am on weekdays and all day on Sunday. (ibid,18)

Sanjek goes on to state that, although this information was little known among the public at large, the *Your Hit Parade* radio show (see chapter two) offered much the same fare (i.e. the most popular ten songs of the week) and so the lives of the songs were judged by their progress and demise on the programme and on 'the sheet': Tin Pan Alley ruled, it seemed.

Despite this apparent domination, however, at midnight 31 December 1940, all ASCAP music went off the air owing to a dispute over an increase in licence fees for radio performances. In anticipation of such a war, the radio industry (frequently 'at odds' with the publishers) had organised, in 1939, an alternative source of licensing music – Broadcast Music Incorporated (BMI). To be successful, BMI had to find songwriters who had not been admitted to ASCAP but were capable of writing songs good enough for radio broadcasting. ASCAP songwriters knew on which side their bread was buttered and, despite the costly radio ban, stayed with their Society.

However, there were many songwriters of 32 bar love songs who were capable but did not have the backing of Tin Pan Alley and song pluggers. Equally, and perhaps more importantly, there were entire genres of music not represented by ASCAP, including both 'race' and 'hillbilly' music published only on record. These genres were actively sought out by BMI and received airplay (much of it on record), while the ASCAP material was excluded. Thus the domination of Tin Pan Alley was overturned, for the first time ever.

By 1941 ASCAP surrendered the fight over fees and their members' music was once again heard on the radio – their (and Tin Pan Alley's) supremacy resumed. But the mould had been broken. Even though BMI was forced to accept that only a small percentage of their licensed music was to be subsequently heard on the radio in the immediate post-WWII era, they satisfied themselves with the knowledge that they licensed an enormous amount of music (blues, hillbilly, Latin) with growing popularity. The lot of the Black and country music songwriter also improved considerably. The truth of the matter is that no other genres of American music were treated as shabbily as blues and hillbilly up until this radio revolt. To this day, the archiving of many of these recordings from the 1920s and 1930s still remains tricky.

However, when in the late 1940s radio downsized and small players began looking for more parochial and relevant recorded sounds for their younger listeners, such as rhythm & blues and country music, BMI were able to take advantage of this gradual transition in tastes. By the mid-1950s it was evident that one musical tradition was pitched in battle against the other. Spencer Leigh:

> The Brill Building songwriters could write whatever you wanted
> – love ballads, show tunes, sambas, fox-trots and novelties – but

they had difficulties in the mid-1950s in coming to terms with rock 'n' roll. Most of the older songwriters detested the music, [...]. (Leigh, 2000:41)

Leigh goes on to quote Brill Building songwriter Paul Evans thus:

They were disgusted with us. With what we were writing, and the tragedy is that some of us bought into that. They kept telling us that we were garbage - that we would be very lucky if we had a hit, and that no one would ever hear of the songs again. (Evans, ibid)

Radical change was evidently in the air for Tin Pan Alley. But on which side of this battle was Burt Bacharach? True, he was regarded by many within the industry as something of a 'young Turk', but he was also steeped in 32, not 12 and 8 bar songs. He had cut his professional teeth within the ASCAP cartel, not the blues of BMI, and the line in the sand had most definitely been drawn between the two. It would not have escaped Burt's attention that his approach to song writing represented the 'wrong' side. It would have to undergo radical change if it was to influence a younger demographic audience and, by doing so, also make a name for Bacharach.

Of course, little did Burt realise that the debate was fuelled as much by institutionalised racism in the industry as by issues over musical 'quality'. In November 1953 the 'Songwriters of America' a nebulous group of 33 Tin Pan Alley composers had initiated an anti-trust action against BMI. The group included the likes of Arthur Schwartz, Ira Gershwin, Oscar Hammerstein II, and Jack Lawrence. The basic charge was that an illegal combination of BMI, radio and TV broadcasters as well as two record manufacturers had discriminated against the plaintiffs (all ASCAP members) by keeping their music from being recorded and played on the air. They stated that they wished to restore 'good music' to the airwaves.

It was actually not much more than racially motivated 'sour grapes', for representatives of BMI stated that, although the music it licensed dominated the minority taste charts, ASCAP still received 85% of all TV performances and 70% of all radio performances – and three times more income from broadcasters than BMI.

Vance Packard was a best selling researcher and author, and a man claimed in 1958 as some kind of expert on popular culture. At the *Hearings Before the Subcommittee on Communications*, he complained about "the manipulation of American Musical taste" especially surrounding "economically cheap hillbilly music [...] rock and roll [...] and a pallid young man named Elvis Presley". His comments make interesting reading, as does his use of language in the next statement – consider the contexts within which the words 'animal', 'raw', 'savage', and 'lewd' are used:

> [...] rock and roll [...] was inspired by what has been called race music modified to stir the animal instincts in modern teen-agers. Its chief characteristics now are a heavy unrelenting beat and a raw, savage tone. The lyrics tend to be either nonsensical or lewd, or both. Rock and roll might best be summed up as monotony tinged with hysteria. (Packard in Sanjek, 1983:47)

The Brill Building – a site of tension

So, by 1956 the Brill Building, located at 1619 Broadway in the heart of New York's music district, and a name synonymous with Tin Pan Alley, also became symbolic as a site for this battle-royal between **old** and **new** Tin Pan Alley. In doing so, it can be seen to have changed the course of music history. In the music business of the 1930s and 1940s it was coined that Tin Pan Alley was 'always located just across the street from the nearest dollar'. In the case of the Brill Building of the 1950s one could also suggest that it was at the confluence of two distinct streams of socio-cultural thought!

The Brill Building is located along Broadway between 49th and 53rd Streets (its address being 1619 Broadway) and is named after the Brill Brothers whose clothing store was first located in the street level corner. They would later buy the building. After its completion in 1931, the owners were forced by the deepening 1930s Depression to rent space to music publishers, since there were few other takers and, via the help of a hit song, the rent could be at least approximated! The first three publishers to occupy the building were Southern Music, Mills Music and Famous Music, but others such as Irving Caesar Music and Fred Fisher Music soon joined these pioneers. By the beginning of the 1960s, the Brill Building contained 165 music businesses of varying sizes on its 11 floors:

> The Brill Building was a rabbit warren of smoky, airless cubicles
> with just enough room for an upright piano, a desk and a couple
> of chairs if you were lucky. (Fiegel, *The Guardian*, 2000)

One could argue, however, that the 'new' ethos of the Brill actually began across the street at Aldon Music. Aldon was Al Nevins and Don Kirshner and it was the activities of these two entrepreneurs in gathering together many of the great song writing teams of the early 1960s that generated real transformation. Don Kirshner's first experiences of the music industry had been as part of an unsuccessful song writing partnership with the equally unknown Robert Cassotto (who later changed his name and became teenage idol and then renowned crooner Bobby Darin). But Kirshner, however, had a plan.

He decided to take the energy of rock 'n' roll music and re-apply the old-fashioned Tin Pan Alley disciplines of craft, professionalism and time management to the art of marketing hits for a youth market. With new partner Al Nevins, the aforementioned Aldon Music was created to exploit this market. One of his first signings was the songwriting duo of Neil Sedaka and Howard Greenfield. Their song 'Stupid Cupid' provided a hit for Connie Francis in 1958 and Aldon (perhaps rather than Sedaka and Greenfield) were on their way.

Sedaka's ex-girlfriend Carole King was also brought on board on a wage of $75 per week (along with her current boyfriend Gerry Goffin). Goffin and King wrote such hits as 'Will You Still Love Me Tomorrow', 'Take Good Care of My Baby', 'Crying In The Rain', and 'The Locomotion', amongst others. Another of the great producers and writers in the Brill was George (Shadow) Morton. He linked Ellie Greenwich and Jeff Barry together and became a 'svengali'-type figure behind the Shangri-Las.

Kirshner's next coup, on the other hand, was to recruit singer/songwriter Barry Mann – who had already enjoyed a hit in 1961 with 'Who Put The Bomp' - and team him up with Cynthia Weil. This duo produced songs like 'Bless You', 'Uptown' and 'You've Lost That Lovin' Feeling'. Describing conditions in the Brill Building, Barry Mann revealed that:

> Cynthia and I work in a tiny cubicle, with just a piano and a chair
> – no window. We go in every morning and write songs all day. In

the next room Carole and Gerry are doing the same thing, with Neil in the next room after that. Sometimes when we all get to banging pianos, you can't tell who's playing what. (Unnamed author: *www.nostalgiacentral.com/music/brill.htm*)

It has been argued, however, that the images of publisher's booths and songwriters in servitude are greatly exaggerated. For example, Hal David enjoyed the luxury of his own office in the 1950s and " […] if stars were factory made, songs were not: images of publishers' cubicles furnished with pianos and slaves writing music was greatly exaggerated […] Pop music [is now] so fragmented […] that some would wish for an institution that seemed to work for everyone's benefit [!]" (Clarke [ed.], 1990:158).

Our man Bacharach had been using a little space – actually in the Brill Building itself – for quite some time. Famous-Paramount was one of the major employers, enjoying the luxury of office space. They had large workplaces with small cubicles attached, and it was in these piano-stocked booths that Bacharach would hammer away at ideas for songs. Burt had also already enjoyed a couple of those hits that the younger rock 'n' roll writers craved. But, unlike the above-mentioned workplace of his collaborator Hal David, this location was by no means impressive or spacious. In fact, Burt's reading of his own situation does tend to reflect the experiences of Barry Mann. He stated to John Williamson:

It was a smoke-filled room with no view, a window that didn't open, and a beat-up piano. Your typical image of how songwriters wrote in those days. (Bacharach to Williamson, *Glasgow Herald*, 2002)

Of course, the post-WWII Brill Building of the late-1950s was a classic model of US vertical integration. Vertical integration explains how commerce controls every aspect of production – in this case from song construction right through to the promotion and publication, the manufacture of hardware and software, and finally distribution. At the Brill Building one could write a song and make the rounds of the publishers until someone purchased it. One could then move to another floor and get a quick arrangement or lead sheet for $10.

Copies could then be made at the duplications office while one booked an hour at the demo studio and hired a few of the musicians that usually hung around. A demo could be cut – tape or acetate – of the song and one might then hawk it around the building to the various recording companies, publishers, artist managers, freelance A&R people or even the artists themselves – some of whom (like, say, Gene Pitney or Barry Mann) were also songwriters. If a deal was made, there were the ubiquitous radio pluggers plus a variety of hucksters ready, willing and able to sell the record at a commission. Burt was working ostensibly with Famous-Paramount music and they were an integral feature of this system.

Famous was founded in 1928 and to this day they remain one of the top ten music publishers in the United States with over 100,000 music copyrights on their catalogue. That catalogue spans over seven decades and includes music from hit movies and television shows, in addition to popular chart and show songs.

They remain an archetypal example of Brill Building/Tin Pan Alley vertically integrated song publishers, being created by Paramount Pictures predecessor Famous-Lasky Corporation to publish music from its 'talking pictures'. Famous Music's history parallels the development of the American music and film/TV industry. They now publish for example, Eminem, P.O.D, and Linda Perry (Pink) as well as Marvin Hamlisch, Duke Ellington and Dave Grusin, and own the rights to such music as *Star Trek, The Brady Bunch*, and *Titanic*.

Bacharach and the Brill

We have already seen that, by the time Burt Bacharach had rented space in the Brill Building during the summer of 1956 he was dedicated to altering the state of popular music composition:

> [...] I thought jeez, I could write five of them a day. I left the Ames Brothers to go to work on songs. I thought it would be really easy. And I didn't get published for a year. It's much harder than I thought. (Bacharach to Cumming, 2001:4)

There was indeed a role for younger songwriters with an eye on the 45rpm market, but they had to work fast, for the 'Jukebox format' adhered to by many radio stations afforded records an even shorter shelf life than that of the *Your Hit Parade* process. The rise of TV meant that live music radio broadcasting was all-but-abandoned by the major players such as CBS and

NBC and radio became a haven for not only small-time players with local markets, but also personality disc jockeys such as Rufus Thomas and Alan Freed. The growth in the popularity of recordings was thus vouchsafed by the disc jockey, particularly once the unbreakable vinyl record went into mass production in 1955. The cult of personality began to surround the person playing the records, and the records themselves became significant cultural artefacts in their own right.

By the summer of 1956 Burt was working in the Brill Building, ostensibly for Eddie Wolpin, the general manager of Famous Music. He had spent something like a year in his rented office attempting to work on around four songs per day - but he met with plenty of rejections. He was hired by Wolpin on a weekly retainer to write for 'B' movies and 'B' singers! However his first recorded work appeared as early as 1954 when Patti Page recorded a song co-written by Burt with Brill Building cohort Jack Wolf, entitled 'Keep Me In Mind'. It was unremarkable, however, and didn't trouble the chart compilers of the day.

A handful of other songs co-written with Wolf followed including 'How About It' and 'It's Great To Be Young' but they were standard fare – 32 bar songs with little to distinguish them from the hordes of popular music songs that Bacharach so criticised. Burt also collaborated with Wilson Stone (Mel Torme recorded their 'Desperate Hours'), Edward Heyman ('Beauty Isn't Everything' and 'Whispering Campaign') and Sammy Gallup ('My Dreamboat Is Drifting' and 'Uninvited Dream'). But none registered with the public.

A major problem for the ASCAP-style of songwriter was that songs were required to reflect the popular upbeat dances of the day such as the jive. But this did not come naturally to many ASCAP writers. By the late 1940s and early 1950s there appeared a generation of young people who had missed conscription, were unmarried, without responsibilities and did not associate with either the jazz rhythms or stylish balladry that had so entranced their elder brothers and sisters – and they wanted to dance. Writers had to be told to write to a dance beat, they did not do so 'instinctively', as it were – not even Bacharach:

> 'they'll never be able to dance to it', the A&R men would complain. If he would just change a certain idiosyncratic three bar phrase to a more conventional four bars, they told him his song would get recorded. (Platt's, 2003:12)

Bacharach, like his ASCAP 'cohorts' (and unlike later writers such as Sedaka, King and Barry) was **not** actually in the front line of those immediately turned-on by rhythm and blues and rock 'n' roll. He has commented that:

> When rock 'n' roll happened the authorities, the second lieutenants, missed it, [...] the teenagers had better taste. They were right about their music, about its beat and validity. (Bacharach to Saal, *Newsweek*, 1970)

As in the opening lines to this chapter, we have Burt citing those mysterious "second lieutenants" once again - but perhaps he, too, should count himself as part of this loose aggregation. Let's face it: very few Bacharach and David compositions of any era could be in any way considered dance records (and there's nothing wrong with that, of course). Unlike (say) Ahmet Ertegun and Herb Abrahamson over at Atlantic Records, Burt was not really 'hip to the tip'.

It's no coincidence that a few of Hal David's apparent pop songs of the same period (such as 'Sea of Heartbreak', 'My Heart is An Open Book', 'You'll Answer To Me') work far better as country music songs. Country songs do tell a story, of course (ideal re David's muse), but one cannot imagine too many urbanites jiving along to 'Sea Of Heartbreak'.

It appears to some commentators that this phase in Burt's career was beset by musical compromise and Bacharach was to later state about this early period:

> To *Newsweek*: "I listened [to the business men] and ruined some good songs." And to *Pulse*: "I became a producer and arranger out of self-defence. I'd write a song, and the record company would come to my publisher and say, 'we like it, but Burt's gotta change this three bar phrase to four bars. If he changes it, we'll give him so-and-so to record it'. And we wanted the record, so we'd compromise. But they came out terrible". (Bacharach to [i] unaccredited, *Newsweek*; [ii] Heller, *Pulse*, 1995)

But it also has to be understood that Burt's material at this stage was very un-ambitious, musically, in any case, and bears few similarities with his later, far more accomplished work. Musicologist Michael Ancliffe:

It's almost as if somebody else has written this earlier material. It is totally unexceptional and surely bears the trademark of somebody other than Burt Bacharach and/or Hal David. (Michael Ancliffe, personal interview, 2003)

One might argue, therefore, that the single-minded Bacharach might have been just a 'tad' over-eager for a hit recording and happy just to get a song published. If so, then perhaps he was also rather too willing to compromise compositional inventiveness and 'bow' to the opinions of those who apparently 'knew better'. Under these conditions, perhaps it was not the men in suits who were entirely to blame for Burt's minimal success. Bacharach was later to admit:

I did really, really bad in New York. And I wrote – I wrote some very ordinary songs. (Bacharach to *CBS TV*, 2002)

Upon being asked which self-penned song he hated the most, Burt's reply was unequivocal:

Well, songs you wouldn't hear, like 'Peggy's In The Pantry' [Q. 'how does it go?'] […] Oh I wouldn't know it […] a dog is a dog. You know, you try to forget about it. (ibid)

Sherry Parsons recorded 'Peggy's In The Pantry'. An article in the *Phoenix New Times* some years later described the track as "a bizarre Sherry Parsons b-side from 1957 in which a jilted girl threatens to scratch her rival Peggy's eyes out for stealing her date". One would, therefore, have to question whether Burt was even taking his popular music songwriting seriously at this stage. For example, in 1968, he admitted to Lillian Ross:

I'd say everything all started five or six years ago [1962] when I decided to stay put in New York and pursue writing **seriously** [my emphasis]. (Bacharach to Ross, *New Yorker*, 1968)

Like all historical conjunctures, the pop process that was encapsulated in the Brill Building was to paradoxically constrain **and** advance the creative potential of the artist. Perhaps it just needed a little getting used to! This Bacharach quote from 2002 appears to contradict his previous comments:

83

You can be happy and write well, or down and write well. There are no specific experiences necessary to write a song. Often it's best when you're told: 'this is the situation, we need the music in two weeks'. (Bacharach to *Independent On Sunday*, 2002)

Ultimately, of course, it was one such pop authority figure – the aforementioned Eddie Wolpin (never a lover of rock 'n' roll, either!) – who, somewhat fed-up with his young charge's lack of success (and perhaps whinging), suggested that Burt pair-up not with a young, upwardly mobile R&B fan, but instead with an ASCAP lyricist 'of quality' by the name of Hal David.

Hal David

"He's kind and gentle: which is important when you have to stay in a room with him all day!" (Burt Bacharach)

Hal David had already been involved in a number of hit recordings and was a man of the ASCAP school, to be sure (he later became president of ASCAP during his time apart from Burt). David (b. Brooklyn, May 1921) was seven years older than Bacharach but looked **much** older. He was also born the youngest son of Jewish-Austrian immigrants but, unlike Burt, grew up in a household that still held and practiced Jewish beliefs. Music was central to family life and young Hal played the violin. But he had an unquenchable passion for words that could not be ignored.

Upon leaving school Hal had a spell as a journalist with the *New York Post*, while his older brother Mack was already in the process of becoming a successful songwriter who wrote both music and lyrics (some of Mack's songs remain as popular today as they were when first written - for example 'I Don't Care If The Sun Don't Shine' and 'Cherry Pink and Apple Blossom White'). But Mack at first discouraged Hal from entering the music business (based on what he already knew, no doubt!).

It was after a stint in the US Army Entertainment Section that lyric writing once more called the young Hal and, in 1943 on the basis of songs, sketches and lyrics he had written for the Central Pacific Entertainment Section of the Army in Hawaii, he became a member of ASCAP.

I did that for almost three years and it was so exciting that I knew that was really what I wanted to do with my life. Songs create an emotion in people that generally seem to be greater than anything else. So when I came back to New York, I started writing songs and knocking on doors. (David to Fiegel, *The Guardian*, 2000)

He continued his writing after the cessation of hostilities at first with comedic songs in partnership with Roger Adams. They didn't get published, as such, but met with some approval from comedians in and around the New York supper club circuit. After associating with other pop songwriters, Hal and Adams changed musical genres and, consequently, were published. From that moment-on, David concentrated upon writing different, very personal lyrics. In fact, right from the off, David's lyrics were imbued with great subtlety and erudition. Inescapably, he was drawn towards the Brill Building:

The Brill Building became my hangout, [...] there was a restaurant, the Turf, where the writers would gather at lunchtime, where I would go and have lunch. I'd meet a lot of other writers – when I could afford to eat at the Turf. Or else I'd be eating at a hot dog stand or something! (David to Platts, 2003:15)

As an aside, in an interview with writer Spencer Leigh one of the 'new breed' of songwriters, Paul Evans, also validated the importance of The Turf Restaurant; but in addition he pointed towards the important cultural divide in song writing that had appeared by 1959!

There were two restaurants in the Brill Building where the writers hung out. The older ones would be in Dempsey's and the younger ones in The Turf. I was in The Turf when the news about the Big Bopper, Buddy Holly and Ritchie Valens came through. The place cleared out as they were all racing to pianos to write songs about the plane crash. (Evans to Leigh, 2000:43)

By 1945 Hal had penned lyrics for a number of songs and, by the titles alone, they all displayed an interesting pictorial quality – a visualization of the counterbalance of bliss and insecurities of domesticity and urban living that also encrypts much his later works. Early titles include the likes of 'If It's For Me, I'm Not Home', 'You Could Sell Me The Brooklyn Bridge',

'The Lady With The Light In The Harbour' and (interestingly) 'The Sands Of San Jose'. The latter two of these were written with his brother, Mack. Hal David stated in a BBC interview with Spencer Leigh:

> The title is a very important part of the song [...] [It] should have that kind of charisma that steps out of the song and you remember it [...] and I've always liked the word 'blue' [...].
> (David to Leigh, *BBC: On The Beat*, 2001)

However, although many songs bearing Hal's name (alongside Roger Adams, Mack David, Don Rodney, and Arthur Altman), were published in the late 1940s, national success evaded him until 1949.

In 1947 Hal sold his song 'Isn't This Better Than Walking In The Rain?' to bandleader Sammy Kaye. Two years later Hal wrote 'The Four Winds And The Seven Seas' with Don Rodney. This number was also recorded by Sammy Kaye and became a hit not only for Kaye but also Mel Torme, Guy Lombardo, Herb Jeffries, and Vic Damone; over 25 artists in total recorded it. This success placed Hal in the premier league at the Brill Building (and The Turf!) and he soon further enhanced his status by having another brush with the Hit Parade when Frank Sinatra recorded 'American Beauty Rose' co-written with Lee Pockriss – another version, by Eddy Howard, also charted.

This activity galvanised Hal's relationship with Famous Music (by then the Brill Building's most active publisher). Hal also wrote with Leon Carr ('Bell Bottom Blues') and Sherman Edwards while with Famous Music, but in retrospect his 'finest hour' was to dawn at the behest of Eddie Wolpin.

Bacharach and David

We have already seen that Bacharach's arrival at the Brill Building was during an era of great reassessment of his own tastes. On the one hand, he was concerned by the overall low quality of popular song, but on the other he was, rather like the avant-garde peers he so admired such as Stockhausen, Cage and La Monte Young, also reacting against the musical over-complexity of the European art music variety.

However, it must be said that his early work at the Brill did not reflect his interests in either developing the pop song or this 'New Simplicity'. In fact, as previously suggested (by Burt himself: "a dog is a dog") his songs were pedestrian and lodged firmly within that Tin Pan Alley school of writing to which he appeared opposed. The likes of Wolpin and the older brigade at the Brill were obviously authoritative figures with prevailing influence. This suggests that Burt's approach to his task of writing himself into the popular song tradition was initially idealistic, and vague enough to be re-formulated by the cartel. Robin Platts suggests that compromise and ambition were actually high on Burt's agenda:

> When Bacharach first set up his office at the Brill, he was happy just to get a song published. (Platts, 2003:12)

Burt Bacharach and Hal David began writing together almost immediately after Wolpin's introduction – they had to, the boss told them so. They wrote the aforementioned 'Peggy's In The Pantry' for Sherry Parsons, 'The Morning Mail' for the Gallahads (with that irritating trademark whistler), the first truly melancholic Bacharach and David song 'Presents From The Past' - a 'Tennesse Waltz' soundalike recorded by Cathy Carr, together with other early items such as 'Tell The Truth And Shame The Devil' and 'Your Lips Are Warmer'. They actually scored a little success almost immediately by placing two of their songs with Paramount movies. Firstly: the theme for Jerry Lewis' second flick without Dean Martin, *Sad Sack* (the song is performed by Lewis: an awful racket). Secondly: 'I Cry More' which was rather fortunately placed with *Don't Knock the Rock* and performed by Alan Dale (not a rock song, it must be noted).

The relative success of these two Famous-Paramount ditties further fuelled Burt's interest in film composition and led to his aforementioned trip to the West Coast (whereupon he met Dietrich), which symbiotically led to a collaboration with Hal's brother Mack on the hit song that accompanied the teen movie *The Blob*. This cheekily daft filmic exposition actually provided the young Steve McQueen with his first major outing. 1950s film expert Mick O'Toole is correct when he states that *The Blob* is "always in everyone's list of the worst movies of all time – a 'Golden Turkey' if ever there was".

There is little doubt that Burt was financially motivated, here. The allure of Hollywood for any songwriter from the ASCAP 'school' was very real in the 1950s. As is the case today, many hit songs were directly related to movies. But we must be careful not to fall into the rock-ist trap of overly criticising Bacharach for this. In its 'a priori' way of recording things, 'rock-ism' usually suggests that in the mid-'50s there appeared clear and obvious 'authentic' alternatives to conventional show business pathways. But, of course, despite a growing interest in Black music, these routes did not appear 'open' as such, and certainly did not appear profitable (as indeed they were not) in such segregated society.

In 1957 'Warm And Tender', the song pitched at Sinatra by Dietrich, became the first of several Bacharach and Hal David compositions to be recorded by Johnny Mathis. Other early songs from the new team included 'The Night That Heaven Fell' recorded by Tony Bennett, 'I Could Kick Myself', 'The Last Time I Saw My Heart', 'Saturday Night In Tia Juana', and 'Third From The Left' – none of which were at all remarkable in either musical composition or lyrical content.

The better-known 'The Story Of My Life' by country-pop artist Marty Robbins, and crooner Perry Como's 'Magic Moments' were both high US charters early in 1958 ('The Story of My Life' actually peaked at no. 15 in December 1957; this was followed by a respectable no. 27 placing for 'Magic Moments' in 1958). But they too remain Tin Pan Alley period pieces and rarely (if ever) reflect later work musically or lyrically, except (perhaps) in rather over-sentimental songs such as 'Blue On Blue' or in unexceptional items like 'Made In Paris' (perhaps one such soundalike is David's 'My Heart Is An Open Book'). Musicologist Michael Ancliffe informed this writer:

> To these ears, at least, there's very little Bacharach in either of these two tunes. One would not really even recognise them **as** Bacharach tunes. The chords are basic and the progressions mundane; the tempo on both is a kind of 2/4 – I don't hear these tunes as Burt Bacharach pieces, to be honest. Bacharach's genius lies in his arranging as much as composing; these arrangements are not his. (Ancliffe, personal interview, 2003)

In fact Hal David later admitted to Don Heckman of the *Los Angeles Times* "our first two big songs 'The Story of My Life' and 'Magic Moments' didn't exactly break new ground [...] we started out writing 'normal' songs" – he wasn't kidding! Burt Bacharach was to interject knowingly in the same interview "yeah, but it sure was great to finally have a hit" – very revealing, Burt! (David and Bacharach to Heckman, *Los Angeles Times,* 1993)

We have in reality, a classic example of songwriters jumping through hoops to accommodate production values associated with a particular sound. In the case of both 'The Story of My Life' and 'Magic Moments', we ought to credit (if that's the correct word!) producer Mitch Miller for effectively re-writing both songs.

Mitch Miller

Miller began his musical career as an oboe player but had already moved into A&R by the late 1940s with Columbia. It was Miller who was responsible for much of the music that Bacharach had actually criticised. Miller personally guided the recording careers of Guy Mitchell, Rosemary Clooney, Jo Stafford and Frankie Laine and in doing so created a 'Mitch Miller Sound' - something that was both detested and adored in equal quantities throughout the 1950s. His 'style' was to take a piece of popular music writing and splice into it a quasi-military-cum-gang show feel. Eventually he had songwriters working to his own soundscript.

The mind boggles, but apparently, Miller could have had Elvis Presley under his wing. Prior to Elvis' appropriation by RCA Victor, Mitch had telephoned Sun Records' Sam Phillips to enquire about buying-out Presley's contract. Upon hearing the price was $17,500 he said 'no new artist is worth that' and put down the 'phone. What a red-letter day in the history of popular music: we were surely saved from a fate worse than death by Miller's parsimoniousness!

Despite his detestable sound, Mitch Miller certainly 'upped the ante' on production levels in the 1950s. His chorus singing, for example, was brought forward in the mix so far that on (say) 'She Wears Red Feathers' by Guy Mitchell, one might have thought that the entire US First Army was in the background. Well before the Phil Spector 'Wall Of Sound',

Miller's records were the first examples of production-led recordings. It actually made very little difference which artiste sang on the records. The sound and mood was already in the grooves before the singer was over-dubbed. For these reasons, Frank Sinatra unwaveringly loathed his work with Miller in 1950 (and made a conscious change in musical direction as a consequence). It was Sinatra's refusal to record 'Feet Up' that gave Mitchell his first breakthrough hit.

As popular as these artistes were (and remain – Guy Mitchell, for example, became an institution in the UK), this was hardly subtle music making. It was inventive, in that its innovation lay in the creation of a system of instantly recognisable sounds, but it was also a musical template into which the composer had to slot, in an almost mechanical way. Listen closely, for example to the inane whistling on both 'The Story Of My Life' and 'Magic Moments'. This is not a sound created by a composer, but by a producer; it is not an aesthetic invention, but a trademark rubber stamp. Stuart Maconie:

> [...] Marty Robbins' 'The Story of My Life' [is] an uncharacteristically folksy ditty complete with cowpoke whistling, it nevertheless has one thing in common with the scores of Bacharach tunes to follow – [...] as catchy as fleas [...] 'Magic Moments' (more urbane but still whistle enhanced for maximum cutesiness), as sung by the monumentally unstressed Perry Como, resided at number one for eight weeks. (Maconie, *Q*, 1996)

Hal David actually admits that the somewhat regimented approach to song writing and production suggested by Miller had many artistic downs. There was certainly an element of Ford-ism in Miller's approach for songs were literally churned out for him with abandon. But, of course, the fascinating paradox remains: a great deal of wonderful material was also produced under such pressure and songwriters were somehow (perhaps in diametric proportion to their workload) able to hone and nurture their talent – something that is, of course, sadly lacking in today's popular music environment. Hal David discussed the process involved in such factory-style composition with Robin Platts:

> We [David and Bacharach] used to meet every day at Famous Music. I'd come in with some titles and some ideas for songs,

lines. Burt would come in with opening strains of phrases or what might be part of a chorus section. It was like 'show and tell': I'd show him what I had thought of and he'd show me what he had thought of. And whatever seemed to spark the other would be the start of whatever song we started to write that day. I'd write four lines or six lines of a lyric and he'd have a melody and, very often, we'd sit in the room and write the song together – sort of pound it out. I'd be writing lyrics and he'd be writing music and, all of a sudden, we'd have the structure of a song, which we'd keep working on. We didn't write songs so quickly that they were done overnight or that day. I'd take home his melody and he'd take home my lyrics and so, very often, we'd be working on three different songs at one time. (David to Platts, 2003:16)

Hal David appears to look back on this period with a level of composure, but this was quite a timetable! And if an artist was scheduled for recording sessions in any given month then the songwriters had to automatically drop 'creativity' and gear their material directly towards that particular artist. Songs were merely 'vehicles' in management eyes for the persona of the artist or, as in the case of Mitch Miller, the sonic whims of the producers. Once a performer or producer had a sound or a groove and had made an impression upon the pop charts of the day his or her subsequent offerings were very often sound-a-likes of the original hit. Under these circumstances, innovation on the part of the writer/s was difficult, but (as has been suggested) not impossible. Hal David, again:

We'd sit in a room and start with maybe a line that I had, or four bars of Burt's music, and we'd build a song sort of like we were building a house. (David to Fiegal, *The Guardian*, 2000)

The inconsistency inherent in the system is an obvious one. The culture industry markets creativity and, historically, there usually follows a time when creativity, spurred-on in some cases by ideas surrounding aesthetic autonomy, challenges the constraint, the 'sacrificial rubbish'.

By 1959 both Hal David and Burt Bacharach were growing increasingly frustrated at their lack of control over their own songs. This growing dissatisfaction did not really surface until the new decade arrived, but it certainly reflected their dissatisfaction with the 'Mitch Miller experience'.

Ron Baron of *Cash Box* later discussed the legacy of Mitch Miller with Burt during the latter's loss of muse, and paraphrased Burt in a somewhat magnanimous tone:

> Burt Bacharach appreciates the relentless enthusiasm of say a Mitch Miller, where Mitch would always claim 'It's a smash', and even when it wasn't always a smash, Mitch, says Burt, never compromised for something like 'well it might make it'. This kind of conviction is what Burt has adopted whether he's right all of the time or not. It's impossible to be right all of the time. There is a hefty gamble to deciding what music the public is going to like. (Baron, *Cash Box*, 1974)

Wise words, of course, but one cannot help but feel that either Baron was putting words into his mouth or else Burt was being seriously misquoted. To think that Burt's admiration for Miller stretched to 'adopting his conviction' beggars belief. Rather, one might suggest that Baron was interviewing Bacharach at a time (1974) when our man was struggling to recapture the elements of his compositional styles.

Despite enjoying some success with Miller, it was obvious that control over material was always going to be compromised under that 'old guard' way of doing things. Bacharach, in particular, wanted to produce in order to shape his material into something that would not be contained by such restrictive formats:

> There was never an ego thing on my end about being a producer. I didn't care if I got the label credit or not. I just wanted to see the songs done right. I'd been shut out of a few record dates while they sat inside and ruined my song. So what I began doing, whether I was technically 'producing' the date or only arranging it, was to go in and make the record however I wanted to make it, whatever 'producer' was sitting at the console. Everything got done right then and there. You got the vocal on, if not that day then the next night. It wasn't like it is now, where everything is staggered, strings one week, brass the next; you got the record made per se. You went in and executed a whole arrangement, right on the spot. Good or bad or whatever, it was there. And I knew that way it would get done at the tempo I wanted it, and

what didn't work with the arrangement, I could fix immediately. (Almo Productions, *Bacharach and David*, 1978)

Notwithstanding his repeated diatribes against the Brill Building/Tin Pan alley system, this particular period of time between 1957 and 1960 also (ironically) appears to have codified Bacharach's future musical direction. With Miller, perhaps for the first time, he had seen the whole aural package in context (hit records force the songwriter to re-evaluate just about everything, one suspects), and Bacharach could see that the recording rather than the performance could become the work of art. Musicologist Michael Ancliffe:

> The record itself was for Bacharach like a cartouche – like the things we see on the side of pyramids! Within the cartouche are all possible worlds, explanations, experimentations – but they **are** also enclosed by the cartouche. For Bacharach, as I see it, his experimentations in, say, modulation and chord extensions began by appreciating the values (as well as the restrictions) of the cartouche. (Michael Ancliffe, personal interview, 2003)

Certainly, it was clear to those interviewing Bacharach that the recording, rather than the performance, had assumed primary importance. Hubert Saal:

> Bacharach is a new breed in more than musical form. For him the song is only the first step. 'I get a greater kick out of making the record,' he says. For him the record is the song and the ultimate goal. 'You can have a hell of a song,' he says, 'and have it spoiled by a bad arrangement or production.' (Saal, *Newsweek*, 1970)

A magic moment, then?

So despite their obvious weaknesses, these two Mitch Miller-produced songs were of massive importance for Bacharach and David for a number of important reasons. Firstly and most obviously, they hit pay dirt. For example, in the United Kingdom alone, there were four hit versions of 'The Story of My Life' and two hit versions of 'Magic Moments'.

This substantial success, sales-wise, certainly placed both writers in some degree of financial security and, according to Burt, "money means freedom to work on what I want and how I want" (Bacharach to Saal, 1970). Michael Ancliffe comments:

> One cannot really knock a couple of songs like those if they lead to a certain amount of financial and artistic freedom which leads, in turn, to songs like 'Alfie' – I mean, come on, what would you rather have? No 'Magic Moments' and thus no 'Alfie'? – I think not [...] some people love them of course! (Michael Ancliffe, personal interview, 2003)

Secondly, they came to understand at first-hand that echelon systems within the record industry were not to be sniffed-at. Despite a level of compromise, the institutions inherent in the Tin Pan Alley schema (song pluggers, production norms, standardisation) had actually worked for them. Hal David, in any case, had worked within this system for some years already, and was probably less idealistic than the young Bacharach. He also had his career to get on with without Burt who was apt to ramble off on another jaunt with Marlene when the fancy took him. So both men came to employ a certain degree of sobering relativism, one imagines.

 Thirdly, It was quite evident that there was a bright future awaiting those in the record industry who embraced technology. There was a cross-pollenization that could not be ignored and it was quite clear to both Bacharach and David that the record, in itself, was now the art form. Progress awaited those who embraced this (as Ancliffe suggests) 'enclosed environment'.

 Yet, between 1958 and 1961, the two men did not work regularly together. Bacharach's live work with Marlene Dietrich was of paramount importance to him, in any case, and David continued to collaborate only as and when it was possible to do so. These collaborations included a single for Jane Morgan 'With Open Arms', that reached a reputable no. 39, a single with Connie Stevens – 'And This Is Mine', the Four Coins' 'Wendy Wendy' (a no. 72 'hit') and a couple of Drifters b-sides. Bacharach also wrote with Bob Hilliard ('Please Stay' by the Drifters being the pick of the crop) and co-wrote the Shirelles hit 'Baby It's You' with Hal's brother Mack and Barney Williams. Hal, meanwhile, wrote lyrics for such chart hits as Don Gibson's 'Sea Of Heartbreak', 'Johnny Get Angry' by Joannie Sommers and Sarah Vaughan's million-selling 'Broken Hearted Melody'.

Burt recalled of this time:

> It seemed everyone was bouncing around. It was almost incestuous. I'd write with Hal three times a week and then I'd switch off and write with Bob Hilliard in the morning, and then in the afternoon Bob would write with the same composer Hal had just finished with. (Bacharach to Smith in Platts, 2003:19)

Little wonder that this period reeks of musical inconsistency! But Bacharach's model for musical composition was to undergo radical change by the turn of the decade. After the 'normality' of his earlier work, his writing came to absorb a variety of differing influences. Firstly, his work with Marlene Dietrich was proving artistically gainful. Michael Ancliffe:

> [...] Discounting the first couple of years, the classical training, Milhaud, cabaret lounge, etc. all of which do contribute artistically, for me orchestral training is very important [...] getting musicians to play this stuff is hard [...] One has to eventually suggest that the Dietrich 'live' period was formative [...] after all, she wasn't a singer, as such, and scoring, arranging is very important in this respect. It has to be precise, minute, bridge units. It has to be subtle – a chord here, a phrase there without interrupting but enhancing the melody. And no matter how much of a classical education one gets, the practical experience of arranging for and then using those arrangements with an orchestra is the real key. His brilliance is in arrangement as much as composition. If I sit down at a piano I don't just play it I arrange it to how I feel at a particular time. That is what Bacharach does, also. Combination of events, yes, but arranging is very significant and there's a history here, in his work with Dietrich. Being a pianist he could interpret the score, himself with complex chord extensions 'in situ'. (Michael Ancliffe, personal interview, 2003)

Ancliffe's comments are certainly worthy of serious consideration. He suggests that the practical value of arranging tends to lead one into chord and tempo experimentation. By merely bridging musical phrases with extended chords (such as major 9ths and 13ths), one adds a delicate flavour between musical units. Songs are often written in units and remain standard by their construction. For example, an AABA pattern is probably the most common of all conventions (and Bacharach uses convention repeatedly). But each unit can be bridged with a chord or an arpeggio that can imply different moods and textures: evoking an atmosphere, setting a scene. Hal David concurs with Ancliffe's analysis:

> Burt was the musician and the arranger [...] in addition to being a marvellous composer, he's a **very good arranger** [my emphasis]. So, I think that when it came to things musical, I would defer to him more often than not. But in terms of basic feelings about the production, my feelings would get expressed and, very often, would be the direction we'd go. (in Platts, *Discoveries*, 1997)

Suspended chords are especially vital to this kind of bridging exercise and Bacharach appears to have used them with abandon for Dietrich. But they are not over-common in popular music (e.g. listen to the unusual suspension after the sung word 'Alfie' as the song draws to a close). Significantly, in expressing tone colour and voicing, suspensions are drawn from a different musical palette: the rhapsody, for example (but also Debussy and Duke Ellington). The Germanic Dietrich, steeped in Romantic Teutonic Art music from an early age, was naturally at pains to preserve such unique arrangements until she could perform no longer.

Francis Davis, writing in *Atlantic Monthly*, certainly viewed Burt's time with Dietrich as seminal:

> As a young man Bacharach studies with Darius Milhaud – a fact duly noted in most early articles about him, as if to suggest that his greater technical sophistication gave him the edge over other pop songwriters of the early 1960s. I find it of greater relevance that before establishing a clear identity as a songwriter Bacharach served as music director for a number of singers and big-time entertainers, including Marlene Dietrich [...] In addition to his formal training, Bacharach's wealth of practical experience set him apart from most other songwriters of the early 1960s. (Davis, *Atlantic Monthly*, 1997)

He continued:

Many of the flourishes that one might think characterize Bacharach as a songwriter turn out on closer inspection to be evidence of his skill as an orchestrator. Bacharach himself might not see the point of such a distinction; he explained in a recent interview that writing a melody and determining which combinations of instruments go where is often virtually a one-step process for him. This may also explain why he has never seemed very interested in orchestrating other composers' songs. Early in his career Bacharach had a reputation for showing up in the studio when one of his songs was to be recorded and gradually taking over every detail of the production. When he and David began producing Warwick's albums, he sometimes entrusted to others the task of orchestrating and conducting those songs he hadn't written. (ibid)

Richard Carpenter also concurred with the significance of Bacharach as an arranger. He stated quite simply "when you're such a great writer the arrangement tends to be overlooked". (Carpenter to *BBC: This Is Now*, 1996)

Burt's expertise in orchestration actually compels us to consider pop as part a continuum extending into classical music. By the late 1950s, there were more and more musicians such as Burt moving, if not effortlessly, then certainly with a degree of confidence, between one tradition and another. Burt was to later consider it "a paradox to be conducting [Dietrich] in Paris and having the Shirelles number five on the charts". But it was less a paradox and more to do with understanding music as existing within a world of multiple realities.

Chapter 6

Hits, Formulae

"You Guys Write Hits!" (Bacharach to Leiber and Stoller, 1960)

ATLANTIC LABELS IN CO-OP DEAL WITH SPARK FIRM. NEW YORK. NOV 12 1955

Atlantic records this week inked a many-faceted deal with Spark Associates, West Coast writing–publishing–talent–recording combine, consisting of Mike Stoller, Jerry Leiber, and Lester Sill. The Spark group, who operated the Spark label and Quintet music, have deactivated Spark and are turning over all masters to Atlantic. Stoller and Lieber, the song-writing team responsible for a number of hits, including 'Black Denim Trousers', will write and acquire song material to be recorded for Atlantic and its subsidiary labels, which will be published in a new firm, Tiger Music, owned jointly by Spark and Atlantic interests. Last year Stoller, Lieber, and Sill were reported on the verge of a similar deal with Decca, but this never materialized. Their negotiations with Atlantic began several weeks ago, when the latter purchased the Spark master of 'Smokey Joe's Café' by the Robins, which is now doing well on the subsidiary Atco label [...]. (*Billboard*, 1955)

For the apparent paradox mentioned at the foot of the previous chapter to have taken place, Bacharach had to receive sustenance from another diverse musical reality: the rhythm and blues of two of the Brill Building's most senior left-field songwriters, Jerry Leiber and Mike Stoller. Bacharach told Alec Cumming:

The stuff Jerry and Mike wrote for the Coasters was really kinda witty. 'Yakety Yak', 'Charlie Brown' [...] extraordinary. (Bacharach to Cumming, 2001:5)

Cumming is eager to point out that the influence of Leiber and Stoller was far greater than this. Bacharach sought advice from them about songwriting and producing more contemporary recordings. They effectively introduced R&B as a musical vehicle to Bacharach, suggesting that writing within this genre would not only sound contemporary, but also give him an opportunity for compositional experimentation:

> Even more extraordinary, for Burt, was Leiber & Stoller's grace and success in bringing sophistication and orchestral drama to the teenage pop music market. Momentously, it would be the exciting world of R&B that would bring out Burt Bacharach's most inspired musical gifts. (ibid, 5)

While many of Leiber and Stoller's songs were indeed 8, 12 and 16 bar blues, based around I, IV and V progressions on the major scale, the pair were able to show Burt how musical space could be created via a 'three chord trick'. For example, while a song can remain within a (say) 12 bar blues pattern, the chords did not have to stay rooted in the blues, but could be extended.

Lieber and Stoller were also sensitive to the 'floating lyrics' of the blues, where phrases common to hundreds of singers and songs were more effective than any of the self-consciously originated couplets of Tin Pan Alley songwriters. Repetition was championed and blues numbers with familiar hooks and themes had long since been enjoyed within the Black community. Mike and Jerry created songs such as 'Hound Dog' and its 'male' response 'Bear Cat' in a continuation of this tradition: openness, honesty, humour, parochialism, and vernacular were all explored by the pair.

Jerry Leiber and Mike Stoller were younger than Burt but had an impeccable pedigree and were an intrinsic element of the new rhythm and blues-based composing phenomenon. In reference to their work with the Robins/Coasters, they have suitably described their songs as 'playlets':

> With the Robins they made a string of individual morality plays into which they distilled a neat and witty combination of guts and well-observed narrative. (Millar, 1974:11)

Furthermore, numerous Leiber and Stoller songs were precision-made musical items with each phrase or unit bridged by a minor 7th or augmented or diminished chord. Many also incorporated a kind of 'Latin' shuffle ('Searchin', 'Down In Mexico', 'Smokey Joe's Café' for example), strings, and tympani. Practically all of them were beautiful little two-and-a-half minute vignettes. Mike Stoller:

> We didn't teach him [Bacharach] how to write music [...] hardly!
> But he was very curious about the effects and rhythms we used
> and the instruments we used. He adopted those in his recordings.
> (Platts, 2003:19)

Leiber and Stoller also claimed "we don't write songs, we write records" and this statement, alone, is of vital importance to the Burt Bacharach muse. Burt was able to observe these little opuses being conceived, arranged, produced and released right before his eyes. Jerry and Mike were effectively the first fully independent producers (Mitch Miller was salaried with Columbia) and are rightly credited with being responsible for converting recorded R&B into an "art form" (Millar, 1974:11). Significantly, they agreed to teach Burt all they knew about production and record-making, as long as he agreed to let them publish his music – a deal was quickly agreed (Bacharach: "they let me go into the studio and gave me creative control").

Pen pictures

Jerry Leiber was born in Baltimore in 1933 and Mike Stoller followed less than three weeks later in Belle Harbor, New York – both to immigrant Jewish kin. Following WWII the families of both moved to the west coast. The pair met in Los Angeles in 1950 and they were soon sharing their love of R&B.

They began writing songs together and artists such as Amos Milburn, Floyd 'Skeet' Dixon, and Jimmy Witherspoon recorded their early efforts. Their first taste of national success came with 'Hard Times' recorded by Charles Brown. They formed a significant alliance with Johnny Otis, the white bandleader who 'passed for Black'. Otis was also L.A.-based and recorded many R&B hits throughout the 1950s. He also promoted a number of R&B acts including Big Mama Thornton and via this connection Leiber and Stoller wrote 'Hound Dog', perhaps one of the seminal popular music compositions of the 20th century. Thornton's recording topped the R&B charts for 7 weeks in 1953.

They formed the Spark label in that same year and continued to write, developing their narrative 'vignettes'. The Robins recorded the first of these such as 'Smokey Joe's Café, 'Riot in Cell Block 9', and 'Framed'. As we have seen, their label was purchased by New York 'indie', Altantic Records in 1955, the Robins became the Coasters and Leiber and Stoller headed east as independent producers. They moved lock, stock and barrel to New York City and set up an office in (none other than) the Brill Building, producing records in the Brill's own studios.

Each production was carefully administered with sometimes up to 50 takes taking place. They produced tracks such as the Drifters' 'Save The Last Dance For Me' and 'On Broadway' for Atlantic but maintained their independence, working for majors such as Capitol and RCA Victor and newly created 'indies' such as Big Top (the recording outlet for Hill & Range publishers). It was during this time (in 1960 to be precise) that Bacharach became predisposed towards their producing and arranging methods (and also by the high quality of their finished product). Joop Visser:

> With the financial security of his early pop successes he left Marlene Dietrich [n.b. but not completely] and joined a small team of arrangers, songwriters, and producers working with Jerry Leiber and Mike Stoller at Atlantic Records in New York. With Leiber and Stoller's background rooted in rhythm and blues and rock 'n' roll, two forms of music with which Burt had not been associated before, it seemed an unusual step. (Visser, 1996)

Jerry Leiber and Mike Stoller had formed one of the most prolific songwriting teams of the 1950s and additionally had learned their trade as record producers. Their formula was to take their love of R&B and transform it into songs that appealed to a wide audience and, importantly, get airplay on white mainstream radio. This meant that the music had to contain unforgettable melodies, well-conceived lyrics and meticulous production methodologies.

However this also meant that they had to hang on to their blue notes and minor pentatonic scales, for these were the style indicators for a generation of US youth. Before this time, Burt Bacharach obviously knew about blue notes, to be sure, but had seldom, if ever, used them in composition.

101

By seeing and hearing what could be done to a 12, 8 or 16 bar blues we have another very formative stage for Burt Bacharach: the realisation that aesthetic autonomy need not necessarily derive from structural complexity. Burt's bourgeoisie art music values were being deconstructed before his eyes.

Appealing

The prospect, too, of being given a free hand in the entire pop process – a kind of personalised vertical integration, mixed with the horizontality of 'shopping around' – greatly appealed to Bacharach. He could express his 'new simplicity' and evolve songs, words and sound in an organic way. It is from these experiences that Burt was able to select and deselect the significant musical areas that were to boost his compositional strength. He was able to pinpoint phrases and sounds that he could use in his own works. Bacharach was able to sidestep the (sometimes trifling) limitations of the Brill by assimilating information and musical material from the most diverse of sources. Leiber and Stoller were indeed mentors but Burt later stated to Dave DiMartino of *Mojo* that context was vital for them all:

> Jerry Leiber was saying one night that if he had to do it again, he couldn't do it. That was a different time in your life. **That fit the time** [my emphasis]. (Bacharach to DiMartino, *Mojo*, 1998)

Bacharach was a quick learner and typically (and somewhat ironically) spotted something in the young Dionne Warwick in 1962 that the blues-bound Leiber and Stoller evidently did not. Stoller was to later concede: "I didn't think he could make a pop record with a voice as high as that" – the student eventually becomes the teacher and even the greatest of Svengalis slip-up.

Bossa Nova

> I love listening to Brazilian music […] the music is fresh, a little manic and always unpredictable. It's in the blood down there – the sound is so sexy and sensual. I have no idea what they are saying, but it is so romantic that I don't care. (Bacharach to Cowan, *The Times*, 2002)

Conceivably the final part of the Bacharach equation to be put into place prior to his meeting with Dionne Warwick is the musical influence of Latin America – particularly via the genre of Bossa Nova. This influence was not 'Bacharach-exclusive', for many hundreds of thousands of North Americans were turned-on to this genre of music in the late 1950s. However, Bacharach works such as 'The Look Of Love', 'Walk On By', 'Reach Out For Me', 'I'll Never Fall In Love Again', 'This Guy's In Love With You', and 'You'll Never Get To Heaven' (and more besides) have specific musical links with Bossa Nova.

'Bossa Nova' means 'new wave [or] disturbance'. It was a dance rhythm created in the late 1950s in Rio de Janeiro, Brazil as a hybrid of samba, baiao, and US West Coast cool jazz. It swiftly became a highly fashionable music for Brazilian poets, musicians, and activists of European descent. By combining the samba with a light jazz feel, there resulted one of the most difficult popular rhythms for the kit drummer, but a most beguiling one for every one else – including Burt Bacharach.

Joao Gilberto, Antonio Carlos Jobim and Luiz Bonfa were the first to create a fashion in Bossa Nova and the Brazilian movie *Black Orpheus* (*Orfeu Negro*), for which they wrote the soundtrack, became incredibly trendy with the arty bourgeoisie across 'the Americas' and western Europe. The film actually received a Golden Palm at Cannes and an Academy Award for the best foreign film of 1959.

A Carnegie Hall concert in 1962 was especially important for changing the profile of Bossa Nova in the USA, and directly influencing Burt Bacharach. Apart from Gilberto and Jobim, there also appeared Sergio Mendes, Dizzy Gillespie (Burt's hero), Charlie Byrd, and Stan Getz. Burt, naturally, was at the concert.

However, in contrast to this rising popularity, back in Brazil, Bossa Nova was becoming decidedly un-trendy with the young Left after Jobim refused to get involved in the student unrests at that time. This re-focused Bossa Nova in the eyes of many critics, leaving it, as the 1960s began to embrace the 'authenticity' of the US folk revival and 'British' beat music by 1964, in something of a 'lounge-lizard' time warp. This 'inauthentic stance', I believe, (created via a mix of sound sense and vague left-wing politics) was one of the first 'uncool' style indicators of the 1960s and facilitated Bacharach's subsequent uneasy distance from the majority of the growing US and UK underground by the late 1960s (and, ironically, his re-embracement by the post modern youth of the 1990s when 'uncool' re-emerged via 'cheesy' as 'cool'!). Let us briefly examine the sounds of Bossa Nova and how they affect the sound of Bacharach.

Sound

Unlike many Brazilian rhythms that tend to utilize different percussion polyrhythms, Bossa Nova has a single, basic pattern. Also it is worth considering that this single rhythm was first conceived for guitar – what has been described as a 'comping' pattern (a 'comp' is a percussive strum). The basic Bossa Nova is also written in 2/4 rather than 4/4; this, like the blues, leaves space.

The most common articulation type in Bossa Nova is a 'drop 3'. This uses six bass notes with a 4 – 3 – 3 voicing above, placing that voicing in a very relaxing mid-range slot: perfect for accompaniment. The bass notes fall on beats one and three. This is significant for this means that the bass notes are rarely, if ever, syncopated. They usually fall on the 'down' beats of each bar. This forms a base from which the three or four note chords on top can be syncopated. The bass sound has to be warm – the style itself was developed for nylon strung guitars, not steel, and it is not uncommon for bass to be dropped entirely, leaving the guitar to voice this sound.

This is the essence of Bossa Nova accompaniment and is also a major feature of Bacharach's 'Bossa-style' work. There is an interaction between bass notes and syncopated chords but the chords are what we really hear rather than any thumping bass. To an experienced pianist such as Bacharach, this would have been exciting for the isolation of an upper rhythm with added bass note is very similar to the basic left and right handed technique of a pianist - leaving one free to extend.

This also means that Bossa Nova can then play around with extended chords. Such extensions that would greatly appeal to the likes of Bacharach in a progression of turnarounds of a typical Bossa Nova I VI II V variety would be (say) C6/9 A7b13, D9, G7b13. We have the standard progression of C-A-D-G, but greatly enhanced by the extended chords. A flattened 13 (as above) in the bass is not only very idiomatic of Bossa Nova, but also of the work of Burt Bacharach (and yet can sound utterly discordant in other genres).

Finally, Bossa Nova juxtaposes dominant majors with rising minors and this helps stir a mix of optimism with regret. One could even describe this melting pot of emotions as a Burt Bacharach trademark: while an Fm7 vies for attention with a Gmaj7 within a rhythmically upbeat backbeat, we never get anything brash or overly sentimental. Apparently, there is a word for it in Portuguese: *saudade* – meaning hope and sorrow, longing and optimism, all rolled into one. Little wonder, this music caught the ear of our hero. What appeared 'sweet' was in fact delicately nuanced.

Of course it was neither Leiber and Stoller, nor 'Tom' Jobim who wrote 'Make It Easy On Yourself'! Ultimately, Bacharach and David were able to create a symbiotic sense of balance: Bacharach's fine melodic phrases often extending and contouring across several bar lines while David's often strangely long and complex sentences worked note-for-syllable. Bossa Nova 'thought' allowed this precious space to appear in the head of Burt – those long hours spent contemplating in the men's room (see on) were Bossa Nova moments.

Where to next?

One feels that Bacharach's critical and analytical skills, combined with his exceptionally broad knowledge of music (and ambition), render this period 1956-1960 of particular historical (if not musical) significance. The skills of the popular music songwriter lie not only in inspiring listeners through creative, original work, but in a kind of assimilation: an assimilation that, ironically, almost inaudibly inculcates a wide variety of musical styles into common aural parlance.

Ben Watson (1995:23) states that composer Pierre Boulez maintained that musical modernism lagged behind its counterparts in literature and painting because of the [unnecessary] stress on originality and the [ambiguous] emphasis on consistency. These bourgeois art concepts linger even in rock music ('one has to be original, man'). But Burt Bacharach was in the process of constructing his music out of what he was learning, in a kind of collage of musical concepts and socio-cultural circumstances. In this way, his work came to symbolise that turning point between the era of musical modernity and that of postmodernity. Robin Hartwell provides a reinforcement of this claim:

> Though the postmodern piece of music utilizes musical language from the past [in this case blues and bossa nova], it is not with the intention of resurrecting this mode as a living language but rather to represent to the listener the artificiality of the language […]. (Hartwell in Miller, 1993:42)

This comment also contributes to our understanding of why his work was later revived but ironized in the kitsch, postmodern mid-1990s.

Burt's time had not quite arrived but by his paradoxical induction into the Brill processes, his successes and failures, his compromises and self-education, Bacharach was close to assembling all of the ingredients that a composer such as he requires in order to communicate via his art. Assimilation was to turn into re-articulation, reflection into re-presentation: that crucial time was about to dawn for Burt Bacharach.

'Magic Potion': The alchemy begins

> Say no to people. I'm not as hard on myself as I used to be – I'm hard on myself – maybe it's become a recognition that I'm gonna get as close to 100% as I can. (Bacharach to DiMartino, *Mojo*, 1998)

During the period working with Leiber and Stoller, Spark, and Atlantic, Burt teamed up with lyricist Bob Hilliard ("one of the few hipper older guys at the Brill Building" Paul Evans to Leigh, 2001). With Hilliard he wrote such songs as 'Please Stay' and 'Mexican Divorce' for the Drifters, 'The Answer To Everything' (released a little later in 1964) for Dell Shannon, 'Tower of Strength' for Gene McDaniels and 'Any Day Now' for Chuck Jackson. He also collaborated of course with Hal David. 'I Wake Up Crying' became a pop and R&B hit for Gene Chandler, "Make It Easy On Yourself" likewise for Jerry Butler and 'You're' Telling Our Secrets' performed well for Dee Clark.

Up until 1962 Burt was still writing in between his stints with Marlene Dietrich. Theoretically, he was also an eligible bachelor around Manhattan

– an attractive sophisticate who enjoyed the company of many beautiful women – but in truth he had little time for any social life of real substance. His sound was changing and his compositions were moving on apace.

Despite his previous successes, Burt was, in the main, not re-using previous formulae. He and his music had moved away from 32 bar standard patterns and towards the 8, 12 and 16 bar blues adapted by his Brill mentors Jerry Leiber and Mike Stoller. One did not need to look far beneath any pop veneer of that era to discover the influences of R&B, of course, but Burt had become more contemporary by linking his aforementioned influences with the music of Black America.

Even so, his songwriting was still somewhat misaligned. There are undoubtedly some great songs from this period (as the above titles testify) but with the notable exception of 'Make It Easy On Yourself' they do not appear at this stage to benefit from the sublime 'Bacharach-David' musical/lyrical 'stamp'. Despite the quality inherent in some of these songs, there also appears a kind of unresolved struggle between conformity and expression going on. As sturdy as (say) 'Tower of Strength' is, there are structural weaknesses in the compositional style (not to mention the production) that seem to be 'flattering' the 'taste' of the public.

The sound of this record is somewhat frustrating; the collusion between commercial success and compositional excellence is still imbalanced. The basic instrumentation serves the song well but, while the sickly horn line in the Gene McDaniels version makes an indelible mark on the receiver's psyche, it is also at odds with the orchestration and the near-triplet/shuffle rhythm remains unimaginative (and the kettle drum corny).

The track is obviously rush produced: it is too loud, overcooked and lacking in subtlety. It appears to be expressing the *zeitgeist* (the spirit of the times) but is still (at least to these ears) only expressing the spirit of the market – it's rhythm and blues for people who don't like rhythm and blues. Thankfully, we seldom ever hear anything approaching this sound again in Bacharach and David compositions, instead "we hear a poky trumpet or flugel horn in many of his songs where in others of the era we would hear a honking tenor saxophone" (Davis, *Atlantic Review*, 1997).

It is still necessary to state, however, that this musical unevenness (particularly evident in the sax in Frankie Vaughan's UK version!) did not discourage buyers. The innovation that Burt introduced into his work after this period allowed itself to be approached, appreciated and purchased by consumers, but his lesser works were also appealing. The secret of both artistic and commercial success resides in the balance between what is surprising and what is 'well known', between information and formula. While the balance on 'Tower Of Strength' was still not quite right – a little prosaic, in fact - it was still sufficiently entertaining to elicit approving responses from myriad sources.

In due course, however, the synchronicity of the pop industry, that somewhat intangible element that brings disparate threads together - something that Burt has seldom discussed ("the business just sucks": October 2002) - was to encourage him in ways he would never have previously thought possible. As we shall see, if we add one young Black vocalist (Dionne) and one independent label (Scepter) - both with an enthusiasm for experimentation with expression, styles and tone colours - we have the requisite 'magic potion'.

Yet, it must be emphasised that prior to the advent of Dionne Warwick, Burt's writing was (mostly) conditioned by less challenging harmonies, forms, colours, and structures. There were songs based around 'classic' turnaround progressions (I, VIb, IV, V; I, IIIb, IV, V), variations on twelve-bar blues forms, foursquare phrases, simpler arrangements, and diatonic and pentatonic components. Most of the chords roots were based around I, IV, and V with some minor sevenths placed in to add, perhaps, the Leiber and Stoller requirements of a blues tonality, but usually many of Burts songs from this period were essentially diatonic, in the major mode.

This is not to suggest that the masterworks were preceded by musical pap – far from it: only to state that the choices (the freedom!) that Burt craved, were not yet fully available to him. In fact, many of the apparent options that he was able to make were never wholly his own, in any case – as we shall discover re Gene Pitney. In retrospect, these early 1960s works can be viewed with a kind of guarded anticipation.

Looking back, one could even argue that there is something of the sublime in the music industry for diffusing this new Bacharach among us. The industry is still unacademic, yet it is also still unanarchic; it remains in one important sense an industry regulated by ideas and risk-taking (an oxymoron, if ever there was one). In attempting to make music subordinate to itself, it only succeeds in presenting us with compositions that are unreachable, subject to mutation and uncertainty. The great compositions were not yet with us, but the seeds of Bacharach's relative freedom and creative activity were planted at this time. The social and historical conjunctures that gave rise to, say, 'Walk On By', were not quite in place, but they were to be along on the next two buses from Hartford, Connecticut.

Early Dionne

> Someday I want the kind of loyalty among audiences that Ella Fitzgerald has. So if I want to stop for two years or ten years, I could come back and still be Miss Dionne Warwick. (Warwick to staff writers *Newsweek*, 1966)

Not until the arrival of Dionne Warwick did a female vocalist achieve substantial chart success for Burt Bacharach. In the years between Patti Page's rendition of 'Keep Me In Mind' (1954, Burt: "it was awful") and Dionne's sublime 'Don't Make Me Over', at least 16 female vocalists recorded Bacharach tunes. Burt, once again:

> I wasn't having hits yet. I wasn't having any success. A lot of these songs, I couldn't give you the first note. (Bacharach to Dominic, *Phoenix New Times*, 2000)

Only one, Jane Morgan (more famous for 'The Day That The Rains Came' [1958]) got within spitting distance of the US Top Thirty (no. 39) with a rather dull version of 'With Open Arms'. Burt even attempted a record with the difficult Etta James in 1962 ('Waiting For Charlie To Come Home') but it was rather bland and listening now, James sounds somewhat disinterested. Marie Dionne Warwick, however, was a totally different proposition!

Dionne was born in East Orange, New Jersey on December 12, 1941 into "a creative and musical family" (Pead, 1983). Her father Mancel was a chef while her mother, Lee, was a manager, handling the family-based gospel group with whom Dionne came to sing on occasions - the Drinkard Singers.

Her family were devout Methodists and the children Marie Dionne, Delia, and Mancel Jnr. were given a very moralistic, but supportive upbringing. Vocalist Cissie Houston, incidentally, was Dionne's aunt. Mary Smith of *Ebony* quoted Dionne in 1968:

> They have always been 100 percent for me. As long as I'm happy and can earn a decent living, they're happy for me. (Smith, *Ebony*, 1968)

Dionne also formed a gospel trio in 1955 entitled the Gospelaires with her sister Delia (Dee Dee) and a cousin. It was as a consequence of visiting a performance of the Drinkard Singers at the famous Apollo Theatre in Harlem, New York City, that Dionne received her first opportunity to sing on a backing session for saxophonist Sam 'The Man' Taylor (the song was 'Won't You Deliver Me').

From an early age music became the most important thing in Dionne's life and in 1959 she accepted a scholarship to study at the University of Hartford's Hartt College of Music in West Hartford, Connecticut (Dionne was later to admit to *Newsweek* in 1970 "You've practically got to be a music major to sing Bacharach music" [!]).

While attending the Hartt College, Dionne and Dee Dee reformed the Gospelairs with two cousins and during the summer vacation of 1961 became session singers in New York providing backup for many of the biggest Black stars of that era such as Dinah Washington, Brook Benton, and Solomon Burke. They also soon found work accompanying acts such as the Shirelles, Bobby Darin, Garnet Mimms, and Chuck Jackson on recording sessions. Throughout this period (say, 1960-1962) she planned to become a public school music teacher.

The Shirelles and Jackson were signed to the independent Scepter label (Jackson to the Wand subsidiary). By the autumn of 1960 both the Shirelles and the Scepter record label were hot property. The Shirelles had scored an enormous hit for Scepter with Goffin and King's 'Will You Still Love Me Tomorrow' and their popularity meant that the label could fish-around the Brill Building for prospective hit songs to furnish the group.

By 1962 Bacharach and Mack David's 'Baby It's You' had reached number 8 on the US pop charts for the Shirelles. It was all very *ad hoc* with Scepter who, although a significant independent player on the singles charts after their successes, were always spectacularly under-capitalised and working from hand-to-mouth, making demos and recycling backing tracks like they were going out of business (they probably **were** on occasion!).

New Jersey housewife Florence Greenberg created Scepter Records. She had no background in popular music but, via meeting a friend of her husband who worked for publishers Hill & Range, she became hooked. Her first label was named Tiara and it was with this imprint that the Shirelles recorded in 1958. Both the Shirelles and Tiara were sold to Decca and Greenberg began another label, Scepter, with the $4000 proceeds she received from the deal. This was a sound business move - Decca dropped the Shirelles after two flop singles and they were back on board with Greenberg by 1959.

It was this kind of almost 'fly-by-night' approach that kept Scepter in touch with the streets (while symbolising for us the difference between the major and the 'indie' label at this time). The Shirelles did not have immediate success with Scepter, but instead of dropping them *a la* Decca (the band having recorded a further three single misses), Greenberg kept faith and invested in better promotion to hustle the group into the public eye. As such, deejays Jocko Henderson and Murray the K became an integral part of the eventual success of the group.

By the turn of the decade Scepter were both familiar and reasonably successful at the Brill – no mean achievement for an independent. So much so, in fact, that Don Kirshner of Aldon went to them, and not a major, with that aforementioned Goffin and King teenage opera 'Will You Still Love Me Tomorrow'. As a consequence, both the Shirelles and Scepter Records inscribed their names in the chronicle of American popular song. But Scepter session-singer Dionne Warwick was soon to surpass even this sizeable achievement.

Gene Pitney

However, both before and contemporaneous to this momentous meeting between Dionne Warwick and Bacharach and David, the latter two had been experimenting with singer/songwriter Gene Pitney as one of their main vocal conduits. Pitney (b. 17 Feb. 1941 Hartford, Conn.) was an accomplished writer of hits for Rick Nelson, the Crystals, Roy Orbison, and others, but tended to sing the songs of other writers for his own chart successes. Gene Pitney later remarked:

> Every time I came up for a session, I didn't have anything good enough that I had written myself, and I would be choosing from the best songwriters around [including] Bacharach and David – tremendous stuff. I would record their songs and then all of a sudden I would write something good. (in Leigh & Firminger, 2001:182)

By 1962 Pitney had already enjoyed chart success as a vocalist with Tiomkin and Washington's 'A Town Without Pity'. He began a brief but fruitful collaboration with Bacharach and David, and Pitney immediately recognised something different about the pair:

> When I first started recording, Bacharach and David were just another two writers coming around when I had a session. [They] were trying to get a song in. But I could tell right away that they were different from the majority of writers. They had that something about them. (in Platts, 2003:20)

There's nothing in their initial collaboration to suggest this however, for Pitney's first major hit with Burt and Hal came in May 1962 with the rather dismal '(The Man Who Shot) Liberty Valance'. This song is a strange affair that has little to do with Bacharach's developing sound, as such. This is because it was actually written 'to order' for Famous-Paramount for the John Ford-produced film of the same name. However, it was eventually knocked-back by Ford. He was not interested one way or the other in the 'ditty' – simply not wanting a song in his film.

But the Burt/Hal/Gene relationship developed positively (they got on well on a personal level, which was a good sign) and Bacharach's skills at arranging and conducting began to take on the required autonomy (and in doing so became an instrument of change). They were mostly working at Bell Sound at this stage and Pitney recalled how he began to notice the care and attention to detail afforded by Bacharach to the overall sound and scoring. His remarks are informative, indeed:

I can always see Burt conducting the orchestras in Bell Sound. His command was electrifying. The musicians had so much respect that they would be absolutely quiet and do his every bidding [...] any Bacharach session was a great one. The air was always crackling with emotion and creativity. [...] To watch the masters at work while I was singing the vocals was a complete rush that prompted that extra 10 percent out of my performance. To see the string section bowing and Gary Chester wailing away on the drums, and Bucky Pizzerelli playing those great licks on guitar [...] it doesn't get any better than that! (ibid, 21)

Burt concurred, but revealed another significant part of the process to Richard Schlesinger of CBS in 2002:

Those were the moments. They were killer moments. They were tense, they were tough. Limited time, expensive, big orchestra sitting there. I'd get stuck [...] what was wrong? Something wasn't working. And I'd break the band every ten minutes. I'd go into the bathroom – into the men's room at the recording studio, and think and try to hear everything in my head. Nine out of ten times I'd come out of there with a solution. It's strange it worked there, but [...] you go in there and you hear the whole thing in your head. (Bacharach to Schlesinger, 2002)

This is an example of not only faith in the usefulness of the men's room but also in the pop process! And Pitney's comments reveal in moving terms a massively important moment in the Bacharach story. We have a classically trained musician (Bacharach) working in the apparent low art of popular music, but he is invested not with the grandiosity of a genius that accompanies his classical training but with an "emotion and creativity" created by the project itself: thus the very process of recording becomes art (remember Gene and Burt are also describing recording as a **live** experience, here) and this art acquires a kind of centrality in modern culture. This brings into focus not the restrictions, but the values inherent in the Brill (and in the new) – Pitney's therefore quite correct: it seldom gets any better than that!

This is also significant when one takes into account the way studios such as Bell and A&R Recordings operated. They were small, quick-turnover demo studios in NYC who, like Scepter, found themselves competing with major rivals for chart placings. Bacharach-collaborator Phil Ramone broke into the business at this time and later sealed his place in pop history by producing Bacharach, Warwick and Barbra Streisand, among others. He states of these early days:

> In those days, we used to do three-hour sessions, and half an hour overtime was considered a sin. In three hours you were supposed to cut at least four songs [...] as an engineer I was constantly looking at the clock and you had to be able to get a balance in an amazingly short time [...] So the clock often determined what a record would sound like. (in Cunningham, 1998:59)

In this testing but creative environment Gene Pitney enjoyed chart success with an additional three Bacharach and David numbers. Firstly, the somewhat mundane tearjerker 'Only Love Can Break A Heart'; Gene was to later remark:

> In 1962 'Only Love Can Break A Heart' wasn't the kind of song that I would pick to record and it was certainly not like the ones I'd been writing. There seemed to be so little to it, but maybe I write too many words to fit the melody of a song. I listened to the producer and to Burt Bacharach and when they said 'Believe us, this is right for you', I agreed to do it. I was uncomfortable with the record as there were so few words in it and I didn't like promoting it. I kept asking the DJs to play the other side, 'If I Didn't Have A Dime', which was written by Bert Berns. (in Leigh & Firminger, 2001:124)

However, the utterly sublime 'True Love Never Runs Smooth' followed this rather drab effort. This was more like it: a song much more in the Bacharach and David cast, featuring a host of beautifully sequenced major 7ths supported by a truly uplifting Hal David lyric. 'True Love Never Runs Smooth' remains an important early high watermark in Bacharach and David arrangements: notwithstanding 'Make It Easy On Yourself', 'True Love [...]' is perhaps the first major musical indicator of things to come.

There isn't much light and shade in the song, it's true - the extended major chords are free flowing and stirring throughout - but it is nevertheless a song of which one could justifiably be proud. It duly scored well on the US singles charts and reached no. 21 for Pitney in 1963. A song of even greater musical contrast and lyrical dexterity, a song that further codified a very specific Bacharach and David genre, was soon to follow.

'True Love Never Runs Smooth' was a fine effort by anyone's estimation, but it was bettered almost immediately by a legendary popular music exposition: the double-timed, mariachi-trumpeted '24 Hours From Tulsa'. This was a truly potent song featuring a lyric utterly conducive to Bacharach's rich, disturbing melody. A significant comment from Hal David revealed the writing process for this particular miniature rhapsody:

> I wrote that to a melody that Burt wrote and that's what the melody said to me. Music speaks to a lyric writer – or at least it should speak to a lyric writer - and that's what the music said to me. And why it did, I don't know; I don't think I had ever been to Tulsa [...] the sound of 'Tulsa' rang in my ear. (in Platts, *Discoveries*, 1997)

We should not deduce from this comment that Bacharach always presented David with a ready-made melody (for there is no such thing as a typical Bacharach and David process). But Hal David is known for this procedure of listening to Burt's part-melodies and musical ideas first. In fact he is on record as stating that he has to like a melody before even considering writing a lyric:

> The music usually says something and hopefully it will be a title [such as 'Twenty Four Hours From Tulsa'] to start me off. I look as to where the title should fall [...] After that I try to hear what it is saying to me. Then I put my thinking cap on and my imagination goes to work to write the best story I can to that phrase. (in Leigh & Firminger, 2001:183)

In this case, Hal must have absolutely loved the melody line for 'Tulsa', for such voluminous vocabulary of space and place is archetypal Hal David at his best. One can weave an entire cinemographic experience into this song. Both the music and lyrics are sweepingly panoramic and represent the very best facets of American songwriting vocabulary. Musically and lyrically, few songwriters **ever** achieve this level of transcodification (turning sound into images, words into pictures). Perhaps only Jim Webb (in his less self-indulgent songs such as 'By The Time I Get To Phoenix' and 'Galveston') and Randy Newman come close to such brilliance. Gene Pitney:

> Hal is so very important in that twosome. I don't know of anyone else, except maybe Bernie Taupin, who can paint a picture so unique and, a lot of the time, do it with very simple words. 'Only Love Can Break A Heart' and '24 Hours From Tulsa' show this very well. (in Platts, 2003:37)

'Twenty Four Hours From Tulsa' has long been regarded as **the** classic Bacharach and David masterpiece written for Gene Pitney. The song was originally intended as a hit in the 'cowboy' vein as per 'Liberty Valance', but without a movie plot Hal David was required to come up with his own 'film noir'. This he did to great effect, creating a southwestern narrative about a man who succumbs to the charms of a beautiful stranger on his way home. It is a piece of American Gothic *par excellance*. Indeed, one half-expects a kind of 'Natural Born Killers' scenario to develop out of this Gothic rhapsody. Hopefully, one day it might form the basis of a film screenplay in its own right (I will always wonder what, exactly, was playing on that jukebox!).

It is quite evident when we examine the enduring success of this song (now almost 40 years old) that the public does understand what it is getting. We are seldom (if ever) consciously aware of the structural reasons behind why we love 'Tulsa', but, paradoxically, it is the musical structures themselves that call forth our responses - and ultimately turn songs such as 'Tulsa' (but not 'Liberty Valance') into long-term classics.

In 1964 Pitney also recorded another Bacharach and David film-related song, 'The Fool Killer', but it flopped. By this time, the British Invasion had halted his run of singles success in the US. Ironically it was in the UK that he was most revered and more hits followed for him there than in his homeland. Gene also recalls hearing 'Trains and Boats and Planes' that year, but remembers that the song, at least in its demo form, left him cold:

> I'm not sure if I ever turned down a Bacharach and David song, I know Burt played me 'Trains and Boats and Planes' one day after he finished it and I told him that it wasn't very good. Yikes, where was my head that day! (ibid, 22)

Gene has also acknowledged in interviews that the moment when Bacharach and David began having commercial success with the sonic talents of Dionne Warwick, he was aware that his own short-lived but fertile relationship with the two writers was destined to end. But he added an interesting aside that illustrates the ever-present commercial/business component of the music industry (then and now):

> I am sure this was publishing coming to the fore again. I couldn't be the vehicle for their songs if they were to keep the publishing so I was taken out of the Bacharach and David picture [...] Schroeder tried to get the publishing on any song I recorded and Bacharach and David were shrewd enough to know they should keep it if they could. You can lose some great songs that way. (ibid)

This absorbing observation from Pitney sheds a somewhat pragmatic light on the Bacharach/David/Warwick 'epiphany'. By 1962, many of Gene Pitney's songs were published by Aaron Schroeder, 'mogul' of Musicor Records, who had also published Pitney's versions of Bacharach and David's 'Liberty Valance' and 'The Fool Killer'.

Schroeder was "an aggressive publisher who wasn't going to sit on the thing for [...] months (in Leigh and Firminger, 2001:182). He was keen to publish any song that Pitney recorded, but Bacharach and David were suspicious of Schroeder and, in any case, did not wish to lose publishing rights over any of their songs. As a consequence of Schroeder being unable (or Burt and Hal being unwilling) to publish songs that may have been intended for Gene Pitney, the man from Hartford lost-out in a big way (e.g. it has been mooted that 'What The World Needs Now', 'Long After Tonight Is All Over', and 'Trains and Boats and Planes' were all originally intended for Pitney).

No compromise with conceptual innovation, no bypassing of ambiguity; the removal of Brill Building jargon, of course, but no dumbing down of ideas (conceptual complexity can be conveyed in the simplest of musical forms). The rules appear to be transparently simple: but it takes a man of his time (and a musical maestro, to boot) to bring all of these elements together in sublime synchronicity.

Chapter 7

Dionne Again

Bacharach and David enjoyed a great rapport with Gene Pitney, something with which Aaron Schroeder was perhaps less than happy. But it was with another, as yet unknown singer for whom the ideal catalyst was formulated. Pitney was already a star – useful sales-wise - but he enjoyed two successful careers (as singer **and** songwriter) and could not be easily controlled. It was therefore problematic for Burt and Hal dealing with pre-existing peripherals such as publishing, personal management, rushed studio schedules and finance.

One had to be able to use studio-time to nurture and hone material, not rush in and out at the whim of a studio engineer. One needed to link-up with an ambitious yet non-aligned talent, but then be allowed time to 'sprinkle the fairy dust'. The appearance of Dionne Warwick on the scene was obviously a major fillip to the careers of Burt and Hal. She was evidently a disparate talent and visibly the youthful crossover artiste they so needed:

> She had pigtails and dirty white sneakers and she just shone [...]
> our first record was 'Don't Make Me Over' – she had to sing an
> octave and a sixth and did it with her eyes closed. (Bacharach to
> Saal, *Newsweek*, 1970)

By late-summer 1962 Dionne Warwick was working principally (although not exclusively) backing the Drifters. She was actually a very busy young lady. For example, she was also demoing innumerable tracks in and around the Brill for Scepter. One such track, 'It's Love That Really Counts' released as the b-side to the Shirelles 'Stop The Music', began life as a demo disc with lead vocals by Dionne. In fact, so professional was that particular demo, it ended up on her first solo album in 1963! Dionne also fleetingly sang with the Shirelles - deputising for the pregnant Shirley Owens.

In between songwriting, Bacharach had been arranging string and horn sections for the Drifters under the auspices of Leiber and Stoller. He was also collaborating with lyricist Bob Hilliard on songs such as (the somewhat unambitious) 'Mexican Divorce' and (the potentially brilliant)

'Please Stay'. He was also just beginning to work on a triumvirate of child-like oddities (utilising Oriental-style 'fourths') that were to prove highly successful for him over the next twelve months or so: 'Blue On Blue', 'Saturday Sunshine' and 'Me Japanese Boy I Love You'.

Back in February 1961, however, the Drifters had actually recorded 'Please Stay' (a sultry disturbing piece of rhythm & blues, the luminosity of which was only finally revealed by British producer Joe Meek with his techno-arrangement for Liverpool group the Cryin' Shames in 1966). Following the relative success of 'Please Stay', Bacharach was further employed as an arranger for the Drifters' next session, which began with Bacharach and David's own song, 'Loneliness Or Happiness'.

It was at this session that Burt first met Dionne Warwick together with sister Dee Dee and Doris Troy. This meeting has been variously interpreted over the intervening years. For example, Dionne's impression was that Bacharach was somewhat desperate:

> We had been doing a lot of background work with different producers [...] Burt approached me and asked if I'd do some demonstration records of songs he was going to write with a new songwriting partner, whose name happened to be Hal David. (Warwick to Platts, 2003:23)

Burt Bacharach prefers a more A&R-like perception of the encounter, placing himself at the fulcrum:

> She was singing louder than everybody else so I couldn't help noticing her [...] not only was she clearly audible, But Dionne had something. Just the way she carries herself, the way she works. Her flow and feeling for the music – it was there when I first met her. She had, and still has, a kind of elegance, a grace that very few other people have. (Bacharach to Smith, *Ebony*, 1968)

Bacharach connoisseur Robin Platts further quotes both Burt and Hal re this meeting of minds. In the first excerpt, Burt continues to highlight his own agency in the formation of the new alliance:

The group [the Gospelaires] was dynamite but there was something about the way [Dionne] carried herself that made me want to hear her sing by herself. After I did, she started to do our demos. (in Platts, *Discoveries*, 1997)

But Hal David views the meeting from an entirely different perspective, stating that it was Dionne who made the first move; this then, he states, led to a more 'formal' invitation to their office:

She was a background singer on a lot of the [studio recording] dates and **she came to Burt** [my emphasis], wanting to do some demo records for him. He invited her up to Famous Music and she sang for both of us. We both were very impressed and we went in and did a couple of demo songs with her. The first one was 'It's Love That Really Counts' and then we did 'Make It Easy On Yourself'. (ibid)

We can see obvious problems for the historian here! Testimony is an odd thing and, often, our first inclination is to think that somebody is not telling the truth. But this is nonsense. We have here illustrated a classic example of perspective. History gives us little more than perspective – a kind of awareness of what has happened rather than the actual facts. We must always remember this when attempting to pin-down specific moments in popular music history.

To further complicate the issue, somewhat (without denying the significance of the above meeting), Dionne was also present at many Scepter/Wand sessions throughout 1961. For example, Bacharach himself recorded the song 'Move It On The Backbeat' as Burt and the Backbeats for Big Top later that year, and the Backbeats? Well, the Backbeats were the Gospelaires fronted by Dionne Warwick.

Actually, in all spheres of life, from personal relationships to music making, we only interpret our experiences. These interpretations are then turned into a collective memory for all of us, a storehouse through which we develop a sense of identity. But even though our identity with the apparent past experiences of pop stars might be of vital importance to us, we must at all times acknowledge that these memories are affected not only by the passage of time (e.g. Warwick's more recent interpretations of past events have also been unfairly criticised because of her involvement in the Psychic Friends Network, and their successful series of 'infomercials' on US TV), but also by multivalent contemporaneous perspectives on the 'one event'. Whatever the 'correct' sequence of events, Warwick signed with Bacharach and David and in turn they signed to Scepter Records.

Did someone say alchemy?

Bacharach and David did not work exclusively with Dionne but one of the first songs to actually sound like a Bacharach and David song ('Make It Easy on Yourself') was demo-ed by Warwick before the hit 'Don't Make Me Over' and one cannot but help feel that the musical matrix was forged by this demo, not the first single release.

'Make It Easy On Yourself' is a very complex song and unlike most previous Bacharach compositions. It is a two-part song that begins with the chorus in a deeply modal minor key. The hook, however ('Breaking Up [...]') moves between major 7th and 13ths. So we have a constant on-going juxtaposition of tone colours between mood enhancing minor tonalities and uplifting extended piano chords; the refrain ('Make It [...]') uses almost one chord per syllable, and requires 5 grace notes on the word 'self', alone. It's only simplicity lies in its time signature, which remains on four. All in all, this is a very difficult song to sing – particularly for a 21-year old female student (both Jerry Butler and Scott Walker's renditions are characteristically baritone)!

Dionne was to later state that what is usually regarded as her breakthrough single 'Don't Make Me Over' was created via her disgust at losing-out to Jerry Butler over 'Make It Easy On Yourself':

> It came about because of a sort of fight I had with Hal and Burt [...] I felt Burt and Hal had given my song away and they felt they hadn't and that maybe I was being a bit unreasonable. Well, one word led to another [...] and finally I said 'don't make me over, man!' and I walked out. About a week later I walked back in. The mad was gone – and they had written the song. (Platts, *Discoveries,* 1997)

121

Hal David was to later relate to Peter Paphides of *Time Out*:

> Ha ha! I've heard Dionne tell that story. I don't remember it
> that way, but it may well be true! (David to Paphides, *Time Out*,
> 1999)

Whatever the accuracy of the story it does at least illustrate that the 21-year old Warwick was confident (nay, precocious) enough to presume that 'Make It Easy On Yourself' would be her commercial debut. In actual fact, it was not really Burt or Hal's fault that the song went to Butler. Eddie Wolpin, the aforementioned executive at Famous, took Dionne's demo to Jimmy Bracken of Vee Jay Records in Chicago. It was the label's A&R man that placed the song with Butler – looking for something to follow up the 'Iceman's' mainstream crossover hit 'Moon River'. Bacharach's demo was used as the backing track – somewhat inadvertently this became the first entire Bacharach record production to be released.

Hal David recalled that Dionne was "much perturbed because she thought that was her song". Yet, by angrily informing them 'don't make me over, man' (slang for 'don't lie to me') her vitriol was organically transformed into a song in its own right, and this, instead, became her breakthrough top 40 hit at the end of 1962. By January 1963 it had reached number 21 on the US chart (but failed to make an impact when released in the UK in February 1963, receiving precious little airplay).

The session for this significant song took place on August 18 1962 at Bell Sound in mid-Manhattan. Warwick already had copious amounts of studio experience with the Gospelaires and took to the session very easily. She was indeed a precocious talent and later recalled that she "was quite accustomed to the studio, the only difference being that I was in the lead vocal booth, while everybody else was in the other booth" (Platts 2003:26). The three tracks produced that day, engineered by Eddie Smith, were 'I Smiled Yesterday', 'Unlucky', and 'Don't Make Me Over'.

'Don't Make Me Over' is a typically testing Bacharach melody. Apart from its varying meter, the song tests the singer to the fullest via its difficult intervals. For example, between verse and bridge the vocalist is obliged to move up almost two full octaves (actually an octave and a sixth). This creates a dramatic musical moment, contrasting the subdued irritation of the verse lyric with the shattering censure of the chorus (used again on the fade-out this achieves *cadenza*-like status). Warwick, of course, pulls it all off with great assurance.

During this period Dionne continued to sing on Bacharach and David sessions in a practically full-time capacity. One of these actually achieved some level of success at the same time as her hit. She backed Timi Yuro on 'The Love of a Boy' late summer of 1962. This reached the number 44 position on the US singles charts later that same year. It's not a great song but it is certainly made more palatable by Warwick's backing. The song was already known to Dionne, in any case, for it was her voice on the original demo (this later became the b-side to 'Anyone Who Had A Heart')

Burt was a noted figure in the business by this time, but Dionne did not appear to care too much about metaphorical forelock touching. In fact, it is interesting to note that, according to Mike Callaghan and David Edwards in the *Scepter/Wand Story* (1999:5), Bacharach was still looking for that really 'big break'. Dionne, it seems, understood this from the outset. Thus, she was undoubtedly unwilling to countenance any potential pomposity with obsequiousness.

Having stumbled across his 'motherlode' Burt, too, was more than willing to put up with a youthful musical savant to get what he wanted – musical autonomy – and so the relationship began and duly prospered. Importantly, too, Callaghan and Edwards flag-up Scepter Records as a significant link in the chain:

> By late 1962, Scepter was well on the way to becoming a label with one artist of note on each [subsidiary] (the Shirelles on Scepter and Chuck Jackson on Wand), much like countless other labels which hit lucky then fade. But then they happened upon Dionne Warwick. Burt Bacharach, a bandleader and songwriter who had only moderate success to that point, had been working with Scepter for some time [...].

123

Hardly a 'bandleader' (!) but most certainly Burt Bacharach was embarking upon a new phase of his career. The session with Dionne singing 'Make It Easy On Yourself' must have been incredibly inspirational for all concerned. But one feels that little of this would have been possible without the chaotic independence of Scepter Records. One man in particular had already impressed Florence Greenberg by his loyalty yet semi-independence. Luther Dixon was a model of 'dutiful friendship' and a template for Bacharach's creative relationship with Scepter over the forthcoming years. His part in this complex play probably assisted Burts' triumph far more than Bacharach could ever have realised.

Luther Dixon

Bacharach's association with Dionne Warwick also led to a very fruitful relationship for Burt with Luther Dixon, a fellow songwriter, who was head of A&R for the Scepter label. Dixon remains an important link in the Bacharach/Brill Building/Scepter Records chain.

While promoting the Shirelles, Scepter boss Florence Greenberg hired one Wally Roker to assist her in promotional duties. It was Roker who introduced Florence to Luther Dixon when they happened to occupy the same elevator. Dixon already had something of a track record as a songwriter and producer. He had written and produced for the Platters, Perry Como, Pat Boone and the Crests - 'Sixteen Candles' was all his own work. Florence asked him if he would be interested in working with the Shirelles and he jumped at the chance.

Several meetings later, Florence was so impressed by the young Dixon that she offered him a financial package with Scepter that allowed him both independence and responsibility. He became an A&R man for the company while, at the same time being allowed his own publishing outlet – Ludix Music. This nonalignment and dependability resulted in some fascinating versions of Bacharach/David songs by Black acts such as Tommy Hunt and Big Maybelle (who both recorded 'I Just Don't Know What To Do With Myself' for the R&B market), Chuck Jackson ('The Breaking Point'), and Maxine Brown ('I Cry Alone').

Following Jerry Butler's Vee Jay success with 'Make It Easy On Yourself' in 1962, other Chicago soul acts such as Dee Clark and Gene Chandler also beat a path to Luther Dixon's door. Dixon was able to recycle the Bacharach and David songs with a variety of artists and labels using the original backing tracks. Lou Johnson, for example was signed to Big Top and their publishing company Hill & Range were also resident in the Brill – and they came to see Dixon.

 By hooking-up with Dixon, Johnson was able to voice-over the Scepter demo backing tracks for 'Reach Out For Me', and 'Message To Martha'. This also happened with the Isley Brothers' version of 'Make It Easy On Yourself', Chuck Jackson's version of 'Lover' (carelessly with Tommy Hunt's original vocal still present!) and Maxine Brown's taped vocal over the Dionne Warwick album track 'I Cry Alone'.

 With the assistance of Warwick, Dixon, and Greenberg Burt had finally succeeded in removing the cement from Brill Building musical form and function. He was free to explore a genre of music entirely of his own creation. This style existed within standardised forms, but expressed far more owing to its adventurous extensions of single sounds or sets of sounds. A relationship between different aspects of these sounds via the voice of Dionne Warwick, instruments such as piano and flugel horn, and his own scoring was created. Yet the 'whistle test' could also still be applied successfully to all of Burt's compositions. But next to this simplicity could be added complexity.

That voice

According to legend, Scepter boss Florence Greenberg enthused about Dionne's voice so much that Bacharach was actually rather miffed. It has been said by some that he and Hal David had hoped to spark Greenberg's interest in the song, not the voice. But this is probably unfair. Burt by this time had no need to prostrate himself in front of the likes of Florence Greenberg to sell an idea (and, in any case, she was not the 'run-of-the-mill' record executive). Song or voice was not an issue: Burt and Hal had come up with something special and Greenberg was wise enough to give them their head. After all, it didn't take an Aaron Copland to realise that Dionne was the perfect vehicle to express both her own and Bacharach's creativity.

Scepter Records signed Bacharach, lyricist Hal David **and** Dionne Warwick to a song writing and recording contract in 1962. This relationship with Scepter was unique for its day. Spurred-on by the successful semi-autonomy of Luther Dixon, Greenberg allowed Bacharach and David total artistic freedom over Warwick's recordings. All, it seems, that Florence wanted (as a kind of rider) were those demo backing tracks.

So, it was quite evident to all concerned that Dionne had the kind of voice that was stylistic, nuanced and persuasive. Bacharach was to later attempt to describe the indescribable by informing *Newsweek* that Warwick's sound "had a delicacy and mystery of sailing ships in bottles. It's tremendously inspiring. We cut songs for her like fine cloth, tailor-made" (Bacharach to staff writers, *Newsweek* 1966). Wow! But one can appreciate Burt's problem, here – music has its own discourse, not always well served by linguistics!

Phil Hardy and Dave Laing [eds.] illustrate this Warwick-Bacharach-David alchemy perhaps a little better!

> Warwick provided the light, lithe voice, David the literate, witty lyrics and Bacharach the imaginative melodies, unusual arrangements and complex rhythms that few singers other than Warwick could have managed: on 'Anyone Who Had a Heart', for example, she deftly weaves into and through 5/4 to 4/4 to 7/8. (Hardy & Laing [eds.], 1992:40)

And Dionne was to later confirm:

> When I first started working with Bacharach and David, they were the songwriters and I was the interpreter. Any of the producers I've worked with since has had to take a similar method. (in O'Brien, 1995:90)

Historically, the great thing about this "light, lithe voice" was that its appeal easily crossed racial barriers. It has been stated that Warwick was to the 1960s what Nat King Cole had been to the 1950s – a mainstream performer who happened to be Black.

Right from the start, it was quite evident that neither Dionne nor her material fitted the artistic template (or stereotype) of African American R&B. For example, following the success of 'Don't Make Me Over' Dionne was placed on an R&B tour in 1963 that included the Impressions. Curtis Mayfield was to recall:

> It [i.e. 'Don't Make Me Over'] was a fantastic hit in the North [but] she was put on the tour when we were touring the South. Hers was a very light type style compared to what [the Southern audience was] getting' down with. And it hurt me so. She came out to do 'Don't Make Me Over' and they would just not accept the music. I remember Dionne crying and everybody letting her know 'hey don't worry about it, you're gonna reach the sky' and of course she did. But the music was so different for those times and those areas. (Mayfield to Heller, *Pulse*, 1995)

These are revealing comments from one of the great soul music composers. There is the indication, here, of a kind of erudition displayed by Dionne somewhat lost on a young audience wanting to dance (as previously suggested there are very few danceable Bacharach songs but there **was** a sizeable dance craze in the US prior to the advent of the Beatles in 1964). As such, the interpretation of Dionne's performance by those Southern Black R&B fans, that so reduced Dionne to tears, was historically very significant. Bacharach, David, and Warwick were evidently giving the public new things to hear.

Dionne Warwick was clearly no 'chitlin' circuit vocalist belting out the latest dance-craze numbers; Bacharach was no longer generating a kind of core product, either. As far as Dionne was concerned, none of the usual Brill Building postulations were working. This was because the work of Bacharach, David and Warwick was no longer part of that 'universal language' of early '60s Brill R&B/pop – the catalyst, the 'magic potion' had moved the musical experiment on apace. Dionne was to presently remark:

> Nobody really understood or knew how to categorize it [...] R&B stations were not really playing my music [...] we were so different musically from anything that was being recorded [...] we kind of carved our own little niche out [...] I was 'colourless'. (www.dionnewarwick.com/Bio.html)

It would be some time before comrades-in-song Goffin and King, and Barry and Greenwich became equally experimental in musical terms. For them it was an enforced survive-or-die stratagem in the wake of the 1964 British Invasion. Burt had pre-empted them.

Perhaps, by 1963 the greatest difference between the songs of Bacharach and those of the Brill cohort was the fact that Burt's numbers could be literally categorised as musical 'works'. The source of the growing Bacharach phenomenon was the record (not the live performance, as such). The record, as the end product, was in itself transcendent. In effect it did not really need a live performance to back it up. Burt's recordings, like those of Phil Spector perhaps, had become 'works' (of art) in their own right. They were self-regulating, and there was absolutely no reason why the recording of (say) 'Don't Make Me Over' or 'Walk On By' should ever have to refer to anything other than itself (including a live R&B show).

Dionne's tour was success measured by failure: another synchronic event tied to the diachronic threads that had been pulling together for the threesome for some time. The unfavourable reception of Dionne's performance happened because the music of one time and place failed to satisfy the needs of another time and place. From these perspectives of composition, performance, and reception we can see that Bacharach's songs could not be aimed at certain modes of reception – they were no longer standard Brill items in the same way that (say) 'Tower of Strength', 'Any Day Now' or 'Baby It's You' had been. Francis Davis:

> Bacharach and David's hits [...] were anomalies in their own day – bridges across the generational divide, built by men born in the 1920s [...] Writers of early feature stories on Bacharach marvelled that his songs achieved great popularity despite offering nothing that the man on the street could easily whistle. A more justifiable complaint would have been about Bacharach's failure to give dancers much of a toehold: [...]. (Davis, *Atlantic Monthly*, 1997)

Concerning 'Don't Make Me Over', he details:

> To that day's teenagers it was simply another 'slow' song: a dreamy record of the sort that a TV dance show host might

designate a ladies' choice. In retrospect it seems one of the most innovative songs of the early sixties, if only for the way its meter fluctuates between 12/8 and 6/8 (each an uncommon time signature in pop) and for the way Bacharach's orchestration spaces Warwick and the background singers so far apart. (ibid)

'Don't Make Me Over' was reviewed in *Cash Box* on October 20 1962. Reviewers used a grading system at that time and the song was awarded only a B+. The reviewer went on to say " [...] this distinctive deck could really go places" he/she called it "a strong ballad". So, it didn't get an A. Perhaps it was explicit that the song and performer had great potential, but implicit that it was somewhat limited in appeal as far as (Black) teenagers were concerned. One can only speculate, really.

In any case, Dionne soon made her European debut performance at the Olympia Theatre in Paris in 1963 – introduced by none other than Marlene Dietrich. This was more like the kind of venue innate for both Dionne and the music. If this 'new/old' music was a link between the ASCAP and the pop worlds, then the venues had to reflect this (and, of course, any great insurrection has to start from within, not out with, the system).

During 1963 Bacharach also worked with vocalist Lou Johnson who charted with 'Reach Out For Me'. But this success was diminutive (no.74) in comparison to his work with Dionne. Although Johnson's versions of Bacharach compositions were quality pieces of work, he failed to make an impact as a kind of 'male Dionne Warwick' (the backing tracks were, well, rather familiar). Lightning does not strike twice – especially when working with backing tracks.

So, towards the end of 1963 Burt decided to concentrate most of his energies into three specific areas: writing with Hal David alone, working with Dionne Warwick as a recording artiste as much as possible, and sporadically releasing a few of his own recordings (having signed a personal deal with Kapp during the summer of 1963). There was no longer a need to 'hustle' tracks, as such. Florence Greenberg and Luther Dixon were recycling backing tracks like nobody's business and artists were literally queuing up to sing Bacharach and David songs.

'This Empty Place': a happy time for Burt, then?

One never really knows. There is no evidence of a romantic relationship between Burt and Dionne, although a certain amount of folklore exists about their bond generally. Leiber and Stoller are on record as suggesting that when Burt first mentioned to them that he 'wanted' Dionne, they understood him to mean in the 'biblical' sense! (Stoller states in a *Biography Channel* interview (2003) that he informed Burt in no uncertain terms that such desires were illegal – Dionne was too young). But this probably has more to say about Leiber and Stoller's social circle than it does about Bacharach's sexual persuasions.

In the same programme singer Steve Lawrence also suggests that Bacharach was one for the strip clubs, persuading him (Lawrence) on more than one occasion to go into a club 'for research purposes'. But Bacharach was possessed by music, not sex, and it is certainly not so outrageous to suggest that he wanted to listen to the live music (as indeed he volunteered to Lawrence). Via this kind of rhetorical 'evidence' we can only speculate about this attractive and wealthy heterosexual's personal life. But one could suggest that his music gives us ample food for thought; for example, Burt was no anti-hero.

Bacharach's music of 1961-1963 is often expressive of loneliness, of optimism, of atomisation but, also of aspiration. The unassuming Hal David created lyrics to echo this: discussing love, separation, home life and devotion – all of the things that Burt had experienced in one form or another, but things from which he had also distanced himself in search of his musical vision.

Both music and lyrics are very revealing of Bacharach's personal life in that we get not really an image of a lonely individual persecuted for his individuality *a la* (say) Dylan from the same period. Instead we have an illustration of his aspirations, his wishes and desires, in addition to his insecurities and his innate sense of shyness. His music is representative of his personal life in that it supplies us with a kind of dualism: what we want and what we achieve is always at the expense of something (or somebody) else. Burt was later at pains to remark on the 'swinging sixties' that he so appears to represent via the post-modern parody of Mike Myers:

In retrospect, I didn't participate in all that or enjoy it too much. I didn't allow myself to, because I was always going 'what's next? Oh, I've got a record to make here, another song to write here' and I was in a pretty strong work mode. Nor did I sit back and evaluate myself and see what or who I was, so I always devalued myself. I didn't think I looked as good as maybe the person I was dating, so I would go for someone, uh, lesser because I thought someone better would turn me down. (Bacharach to Williams, *NME*, 1996)

There are no hidden histories here, no skeletons lurking in the closet to shock and outrage. Burt was probably no angel, but we must not sacrifice him at the altar of 1960s excess and alienation. Sure, he had plenty of female 'trophies' on his arm during this period. At rapid pace he went from behind the scenes to being a star – an astonishing transformation for him (occurring as it did at a time when assembly-line songwriters were being told that their services were no longer required).

But remember: the man in his bachelor pad is a lonely man; the penthouse scenario involves TV dinners as much as it does Martinis; as Burt himself suggests, the touring schedule is often a way of avoiding self-reflexivity; the 'magic' of live performance often obscures some kind of safety-net for myriad insecurities. Strange as it may seem to modern eyes, this was the private life of Burt Bacharach in 1963.

Perfection

"A Perfectionist? We drove each other crazy" (Hal David, 2003)

From 1964-onwards Bacharach thrived vividly as a composer, arranger and producer. He did so by appearing to break all of the accepted rules of Tin Pan Alley. On the one hand, he never forgot the Darius Milhaud cardinal principle that melody must be accessible to the man in the street, but, on the other, he was also attempting to make popular music few people could actually whistle. Certainly, via the voices of Dionne and (to a lesser extent) Gene Pitney, he was able to codify the sounds in his head and in the men's room at Bell Sound.

But, in truth, there was very little rule **breaking** going on. Burt had embraced the Ford-ism of the popular music industry but had done so in such a way as to deplete the vertical integration of the major labels and 'go it alone' into the realms of horizontal integration. He was a maverick, using all methods possible to organise the quality of his final product. So, while considering his actions to be relatively subversive, we must also appreciate that he was actually replicating the structures of the macro industry by attempting to control every aspect of the songwriting and distribution process on his own.

He was, like Leiber and Stoller, working with labels such as Atlantic, Scepter, Big Top, Vee Jay, Kapp, Musicor and UA; he was producing at the Brill's own studios and at Bell Sound and A&R Recordings (the latter founded in 1961 by Phil Ramone and Jack Arnold); he was hiring his own musicians, advancing the career of his own model performer (Dionne), and retaining wherever possible his own publishing rights. He was, in many respects a one-man music factory. He and Hal even took trouble to search for the correct pressing plants for his recordings, overseeing the vinyl process. No wonder there was little time for a private life. The following somewhat obsessive information supplied to *Billboard* in 1964 certainly reveals two things: firstly someone learning 'on the hoof', and secondly that same person displaying more than a tad of neurosis about his vocation:

> Unfortunately there has to be a gradual diminishing of sound quality from the original tape to the sound of the 'date' [meaning the mastering on to acetate session, here] - down to monaural mix, then the 'final catastrophe' when it goes in and out of the pressing plant. [...] We find that there is a difference in various songs and 'dates' we do [this can depend upon] whether a compression or injection pressing method was used. Thus we always get pressings from at least two plants on every 'date' and we choose the record closest to the original tape sound. Not many songwriters and producers go out inspecting pressing plants. (Bacharach to *Billboard*, 1964)

How very true! This quote, of course, also highlights just how much Burt was interested in the 45 single as a cultural artefact. It was to be at least another five years before popular music academia (via the likes of Mellers, Laing and Mabey) even began to identify the 45rpm record as a meaningful material asset. By 1962, however, Bacharach was already in full appreciation of the significance of the single. After all, nothing had ever been achieved by composers who could not hear their ideas realized.

However, despite Burt's employment of the Royal 'We', above, Platts (2003:33) accurately suggests that Hal David did not entirely share this control mania with Burt in quite the same way, which further emphasises that Bacharach's fixation was in reality a rather solitary affair:

> Unlike Bacharach, David preferred the writing process to the recording process. Hal said that working in the studio "has never been as satisfying as writing a song [...]".

Although Hal did recall in an interview with the *Biography Channel* in 2003, "we were as painstaking with our records as we were with our writing", he did not share Burt's obsession, as such.

It was no coincidence that Phil Ramone came to be Bacharach's preferred collaborator when recording and that A&R studios (sited at 112 West 48th Street) was his favourite place to record. Not only was Ramone a first-class engineer (and classically-trained violinist), he was also equally engrossed in recording developments. A&R became the first independent studio to house a four-track recorder and, even though most Bacharach sessions were actually conceived and recorded live without overdubbing, this investment sent out an important message to songwriters such as Bacharach and David that Ramone was a serious player. Phil was later to affirm:

> They had made some big records at Bell Sound and it was booked, or something, so they came over to A&R and tried me. My reputation as an engineer was starting to get some good marks. I had been working with Leiber and Stoller, Jeff Barry and Ellie Greenwich. I'd had a couple of years under my belt to get me to a place where people actually knew who I was. There was an instant feeling between Burt and Hal and myself – plus Dionne; we got a great sound on her. (ibid, 45-46)

A&R Studios moved to a larger space in the mid-1960s on Seventh Avenue but Burt continued to record with them right up until his split with Warwick in the early 1970s.

133

Gnosis

Bacharach had certainly come a long way from his judgemental pronouncements on the jukebox and radio music of the mid-1950s. At that time he could see the mass market as only a degradation of the uniqueness of composition. He vilified the song pluggers for peddling tarnished wares. By at first becoming his own one-man watch dog committee, then capitulating somewhat to the system, then in due course carrying the baton so generously passed to him by Leiber and Stoller, Burt had come to appreciate the dialectics of popular music and, as such, was responsible for tracing its future material orientation.

It is via this presentation of the history stored up in Burt's changing compositions, attitudes and critical approaches that we can appreciate him as being at the nexus of most of the classic struggles within popular music. For example, Burt still wanted to remove 'bad songs' from the popular music sphere, to challenge the anaemia he felt was lurking within the pop process, but he also wished to do so on terms both he and the public could understand. He wanted the public to be knowledgeable about the pleasures of the text. He remained concerned about musical 'quality', but also identified that meaning was ultimately made by the consumers (even if this reception was formulated under conditions not of their own choosing).

This 'gnosis', however, was by necessity a gradual process: one of orientation, familiarization and then origination – it could not be hurried (as we have seen, it took Burt years to develop). Thus there can be no easy way to describe how both he and his music went from the predictable ('Magic Moments') to the complex ('Anyone Who Had A Heart'). Certainly the influence of different musical forms contributed, but so too did the times in which they were made.

Bacharach's music was (like all great art) steeped in context and a classic socio-cultural construction. It was not spontaneous or 'arc-ing with nature'. If we allow his art to lose some of its mystique by suggesting as much through this non-romanticised form of analysis then, so be it. Something is gained as a consequence: the realisation that Burt's music provides us with a means of establishing a dialogue with the contexts of the day – it is a direct route into that era. This surely reasserts its position as great art.

He wanted his songs to fibrillate without conceding to the *a priori* predispositions of the dance floor. He was actually keeping the American popular song tradition alive by its usual routes i.e. feeding the musical mainstream from a specific refraction, but his hits came to be full of surprises (whereas his earlier works were exactly the opposite): they became living organisms, keeping the listener off balance, going into the unexpected. Harnessing this conviction to new sounds, however, had to be well conceived, planned like a military operation.

In that 1964 interview with *Billboard* quoted above, Burt conceded that his muse was not one of inspired spontaneity – far from it, in fact; it was 1% inspiration and 99% perspiration and represented a level of fundamentalist zeal hitherto usually only associated with the volatility of a Phil Spector or Shadow Morton:

> We do maybe 24 takes in the studio […] we listen to the playbacks, remix and listen to the acetates. After 1000 listenings we must force ourselves to listen to the record as if we had just thought of it and were hearing it in completed form for close to the first time. Believe me this is the hardest thing of all. (Bacharach to *Billboard*, 1964)

This is an astounding admission – a quest towards perfection. One can only imagine what it was like to be a jobbing musician on these sessions. Regular Bacharach session player Russ Savakus later admitted to Hubert Saal in 1970 that he thought Burt was "possessed […], and a little of each man's flesh is left in the session". In the same interview long-term Bacharach sideman Gary Chesters stated "we're all extensions of him […] mostly the problem is to find out how to do it his way". Burt undoubtedly drove his musicians unremittingly. But he loved the studio with a passion seldom ever imparted to another human being:

> The most exciting thing musically for me is getting into the recording studio and making a record. So fantastic! Or disappointing! But it's all in your hands. (Bacharach to Gussow, *Newsweek*, 1968)

Yet another very revealing comment: either fantastic or disappointing, eh? Real people are not usually quite so binary in their emotions! This devotion to duty is all the more astounding when one considers the musical and socio-cultural climate of the US in the early days of 1964. Like the Beatles, Burt was a physical embodiment of change.

Cultural temperature, British Invasion

The Beatles arrived in the United States in February of 1964, further turning the accepted Tin Pan Alley ways of doing things on their heads. The cultural regicide of American popular music committed by the Beatles, Herman's Hermits, the Dave Clark Five and the Rolling Stones was not without a quirk of fate, for their inspirations were, of course, American recordings. Here were young men from the suburbs and provinces of the United Kingdom singing R&B, Carole King songs, Burt and Hal compositions, and describing copious experiences about which they could only fantasise.

They were in many respects the bastardised cousins of Burt Bacharach, for like Burt they considered the record to be the thing. They learned everything they knew from records, not from their own lives. They were absorbed in the recording experience, from both footage and reception perspectives. Andre Millard states, "nobody could have imagined [the records] power to diffuse culture. Yet exports of records helped to define the culture of rock'n'roll [as] 'sacred artefacts'". He goes on:

> The record was supposed to follow in the wake of a great musical career, not create it. But all this happened in the 1960s. Paul McCartney of the Beatles put his finger on it when he said that the 'record was the thing. That was what we bought, that was what we dealt in. That was the currency of music: records'. (Millard, 1995:257)

Never one to praise, Paul McCartney was also to admit with grudging admiration that Bacharach's "songs are a lot more musical than the stuff we write and a lot more technical. None of us can read or write music." McCartney had identified, one suspects, a dynamic interrelationship between Burt's work and the receptive audience. But, of course, this "technical [...] stuff" was also the result of Bacharach, David and Phil

Ramone moving "into a more collaborative relationship with the artist working in the studio" (Longhurst, 1995:77). McCartney, too, was to benefit from this formally trained studio perfectionism via his association with the **real** 'fifth Beatle': George Martin.

The Beatles, it must be noted, also arrived during an extraordinarily significant historical moment in US history – only a matter of three months after the assassination of US president, John F. Kennedy. This was a time when the United States was in a deep sense of mourning (even seasonal fluff like Phil Spector's *Christmas Album* was considered bad taste and pulled from the shelves). The Beatles (and Bacharach) both contributed to bringing the country around from this depressed somnambulance. Broadcaster and writer Paul Gambaccini:

> I have my own theory about this, which Paul McCartney doesn't agree with, but he needs an American perspective to judge it. The country had been in deep mourning over the assassination of John F. Kennedy – deep, deep mourning and it had really needed an up. It was such mourning that the Singing Nun was no.1 – this was like penance. Everyone wanted to be happy again and the Beatles with 'I Want To Hold Your Hand' were the first positive thing to come along. (quote no. 159 in Leigh, 1991:31)

Burt had produced some pleasantly uplifting music during 1963 but ditties such as 'Me Japanese Boy' on the one hand and 'True Love Never Runs Smooth' on the other were actually complemented by a handful of incredibly downbeat songs that reflected more accurately the latter months of 1963. Perhaps this is why, as pleasant as (say) 'Me Japanese Boy' or 'Saturday Sunshine' are, they do not represent the mood of the times, the important *zeitgeist* mentioned previously. They are only occasionally remembered and then with no more than a mixture of affection and affectation.

'Anyone Who Had A Heart' on the other hand reflects truly the mood of the people upon its release in January 1964. It is a monumental musical event tied, as it is, to this disturbing time in US domestic history. Although this writer has never seen any comments from Burt about any direct connection with the post-assassination mood, historically it shares and reflects this ambience perfectly, traversing as it does, the cultural topography of the United States of 1963/64.

Burt's (and the Beatles') songs undoubtedly began to refract the times in which they were written. By doing so they are now able to emit to us information about that catastrophic period in US history (and the generation gap that followed - for many Americans the 1960s began in November 1963). But while these two giants of the 1960s appeared to enjoy massive generational crossover appeal, they were also rooted in differing and diverging demographic audiences.

Via his obscure Latin rhythms and his gloriously asymmetrical approach to composition, Burt demarcated his listeners. Popular music was already fragmenting: there were new genres such as surf, soul, Motown, high school, etc replacing the older metanarratives of popular music (including rock 'n' roll) – the era of postmodernity had dawned and Burt's music was being identified by what it contrasted with, as much as by what it represented. The essentialist tendencies of Tin Pan Alley were no longer referential truths. Burt had blurred the distinctions between high and low art, he had effaced the boundaries of what could be done in popular music composition but, via a cocktail of chord progressions and radio legislation his music was to be pigeon-holed as 'adult-oriented'.

Chapter 8

Recordings

To think of him without his music is to see him in two dimensions [...] to watch and hear Bacharach performing his music is to see him literally in living 'color'. (Bruce A. Lohof, *Popular Music and Society*, 1972)

Post-November '63 Bacharach's songs were never the same again. Even those numbers that appeared to canter through 1964, such as the gorgeous 'To Wait For Love', secreted a curious tension between introspection and outright commerciality. The plodding 'one and two and' piano vamp tempo of this song suggests an almost childlike simplicity. But Hal David's lyrics succeed in enhancing an immensely sad refrain consisting of bars of sixths mixed with minor 7ths, suggesting a character study of loneliness rather than a straightforward love song. The minor chords are achingly heart-rending, and, mixed as they are with the beautiful accordion on Tony Orlando's superb version (and the deliberately ambivalent middle 8), present an image of an insecure young man forever doomed to kissing his pillow.

Dionne's recordings towards the end of 1963 were something of an anti-climax. 'This Empty Place' and 'Make the Music Play' – the latter number previously recorded by the Drifters - quickly followed the 1963 triumph of 'Don't Make Me Over' but neither were overly successful. This was hardly surprising, for both were sonic leftovers from Bacharach's now receding R&B period, rather than part of the new 'Bacharach-David' genre. Meanwhile – and perhaps as a consequence of Dionne's lowly chart placings with these two singles (no.s 84 and 81, respectively) – Bacharach hedged his bets somewhat by recording with a few other artists.

For example, Gene Pitney was, as we have already discovered, enjoying a good run with Burt and Hal material in 1963. Furthermore, Bobby Vinton ('Blue On Blue') and Jack Jones ('Wives and Lovers') both made the US Top Twenty - whereas Bobby Vee's 'Anonymous Phone Call' remained anonymous. Hal David was to later state of 'Blue On Blue': "We didn't play that for Dionne – it didn't sound like Dionne at all". It most certainly did not fit the genre that had been established for her and so the track was given to Bobby Vinton whose career was revived somewhat by its US Top Ten success. Burt liked the song for he conducted the orchestra and played piano on the session. His involvement with this project was decidedly 'hands-on' - attempting, no doubt, to secure the success of the song.

'Wives and Lovers' was inspired by the movie of the same name but was not directly linked. Hal David:

> *Wives and Lovers* was the title of the film [...] it was an assignment from Paramount Pictures. As we saw it, the only honest approach was to do it offbeat, musically. So we wrote it as a jazz waltz [...] We were asked to write what would be called an exploitation song. It wasn't going in the film, but it was meant to come out and every time it got played the name of the film would be 'performed'. It was a song made to promote the film, but it was never in the film [this was] very common in those days [...] I never thought for a moment it would be a hit, it just seemed too hip and sophisticated for its time. (Platts, *Discoveries*, 1997)

'Wives and Lovers' (the song) is worthy of further note even if the film most decidedly is not! It is unlike other material from the Bacharach and David camp and yet, ironically, over the years has been regarded by many as something of an archetype. Perhaps it is one of those songs that can be (historically) easily stereotyped and ironized. Both its arrangement and its lyrics are an odd mixture of brash musical confidence and (apparently) misogynistic intent that can often be mistaken for socio-cultural cockiness, but the song is much more challenging and complex than at first appears.

To Bacharach and David connoisseurs the differences are immediately noticeable via the big band arrangement. The brass stabs on the 'one' in a 3/4 time signature ("A jazz waltz" – Hal David) are not unlike those in the classy arrangements of Percy Faith and Nelson Riddle (e.g. consider the latter's theme from the TV series *Route 66*). Furthermore the vocals of Jack Jones add great interest as they, too, are obviously 'adult'. The song is actually a Bacharach rarity in that it swings with an economy not usually associated with our hero. Burt remains philosophical about the latterday stereotyping of his work via songs such as 'Wives And Lovers':

I guess that's what they mean by the Bacharach sound [...] or something about the orchestration or the rhythm flow [but] I've never really understood it because 'Walk On By' is so different from 'What's New Pussycat' and 'Wives and Lovers' sounds nothing like 'Anyone Who Had A Heart'. (Bacharach to Maconie, *Q*, 1996)

And concerning a possible answer to this specular pigeonholing he proposes:

[...] I think it gets into the arrangements, when whatever the sound that I had in my head got translated [...] that seems to be the link [...] something in the rhythm patterns maybe, was consistent. But I've never been able to, or really cared to analyze it. (Bacharach to *Almo Productions, 1978*)

Hal David, however, continues to remain sceptical about an overall 'Bacharach and David sound':

I don't think we've ever tried to write in such a way as to be recognisable. The 'sound', the 'personality' of our work grew from a natural evolution. (Hal David, ibid)

So different was 'Wives And Lovers', in fact that (as with a few other Bacharach and David musical timebombs) it was originally scheduled as a b-side. However West Coast promotion man for Kapp, Gil Frazen, had other ideas. He loved the track and took it upon himself to plug the b-side until it became a smash. It is not without significance that it was first a hit on the West Coast. The song is a classic example of a kind of mature jazz-oriented pop music that comfortably dovetails the 'West Coast' and 'Cool Jazz' grooves – what was later to be described by 'easy' radio guru Jim Schulke as 'beautiful music'. Burt in fact re-recorded the song in a 'cool jazz' mode. Music journalist Stan Britt was to remark on this later Bacharach-plays-Bacharach re-working thus:

'Wives And Lovers' is certainly the most exciting track Bacharach has ever recorded. It's chameleon-like in that it switches tempo, feel and instrumentation throughout: one minute it's proceeding, orchestrally, at a sedate 3/4; the next we're being uplifted, in jazz-waltz fashion, with a blistering freewheeling alto-sax solo from Jerry Dodgion, followed by sparkling trumpet from Marvin Stamm; there's an intriguing chamber music section featuring strings; a fascinating passage utilising some Jean-Luc Ponty-inspired violin from Gene Orloff; and a gloriously funny ending that has to be heard to be really appreciated. (Britt, *Record Collector*, 1972)

'Wives And Lovers' has also created quite a fuss over the years. Feminists have singled-out the lyric (concerning how the woman in the home should please her husband) for severe criticism. It has also been cited as a typical representation of Hal David's lyric writing. But both paradigms are unfair. As for the latter of these denigrations, the song is an atypical effort (it was meant as a quickie hit), and does not represent the main body of David's work.

While 'Wives And Lovers' expresses sentiments within a domestic setting – a familiar subject to David - it in no way represents the usual sensitivity of his lyrics. As for the feminist diatribe, this appears (to this writer at least) somewhat humourless and lacking in imagination. Perhaps we should read both the lyric and the crooner-like vocal rendition by Jack Jones as ironic statements about Middle America – a redefinition of the home in the wake of the polemics of the sixties!

For his part, after BBC DJ Sarah Kennedy found the song offensive in 2002, Burt repented, expressing 'mia culpa':

She was totally right. I like the song, but it would be wrong if it were written now. It's unacceptable. (Bacharach to staff writer, *Independent On Sunday*, 2002)

Despite the only minimal success of both 'This Empty Place' and 'Make The Music Play' the triumvirate of Burt/Hal/Dionne were not easily put-off. In fact, throughout 1963 they were meeting on a regular basis and planning for the future. They would often rehearse in Burt's New York apartment and then move the songs quickly into the studio to test their strength. By the summer of 1963 Burt's melodies were usually specifically designed for Dionne. To paraphrase a number of interview comments, he was able to 'hear' Dionne singing in his head when a melody or part-melody would come to him, making the music very specific, very focused.

Part-songs were often attempted and occasionally shelved for later development, but after hearing one such effort in the fall of 1963 Dionne insisted that the song be finished off immediately, for she heard herself in it instantly. It was duly completed over the next 24 hours and the polished gem was entitled 'Anyone Who Had A Heart'.

The next recording session had already been advance booked at Bell Sound with three songs scheduled: 'Anyone Who Had A Heart', 'In The Land Of Make Believe', and 'Walk On By'. Typically for the three, the session duly ran behind schedule and rather than run through the allotted three songs in one hour, they concentrated instead on two and 'In The Land Of Make Believe' was shelved. As a result of their own attention to detail, inadvertently the next two Dionne Warwick singles were pencilled-in. Hal David remembers:

> We had done 'Walk On By' and 'Anyone Who Had A Heart' at the same recording session and we couldn't make up our minds which record to go with first. And we went back and forth and back and forth and finally elected to come out with 'Anyone Who Had A Heart'. And so 'Walk On By' was always meant to be the next one. (David to Leigh, *BBC: On The Beat*, 2001)

'Anyone Who Had A Heart' was released in January 1964 and became Dionne's first top ten hit in the US. Even after almost forty years it remains a wonderfully creative and moving experience. Its meter begins in sixteenth-note triplets in 3/8, moves into 6/8 and occasionally runs in 5/4 (which in 1964 was only just being adopted by fellow Milhaud student Dave Brubeck!). Burt later disclosed on a 1979 press release: "bands couldn't play 'Anyone Who Had A Heart' at first because they couldn't play the time changes".

Here, the string arrangement is far more typically Bacharach than the aforementioned 'Wives And Lovers'. It links directly to the meaning of the text via the 'trademark' juxtapositioning of minors and majors. The exquisite piano vamps tap-out a kind of Morse code of despair intimating tension inherent in Dionne's voicing. The backing singers are delicately arranged and their 'oohs' are perfectly mixed between the main voice and the orchestra. The reverbed guitar chording of an Fmaj7 at the end of each phrase is like an intake of breath: incredibly affective.

There is also a beautiful and uncertain detachment between the voice and the middle 8 as the saxophone (by this time a somewhat redundant instrument for Bacharach) repeats the forlorn melody as a kind of requiem. There's not much hope, here, that's for sure – the 'so' (Ab) is sobbed rather than sung and the final pleading of 'why (Bbm7) won't (Eb7) you (Ab)?' graduates from a deeply minor chord into a turnaround 7th and then a defiant major as a musical exclamation of despair; it seals the singer's fate via a kind of anti-*morendo* - it's not going to happen.

'Anyone Who Had A Heart' is an extraordinarily moving song that confirms Dionne's 'grown-up' status in the time it takes to listen: 3 minutes and 13 seconds. It is pure majesty – could this be mono 45rpm perfection?

The U.K., Dionne and Burt

The year of 1964 was a very significant one for Burt Bacharach but there were also inconveniences. Burt was a regular visitor to the UK (at first with Dietrich) and was a confirmed Anglophile. He loved London, enjoyed theatre land and the lavish opulence of the 'American in London' lifestyle often afforded to visiting Yanks:

> Even more so than his home country, Bacharach's sound has always been appreciated in Britain, an affection he returns warmly. 'Before they knew me in the States they knew me here', he says [...]. (staff reporter, *Independent On Sunday*, 2002)

Burt was, therefore, fully aware of what was going on 'across the pond' and kept a close eye on the UK charts. He had been conscious of the progress of the Beatles – royalty accounts brought to his attention their cover of 'Baby It's You' - and he was already savvy with their home city of Liverpool. 'The Story Of My Life' was a UK number one for the tragic Michael Holliday who it is said came from Liverpool (although this remains a little unclear owing to his Irish background). Frankie Vaughan ('Tower Of Strength') also came from Liverpool.

Bacharach actually sold 'Story Of My Life' directly to the British publishers and so kept a close watch on the song's (and Holliday's) progress. Hence, when Cilla Black recorded 'Anyone Who Had A Heart', Burt was one of the first to guardedly congratulate the singer on her version. Dionne was (rightly) miffed, for Black's version was identical in every way – except, of course that where Dionne's version appeared effortless, it was obvious that Cilla was straining her garters. This is not a criticism of Cilla (who has made some wonderful recordings over the years), merely a comment upon the very distinct vocal styles of these two great chanteuses.

Problems loomed, however; in the UK the early Dionne singles appeared on EMI's US imprint Stateside, but immediately after 'Make The Music Play' was released, Scepter's UK distribution passed from EMI to ATV-Pye. All of the Stateside-labelled copies were withdrawn from the shops. This began a protracted and largely unresolved dilemma for Dionne Warwick releases in the UK. It's a travesty that, despite her enormous popularity, Dionne scored only two Top Ten hits on the British Hit Parade throughout the entire 1960s ('Walk On By' and 'Do You Know The Way To San Jose'). Much of the blame for this sinful miscalculation must be laid at the feet of the ever-inefficient Pye Records.

For most of the decade Pye lacked decent proactive distribution and, coupled with the continual leaking of Dionne's originals to other producers, a stream of usually substandard UK covers was able to 'compete' in an already uneven pro-British marketplace. The upshot of this was not only did her records sound different they were also difficult to obtain! In fact, the UK issued 'Make The Music Play' is now considered to be the rarest Dionne single of all – one for the collectors.

Cilla

Dionne was aware of this mismanagement and angry about her powerlessness. In fact, When Cilla Black's name was mentioned in a more recent (2000) interview with *The Observer* Dionne still expressed a level of bitterness about Cilla's cover and that period of the 1960s:

> I could have killed her [Cilla] when she did the song in the beginning, of course, but time has a wonderful way of putting everything in perspective (Warwick to *The Observer*, 2002).

Indeed, Dionne never really forgave **any** of the British cover specialists:

> I just felt that it was very expensive demonstration records that I
> was making for European artists to enjoy and reap success from,
> but subsequently it got to the point where the audience became
> curious as to where the original came from [...] if I had during
> the course of the recording coughed or sneezed, that would have
> been an intricate part of what they recorded. (in Howes, 2001:
> 159)

Via a trip to New York, Cilla's manager Brian Epstein (always a man of
exceptional taste) had spotted the potential of 'Anyone Who Had A Heart'.
He purchased a copy in the States and upon his return to London gave it to
George Martin. The EMI recording manager felt that the song was perfect
- for Shirley Bassey. Epstein replied unequivocally 'I wasn't thinking of
Shirley Bassey'.

Martin was not initially optimistic about Cilla's vocal abilities, and the
scoring was left to Johnny Pearson. As it turned out this proved to be
a winning combination: Pearson's delicate arrangement of strings and
French horn contrasted well with Black's emotional rendition. 'Anyone
Who Had A Heart' was a UK number one before Dionne's version even
had a chance to register.

Cilla put her foot in it almost immediately stating to the British musical
press that she preferred to sing: "good numbers recorded by lesser-known
American artists". Oops! Whatever her motives, Ms Black did not endear
herself to Dionne by such pronouncements. Furthermore (and to add
insult to injury) considerable hype from EMI (who had lost the Scepter
franchise to Pye but held Cilla's Parlophone recording contract), coupled
with the institutionalised cultural elitism of the BBC (never known to
play an American record when a British one would do), ensured that Cilla
sold a million copies in the UK alone of 'Anyone Who Had A Heart'. She
courteously said of Dionne's original:

> I love her version, but the song was too good for me to turn
> down. (in MacAleer, 1994:91)

And much later admitted:

Dionne was dead choked and she's never forgiven me to this day. (Black, *BBC: This Is Now*, 1996)

Dionne was evidently peeved at her lack of success in Britain but she need not have worried too much. Within a matter of months she was enjoying her first transatlantic success with 'Walk On By'. This time Pye were forced to rush-release the single. Scepter insisted that it was released on the same day as the American version to prevent another cover version from stealing Dionne's thunder (in this case Helen Shapiro was waiting in the wings).

'Walk On By' was issued in Britain in April 1964 and reached no. 9 on the UK charts. It won Dionne wide recognition in the UK, beautifully demonstrating her vocal dexterity. Warwick authority Debbie Pead writes:

Within her note-perfect performance Dionne managed to convey a restrained anguish that, coupled with Bacharach's skilful orchestral arrangement (he also played piano on the track), resulted in a highly moving recording, which is just as powerful today. (Pead, *Record Collector*, 1983:47)

But the Cilla Black saga illustrates perfectly the way in which British covers pre-empted the American originals and continued to frustrate the commercial progress of US artists in the UK.

Lou Johnson was especially unfortunate in this respect: no sooner had 'Message to Martha' been released in the States than there was (an albeit tolerable) cover from Adam Faith in the UK. This was less than three months after Sandie Shaw's cover of '(There's) Always Something There To Remind Me' had topped the UK singles charts, condemning Johnson's superior original to British obscurity (Scepter/Pye released the retitled 'Message to Michael' in April 1966 and 'Always Something There to Remind Me' in August 1968 as singles for Dionne, but both stopped short of the British charts – more negligence, no doubt).

Burt was largely unconcerned, however. His songs remained very popular in the UK via airplay on both Radio Luxembourg and the BBC Light Programme. On the one hand the land-based 'pirate' understood the trendiness of Burt's music (and many Radio Luxembourg shows were record company-sponsored, in any case); on the other the songs fitted the somewhat anti-teen Reithian attitudes of the BBC Light Programme producers. Burt enjoyed the best of both worlds – he had no control over the cultural interpretation of his material. As far as he was concerned, if British covers outflanked his US artistes while these originals were still able to get into the lower reaches of the UK charts then his publishing and songwriting royalties were boosted.

Success

By 1964 Dionne was on the road for much of the year in the US and Europe. After her successful Marlene Deitrich-encouraged demographic relocation, she was booked for more 'stylish' venues (together with considerable TV work) than those previously encountered on tour with the Impressions: her audience sector was thus confirmed. Dusty Springfield actually watched Dionne perform 'Anyone Who Had A Heart' at the aforementioned Dietrich Paris Olympia show and said that it was the only time she had ever cried in a theatre. But Dionne was only able to fit recording into her busy schedule as and when her touring allowed – usually at the very last minute. But, because of the symbiosis with Burt and Hal, it didn't really matter:

> " […] when I was available, because I was also on the road. I'd
> go over to Burt's apartment or to Famous Music, usually the
> day before. Sometimes it was a couple of days before and we'd
> have the background group in too. But it didn't really take that
> much time […] sometimes we would come up with something
> in the background that would cause a reaction to either change
> a melody and/or time signature or something of that nature, but,
> by and large, whatever they wrote was what they wrote and that's
> what we sang. (in Platts, 2003:32)

However, her lack of availability did mean that Burt and Hal accepted a few film music contracts from Famous-Paramount to further 'magnetise' their own 'fame and fortune'. Two song contracts in particular meant that work would continue to flow: firstly the theme tune to the Shelley Winters film *A House Is Not A Home* and secondly the Doris Day and Rock Hudson frolic *Send Me No Flowers*. Neither movies were remarkable, but the songs were suitably impressive – particularly the former which has since become something of a standard. Burt's attention was also redirected towards another vocal perfectionist.

Dusty

From the summer of 1964 until the end of the year, Bacharach enjoyed an exciting run of successes with his songs. First, UK vocalist Dusty Springfield came to his attention by recording a US number 6 hit with 'Wishin' and Hopin'' (a song previously on the flip-side of Dionne Warwick's 'This Empty Place'). It was the very first Bacharach and David song recorded by Dusty, who later admitted that she had "swiped" 'Wishin' And Hopin'' after 'This Empty Place' proved "too rangey" for her: "I don't think Dionne ever forgave me for this" (in Howes, 2001:159).

Actually Dusty gives herself little credit, here. Of the two numbers, 'Wishin' And Hopin'' is the more complex, at least for a vocalist. The song appears to move from *staccato* to *legato* very smoothly, but the singer has to open out into longer notes halfway through each verse: a difficult manoeuvre. Thus Burt was magnanimous about Dusty's achievement:

> Then Dusty recorded it ['Wishin' And Hopin''] in England and she knocked me out. I believe that Dusty is not only the best pop singer in England but one of the top singers in the world. What she has is the power to command attention. Her performance of 'Wishin' And Hopin'' just walks right off that record. She really takes charge. (ibid)

In the UK this song had actually charted for the Merseybeats while Dusty enjoyed a hit with a version of Tommy Hunt's 'I Just Don't Know What To Do With Myself', released at the end of June '64 (Hunt, incidentally, was never destined for great success: Scepter's Florence Greenberg hated him so much owing to his two-timing 'Shirelle' Beverly Lee while simultaneously being 'kept' by a mafia madam, that she would not promote his singles!).

The highest tribute paid to Dusty must have been when Bacharach admitted that the quality of her recording exceeded the one he had made with Hunt. The two versions were actually very different – for example, Dusty's version is extended, with a passionate reprise of the third verse. Bacharach was not damning Springfield with false praise, here, for on that 1962 Hunt original, his 'dream team' were assembled: he conducted the orchestra, Phil Ramone engineered, while Leiber and Stoller produced!

However, in truth, Burt was already coaxing Dusty into covering his songs well before the recording of 'I Just Don't Know What To Do With Myself'. During the spring of 1964 he arranged a meeting with the young diva. That April, Dusty's first UK album had been released and included renditions of '24 Hours From Tulsa', 'Wishin' And Hopin'' and 'Anyone Who Had A Heart'. Bacharach was mightily impressed and wanted Dusty to record more of his songs. At this meeting, as part of an evening's sampling of Bacharach and David tracks, Burt played the Tommy Hunt recording (among others) to Dusty and she was invited to select her preferences. She stated to the British pop press:

> I was falling off my stool in ecstasy. He gave me four nice songs and now I'm thoroughly concussed. For once I've got too much good material. (ibid, 63)

And:

> Who wouldn't want to sing a song like that? Here, at last, was a writer who was dramatically changing the way pop music sounded. No wonder we all wanted to sing them. (Springfield, narration, *BBC: This Is Now*, 1996)

She also stated - apparently in more detail:

> 'I Just Don't Know What To Do With Myself' was Tommy Hunt, and I hadn't heard that record until Burt Bacharach played it for me [when] I flew over to have dinner with him. I was at the Liverpool Empire and I remember leaving there and catching a plane on Sunday and having dinner with Burt on the Sunday night and we went to his apartment, he played me that song [...] I was crazy about 'This Empty Place' which was the a-side of Dionne's record. When he played it to me he said 'here's the other side' and that was how 'Wishin' and Hopin'' came about. So it was a very productive trip. I remember exactly where we ate. A place called Dawson's Pub, probably not there anymore. It's on Third [...] yeah. He was really handsome. Still is. (in Evans, 1995:76)

However, if, as Evans also states, Dusty was back on stage at the Liverpool Empire on Monday night, it is highly unlikely that a trip to New York took place on that particular occasion. Furthermore, Dusty had already recorded 'Wishin' And Hopin'' prior to her first meeting with Burt. Perhaps Springfield remembered the pub in New York and pushed a couple of memories together to create one event – as we all have a tendency so to do. It's far more likely that her meeting with Burt was in his Belgravia apartment in London.

When Dusty's hit version of 'I Just Don't Know What To Do With Myself' was released in the UK that June, Burt's admiration was palpable:

> That girl listens with an arranger's ears. She's a fine musician and it must be a great pleasure to work with her on a recording. I only hope that her next American release will be 'I Just Don't Know What To Do With Myself'. I think it could be a monster hit. (ibid, 63)

Sadly for Bacharach and Springfield, Philips didn't release the single in the US. His strategically laid plans for Dusty's international stardom via 'I Just Don't Know [...]' were foiled.

It has been occasionally suggested that there was a deeper attraction between Burt and Dusty, but again, this might be the wrong conclusion to draw. Of course, while Dusty did date men at this stage, her latent lesbianism decreed that her friendship with our hero remained platonic. Nevertheless their relationship was strong enough for Dusty P.A. Pat Rhodes to state to Lucy O'Brien:

> Had the time been right, they would have had a relationship. Burt was married to Angie and Dusty would never have broken up somebody's relationship. Then when Angie and Burt split up, Dusty and Burt were on the other side of the world from each other. It's a pity because I thought there really could've been something there: they were so musically tuned. (Rhodes to O'Brien, 1999:107)

It is the opinion of this writer that Bacharach had visions of grandeur here. Like two pillars of excellence bestriding the Atlantic – one Black, one white - he could see Dionne and Dusty bridging the US and UK pop establishments in a bulwark against mediocrity.

The British pop press reported during 1964 that there were plans for Dusty to record with Burt in New York but, sadly, these plans never materialised. Initially, a commitment by Burt to a short tour of the Soviet Union with Marlene Dietrich shelved the idea; thereafter the timing was never right. Bacharach went on to produce only one of the ten Bacharach and David songs recorded by Dusty: 'The Look Of Love' (with Phil Ramone) in April 1967: a great pity that these two purists were never able to work together on at least one album. A 'meeting of minds' brought about their mutual admiration and Howes quotes Burt's later self-reflexively in identifying further Dusty idiosyncrasies:

> Dusty's very hard on herself. I recorded her sometime afterwards ['The Look Of Love'] and I saw what she was about – she's just a real perfectionist [e.g.] She doesn't want to be in the same room as you when she's listening to a playback. (ibid, 159)

A perfectionist, eh? Now where have we heard something like this before?

> I've always had this thing of really being scared to hear the record on the air for the first time because it never sounds as good as I thought it would sound, or hoped it would sound. (Bacharach to Ward, *Ottowa Citizen*, 2001)

Ipso facto: my case rests!

Demographics, genre, radio

The latter months of 1964 witnessed Burt racking-up more successes – occasionally with belated stuff. Dionne charted with two more Bacharach-David compositions 'You'll Never Get To Heaven (If You Break My Heart)' a beautiful bit of fluff that is almost like a reduced 'jus' of melody, and 'Reach Out For Me' – a song originally recorded by Lou Johnson the previous year. Both Warwick releases charted (no.s 34 and 20, respectively). During August Brook Benton's excellent version of 'A House Is Not A Home' reached a somewhat disappointing no. 75. Warwick also released the song as a flip to 'Reach Out For Me', and this version received enough radioplay to also chart – a little higher at no. 71.

Despite this succession of chart entries, these lower placings evidently tell a story – this kind of unusual and carefully constructed popular music was not the type AM radio deejays launched into the top ten (even Bobby Goldsboro's overtly commercial 'Me Japanese Boy' stalled at 74). Maybe younger audiences – expecting the iconic blues cliché via a mixture of 'Tower of Strength' and 'Don't Make Me Over' - disapproved of this journey towards adulthood (and consequently preferred the British beat groups and a smattering of Motown). But it's equally likely that the generic reconstruction of US radio broadcasting also played a part in the dissemination and thus reception of Burt's music.

Whatever alternatives were preferred by the American youth of 1964, it is quite obvious that the role of genre was of paramount importance to the US charts. According to Roy Shuker, there are three interconnected elements through which a genre can be defined: musical stylistic traits (compositional conventions, instrumentation, performance), non-musical stylistic attributes (iconography, dress codes, locale, etc.) and the primary audience defined by these stylistic features (Shuker, 1998:147-8). Keith Negus also states "genre is not a form of textual codification, but a system of orientation, expectations and conventions that circulate between industry, text and subject" (Negus, 1999:25).

Like Dionne's performance failure in the Deep South, Burt's modest chart activity represented not merely responses conditioned by his musical stylistics, but also the expectations of elements of the public. The connotations, therefore, of a kind of meta-genre, by which one could place this music were coming into force – i.e. 'easy listening'.

Technology, however, also played a significant part in this codification. For example, in 1964, the Federal Communications Commission informed owners of AM & FM combined stations in markets with populations over 100,000 people that as of July 1965 an enforced diversity was to dawn: too many stations were pumping out the same stuff on a crowded waveband (AM) and it had to stop.

The upshot of this was musical division. FM stations began to develop their own generic underpinning and in doing so immersed themselves in discrete genres: on the one hand jazz and light orchestral music, on the other rock album-oriented music. Jim Schulke, the 'Godfather of 'Beautiful Music' radio' (Lanza, 1994:169) developed seamless segues and studied the tempo of certain tracks. Burt's music (particularly in instrumental form) was ideal for Schulke. It was not overbearing, did not draw attention to itself and fitted together with the likes of Andy Williams, Johnny Mann and Anita Kerr.

Therefore, despite Burt's music reflecting a certain autership, the genre into which he was placed by FM radio contributed to the audience's 'understanding' of both the man and his music – genres continue to be discourses through which expectations and meanings are established, negotiated and renegotiated. The parameters of Burt's generic areas were connoted at this stage largely by radio broadcasters, A&R men, song pluggers and the like (due to a variety of socio-cultural reasons – not simply because the music was 'easy'), and, as such, were being denoted by US youth. Genres were vital to the fragmenting social identity of young Americans of the 1960s.

Counter culture

For example, the folk revivalists were in the process of getting into the rock of the Beatles, the counter culture of Ginsberg, and the radicalism opposed to the USA's increased activity in Vietnam. Motown boss Berry Gordy adorned his singles bags with the slogan 'The Sound Of Young America (not young Black America) in an attempt to confirm the trendiness of his label. Garage bands from as far away as Texas and San Francisco were pretending to be English! The youth of America had lost a President and gained fragmentation. Anyone who could apparently sentimentalise art in such a way as Burt Bacharach could not possibly resonate with the counter culture!

There were many such musical pronouncements emanating from the folk revival and counter culture. Fallacious oppositions abounded far more among the underground than they did in the mainstream about musical authenticity (organic folk and rock) as opposed to inauthentic pap – essences to categories again! In this Manichaean scheme of things modern life was found guilty of having destroyed the characteristics of true identity and Burt was guilty by association. Ironic that Burt was a popular music auteur condemned for little artistic weight by so-called 'alternative' evaluations of music.

Many counter cultural criticisms were tantalisingly vague. As such there appeared little self-reflexivity about the hippie's **own** social position (from which much of their bourgeois hippie proclamations about auteurship actually emerged). While attempting to rubbish the kind of society in which Burt moved, the underground equally owed its own existence to the bourgeois, purblind, self-indulgence of the 'Great Society'. It was always ill considered to take as axiomatic that authenticity and commercial success was antithetical, since both can logically be components of the same accomplishment. Despite great musical gains from the US underground of the 1960s, there also existed a kind of terror of the truth, an arrogance of its assumptions that led inexorably towards Altamont.

In fact it remains ironic (and to this writer somewhat satisfying) that the one white US songwriter to whom most Black American singers cleaved throughout the 'long '60s' (say to 1974) was Burt Bacharach (From Gene McDaniels to Isaac Hayes). The counter culture's sniffy response to this 'easy listening' (as it came to be dubbed) was basically a litany of small-minded prescriptiveness. Black America – surely the most neglected area of US society throughout this period - actually embraced Burt Bacharach like a 'brother'.

The minor hits kept on coming, brought about by radioplay as much as anything. In September '64 Lou Johnson released the first recording of '(There's) Always Something There To Remind Me'. This version made 49 on the US charts whereas, as we have seen, Sandie Shaw's version topped the UK charts that October. Popular music writer Barney Hoskyns highlights this incongruity by stating:

> Is there any more perfect pop-soul record than the unsung Johnson's original 1964 version of 'There's Always Something There To Remind Me', a 45 whose considerable thunder was undeservedly stolen by that shoeless Shaw creature? (Hoskyns, *Mojo*, 1997)

Later that year the first single release of the Marlene Dietrich-tested 'Kentucky Bluebird' peaked at a modest 104 for Johnson, Jerry Butler's version didn't show. October '64 also witnessed the release of Paul Anka's mawkish 'From Rocking Horse to Rocking Chair' and Doris Day's aforementioned lively and appealing movie theme track 'Send Me No Flowers' – neither performed well on the *Billboard* charts.

Swinging London

It is not really surprising that the British invasion of 1964 did not have the adverse effect upon Burt that it did on his younger Brill Building cohorts. While the US public generically characterized his style/s, the British Invasion assisted rather than hindered Burt: a kind of bridge into Europe was erected for him to cross at will. Those British groups had a beat but they also appeared to enjoy massaging melodic and often complicated numbers into group arrangements, incorporating Burt's material into their live (and recorded) repertoires. Under these circumstances, what could be more flattering to an Anglophile composer than seeing his compositions on the British charts?

Burt occasionally released his own orchestral material on the US Kapp label. He never really expected the singles to perform well on the singles charts but was aware of the fact that FM radio was being taken over by more adult oriented popular music. In March of 1965 he released another such 45. This was a semi-orchestral version of 'Don't Go Breaking My Heart' that contained vocals, but by a session singer – as was Burt's wont. Of course he could not have used Dionne even if he had wanted to – she was signed to Scepter on an exclusive contract and Kapp was Decca-based.

Predictably, the single did not chart, however the b-side 'Trains And Boats And Planes' was aired by the BBC Light Programme and reached number 4 on the UK singles charts that same month, eventually spending 11 weeks on the chart – a sizeable hit by anyone's standards. As luck would have it, unlike the majority of American artistes covering Burt's material, his own release outpaced a later UK version! (May 1965 by Billy J. Kramer - Brian Epstein also managed Kramer and George Martin produced the session). The one artist to knock the British covers debacle was the man himself – how very gratifying.

As a consequence, Burt was invited to record a television special by UK independent TV giants Granada in April '65. Entitled *The Bacharach Sound* it was directed by Philip Casson and produced by the influential Johnny Hamp. The show was recorded at the Chelsea Palace Studios in London and Burt's guests were Chuck Jackson, the Merseybeats, Dionne Warwick and Dusty Springfield. It was broadcast on the 14 April and was a comprehensive success with the British public. So well, in fact, that Burt decided to record his own album in London.

Bacharach certainly enjoyed his time recording, writing and generally 'larging it' in London. Although one would always wish to avoid stereotyping eras, 1965 was certainly an important year for British culture and London appeared to be at the heart of everything. Burt's compositional impressions of London (e.g. 'London Life', 'Bond Street') are drawn from his 1965 'Swinging London' experiences.

The *Hit Maker!* album was released mid-1965 and charted in Britain but failed to sell in the States, and the composer spent a great deal of time in the UK. There was talk at one stage of him moving to London on a semi-permanent basis, but New York (and Angie Dickinson) called. The album included several cleverly scored reworkings of his most popular songs and featured two guest vocalists: cabaret-men Tony Middleton and Joel Grey. The very best session men that London could offer played on the record, including two future members of Led Zeppelin: Jimmy Page and John Paul Jones.

During 1965 Dionne Warwick's fourth album *The Sensitive Sound Of Dionne Warwick* was also recorded in London, this time at the Pye-ATV studios. Warwick was already touring in Europe, and Burt's affinity for the UK meant that they could meet up for those long-scheduled but now overdue sessions. Dionne remembers this period with a mixture of affection for the sessions but puzzlement at British Trades Unionism:

> I was on tour, and Burt was in London, so it was very timely. We did sessions at the studios of Pye Records, which was the British licensee for Scepter. Of course, Burt and I were not quite accustomed to stopping in the middle of a song while the entire orchestra put down its batons [...] and went for a tea break! (Warwick, 2001, liner notes to *Love Songs*, Rhino Records)

Bacharach actually composed a number of songs and part-songs while in London. For example, Burt and Hal were in 'the smoke' for the Dionne Warwick Pye recording sessions when they met old-style Hollywood producer Charles Feldman, the man responsible for *What's New, Pussycat*. Feldman had sunk a lot of his own money into the project and it wasn't going too well. He had already assigned the score and songs for his movie to others but was less than happy with the results. At the suggestion of his then girlfriend, Feldman asked Bacharach and David to step in. That early spring of 1965, Burt cracked the opening melody for 'What's New, Pussycat' and sang it over the telephone to Hal David. Hal set to work on the rest of the words and finished the song with Bacharach in a London Hotel suite on Easter Sunday, 18 April 1965.

The film is a strange affair, filmed by a French cameraman in Paris by virtue of American money under the direction of British TV man Clive Donner, but it is probably most significant to film buffs in that it marks the first time Woody Allen appears on screen in a script drawn from his own writing. His script was actually butchered, but the film made a great deal of money for Allen. Both film and score are good indicators of an American 'take' on the 'swinging sixties'. Peter Sellers is the freaked-out Beatle wigged analyst attempting to assist Peter O'Toole deal with his neuroses.

The movie was released on 23 June 1965 and was the biggest international comedy success of the year, but, in truth, it hasn't worn as well as the music. Sets and costumes are superb and the movie itself remains a good example of the '60s fashion for international coproductions, but Burt and Hal's music and lyrics greatly assist this rather moribund appropriation on *La Ronde*. Tom Jones delivers the title song, which was also very timely for him: his singles career had stalled somewhat in the UK but was given a substantial lift by 'What's New, Pussycat'. Furthermore, of course, it launched him in the US, where he became an even bigger star than in his home country. The song was not without its critics, however. Burt was to later admit:

> With 'What's New, Pussycat' someone said, 'this is in ¾, it's a waltz, how is somebody in a disco in Paris going to dance to this?' I said 'they'll find a way, it feels right the way it is, they'll find a way to move to it'. You can't think about things like that. I never bothered counting bars, about seeing whether or not there

were eight bars in the first section. Sometimes there'd be nine bars, sometimes twelve: I never paid any attention. I never paid any attention to a changed time signature. I think it was Dionne who told me that the turnaround bar on 'Anyone Who Had A Heart' was in 7/8. She counted it out, and I couldn't believe it. It wasn't intentional, that's just the way it came out. (from 'Bacharach & David', *Almo Productions*, 1978)

Burt and Hal received the Academy Award for best song with 'What's New, Pussycat' but they actually included in the movie arguably two superior songs. Firstly the superb 'Here I Am' (sung by Dionne) and secondly what was to become a dazzling garage/punk classic 'My Little Red Book' (performed rather awkwardly in the film by Manfred Mann). It was not the Manfreds' version that became the touchstone for punk, however, but a rendition by Bacharach aficionado Arthur Lee. His group Love recorded a storming adaptation of the song on their first Elektra album in 1966. Burt Bacharach:

That was an odd [song], really atypical of what I wrote. Then Arthur Lee came along and cut his version and I had a hit. I've just had to get used to people making radical changes on my songs, stand back and objectively look at it and see if I liked what they'd done. (Bacharach to *Los Angeles Times*)

Back in the USA

Meanwhile, back in the US, Jackie DeShannon had recorded an old Bacharach and David song 'What The World Needs Now Is Love'. Hal David remembers this sleeper with great affection:

There wasn't great enthusiasm for it […] I had great enthusiasm for it. We were asked by Liberty Records to record Jackie, who was a great singer – and a good songwriter, too. I remember we were in an office in the RKO Building and played a number of songs for Jackie. And I suggested to Burt that we play 'What The World Needs Now Is Love'. And we did and Jackie said 'that's the one I want to do'. Jackie was the catalyst – she was excited about doing that song. (David to Platts, 2003:147)

Excited with some justification. 'What The Word Needs [...]' is probably one of Burt and Hals' most durable songs and DeShannon's rendition remains the seminal text as a kind of cross between Greenwich Village folksiness and Brill Building accomplishment – more perfection, perhaps?

Following the triumph of the *What's New, Pussycat* film project, Bacharach and David were hot property among moviemakers. For instance, they were asked to compose the title song to the new Peter Sellers movie entitled *After The Fox*. This interesting but flawed movie was released in 1966 and is delightful and frustrating in equal doses. The critics were less than impressed, however, affirming it an:

> [...] Unlikeable and unfunny farce which sets its star [Sellers] among excitable Italians and hopes for the best.

And:

> [...] Never even begins to get off the ground [...]

The script (and Sellers' performance/s) is certainly uneven, but Victor Mature is genuinely hilarious and deserving of at least an Oscar nomination for mocking his previous 'film noir' persona. The Italian director Vittoria De Sica parodies filmic and national stereotypes throughout the movie with great aplomb but not always, it must be said, with great comedy. Burt's music is also at times somewhat anachronistic but, then again, in a movie such as this, it's just what one might expect.

Sellers also appeared on the recording with the Hollies. The sessions took place in London with George Martin on hand to produce Sellers (whom he knew via his recordings for the Goons), Hollies producer Ron Richard there for his charges, and Burt present to put his own personal imprint on proceedings. Bacharach contributed a nice harpsichord phrase or two and an interesting vocal percussion.

So, by the end of 1965, Burt and Hal were truly at the top. Their songs were making the charts, being featured in popular movies, and becoming radio standards. Burt was both talented and fortunate. He was able to fuse music with context, reflecting all things to all people; but he had also been

Young Burt

With Marlene Dietrich

The Playboy

With Hal David

With Dionne Warwick

With his Mother and Father

With Angie Dickinson

With Angie Dickinson

In the studio

The singer-songwriter

With Carole Bayer Sager

With Elvis Costello

With Dionne and Hal

The Rock'N'Roller

With Noel Gallagher

With wife Jane

lucky in finding a diva in Dionne ("she had a perfect voice") who knew what he was thinking and was a unique talent in her own right.

He had also become something of a sex symbol and was a natural on television and in concert. In an absorbing comment, Albert Goldman writing for the *New York Times* described him that year in God-like terms, sporting a "handsome, purely American face, an image blown back from the Kennedy years, with those sun crinkles in the eyes, that trace of silver in the thick, choppy hair".

Importantly, as a kind of beautiful coda to the year, Burt was also no longer alone. After a rather gauche blind-date set-up for him by his parents Bert and Irma, he had fallen in love with and married actress Angie Dickinson.

Chapter 9

Angie, Alfie And Alpert

It has been mooted by some that when Burt married 'rat packer' Angie Dickinson in May 1965, she was regarded by him as a thinking man's 'trophy blonde'. It was actually more typical of the man that his parents had arranged their first date in 1964! The relationship worked well for some time, but seemed to at first prosper and then later dissipate on a similar premise: for a married couple, they actually spent little quality time together. Angie was to inform the *Biography Channel* in 2003 somewhat ironically "he's an incredible guy. We had a wonderful combination for weeks [...] for weeks on end we were happy!" suggesting, perhaps, that the times spent in between their various individual projects were something akin to annual holidays.

The reason for the eventual demise of their marriage was their self-absorption, not because either partner 'played away from home'. Bacharach latterly admitted (in reference to all of his four marriages) that the sudden arrival of (say) a G natural or Gb into his thoughts could disturb even the most intimate of moments!

For example, the year of 1970 should have been one of rejoicing in the Bacharach household. Burt had a young family, enjoyed two US number one hit singles in 'Close To You' and 'Raindrops Keep Falling On My Head', was awarded two Oscars, and his musical *Promises Promises* was in its third of a four year uninterrupted run on Broadway. But he had increased his workload by beginning to perform his own concerts and admitted to Hubert Saal that his marriage to Angie was, even at that stage, showing hairline cracks:

> You have to pay a price for being what you are. If I could put my head down at night, go to sleep like everyone else, I wouldn't write the music I do. The trouble with being busy is that you either neglect and thus hurt people – or yourself – by trying not to hurt them. (Bacharach to Saal, *Newsweek*, 1970)

He continued:

> Maybe work is a private little torture chamber you inflict on
> yourself to shut out the world. Sometimes I have this fantasy
> that I'll just stop, go into one of the restaurants, greet the people,
> play the piano a bit and go to the track every day. A man's a fool
> if success is more than trying to forget the day that just passed.
> Happiness is a question of percentages. You're lucky to get a 50-
> 50 split.(ibid)

Much later, he was to add a somewhat profound postscript by admitting:

> I don't think I was any bargain to be married to at that time – or
> even now. (Bacharach to Schlesinger, *Sunday Morning On CBS*,
> 2002)

While this work does not intend to rake-over personal matters that have
little or no consequence to Burt's compositions, his marriage to Angie
Dickinson was a major event in his life. Historically, however, it has been
largely disregarded; perhaps marriage is simply seen as something people
'just do'. But people don't **just** do anything and it is congruent with the era
being chronicled that issues such as marriage, relationships, sexuality (and
the post-war settlement of which I wrote in earlier chapters), are brought
to the fore in the reader's consciousness, for the times within which this
marriage took place were, indeed, turbulent.

For example, *Alfie* the movie was released in 1966; owing to the rise of
new feminism, this film could never have been made after 1970. Between
these two dates, alone, the libertine trendiness of Michael Caine's character
came under severe social pressures, ultimately representing a bygone era
almost before it had passed. By the 'high sixties' of 1964-69 (Marwick,
1998) it was hoped that relations could gain new depths and subtleties (to
which Michael Caine's Alfie was, of course, oblivious).

Dr. Arthur Janov was prescribing primal screaming, while Dr Timothy
Leary was telling his faithful to turn-on, tune-in and drop out. The strident
male chauvinism of both the mainstream and the underground inadvertently
became a great motivator for the nascent women's liberation movement.
Yippies became a radical and militant sector of the counter culture – a

political party, really, with a leader in Jerry Rubin. Their finest moment was the Dada-inspired event in Chicago in 1968 when they put forward a pig for the presidency of the US. Of course, Hollywood, that yawning abyss of compromise, in its 'infinite wisdom' either ignored or parodied most of this important era in US history.

And yet, Burt decamped to Hollywood! Context, therefore, has great bearing upon artistic creativity. Myriad different elements come into play, for individuals are products of their social environment, and when that environment changes, so too do the individuals: issues such as political discourses, 'progressive' thinking, groups of neurotics, cultural geography, etc., all have significance even on a personal level. Such specifics need to be at least highlighted for their significance, (posited with value, so to speak) for any compositional 'identity' experiencing a series of collisions with changing social and geographical contexts will at the very least modify, and perhaps even destabilise.

To what extent this loss (or 'lack' perhaps) of stability decentred Bacharach's creativity is, of course, always going to be open to debate: Burt himself may suggest that this was simply not the case (and many of his post-1966 compositions were of the very highest quality and originality). Yet, for this writer at least, it appears that some kind of untranslatable residue collected for Burt on the West Coast that was eventually to confer its own creative death warrant.

Angie

Angie Dickinson was born in 1931 in Kulm, North Dakota. Her moniker at birth was Angeline Brown but she continues to use her name from her first marriage. Her parents ran a small town newspaper and she and her two sisters were local favourites. Her dad ran the movies one evening each week and she became fascinated by the silver screen. Her father became an alcoholic and her mother took him and the children away from Kulm to Burbank, California in an attempt to start a new life (sadly, Angie's mum ended-up supporting all of them, financially).

By 1953 Angie had come of age and was appearing regularly on the Jimmy Durante TV 'Colgate Comedy Hour' and playing bit parts in movies – mostly Westerns. In 1959 she hit paydirt with an appearance as

Feathers in the Howard Hawks *tour de force* rebuttal to *High Noon: Rio Bravo*. Dickinson was cast in this excellent film featuring very human characters supporting and understanding one another under great strain, but she was somewhat feeble in her role.

Despite being given all of the right dialogue as the quintessential Hawksian woman, she possessed neither the oppressiveness nor the spunkiness to match the John Wayne and Walter Brennan characters. The real revelation of the film was, of course, Dean Martin (in a part he obviously understood well). Nevertheless, Angie was critically acclaimed (perhaps, if the truth were told, for her sex appeal) and received the Golden Globe for 'Most Talented Newcomer' in 1960.

Angie had already married a semi-professional football player Gene Dickinson in 1951 but they split amicably in 1955, divorcing in 1960. Following this, she was linked romantically to a number of stars including the leader of the 'rat pack', Frank Sinatra. Dickinson was later to propose that Sinatra was rather disinterested in female company:

> We had dinner alone, certainly over the years. But he preferred groups because it meant stimulating conversation and let's face it, it's more fun. Frank loved to drive, usually his beautiful Dual Ghia. He would pick you up and take you home. He had so many cars, but he never drove me in a convertible – not with my hair. He knew better. (www.swinginchicks.com/angie_dickinson)

After meeting and discovering the good company of Bert and Irma Bacharach, Angie agreed in late-1964 to a blind date with their son. On the surface this appears an odd thing for such a glamorous and sexy actress to do, but again suggests that the lifestyles of movie stars and musicians can be somewhat solitary affairs: plenty of parties (plenty of anything really), but seldom any really close relationships. If one is 'driven' there is very little time for anything else.

But stars have needs, too, and Angie, already aware of the sophisticated bachelor via his music, agreed to meet when they were next both in New York. During the early months of 1965 their on-off relationship blossomed in a kind of symbiotic way. Burt's absences in Europe and Angie's work in Hollywood cemented their ties – 'absence makes the heart grow fonder', as the old adage goes.

As previously suggested, Burt was regarded as something of a ladykiller and was romantically linked with Dusty Springfield by the UK pop press on more than one occasion, but by the time of his first one-to-one meeting with Dusty in April 1964, he was already deeply in love with Angie. In any case, as Edward Leeson (2001) suggests, Dusty always quashed any such rumours, and as Dusty companion Penny Valentine commented:

> [...] there were some heterosexual people in [Dusty's] life who believed that [...] if songwriter Burt Bacharach had not been happily married to Angie Dickinson Dusty would have been overjoyed. It's likely that Dusty did have a crush on Bacharach because he was one of the few men who understood her, was gentle and just as finicky in the studio as she was. But it was, in fact, to Angie that Dusty ran to pour her heart out when things got tough. (Valentine with Wickham, 2000:7)

Within months of that first meeting, Burt and Angie eloped to Las Vegas and married at 3.30 in the morning one day in May 1965. It was a whirlwind romance and featured in an already exciting year for Burt. Angie recently (2000) informed *People* magazine that a combination of personality and looks succeeded in attracting her:

> He woos without even trying. Not only is he devastating looking, but he has this gentility about him, with lots of strength but also softness, like a prizefighter carrying flowers. (Dickinson to *People*, 2000)

Perhaps it was rather more functional than this. Certainly the two were deeply in love, but they already loved somebody else: themselves. So conceivably there was a level of salutary relativism going on here. Unlike his previous unfortunate liaison with Paula Stewart, when Burt claims that songwriting was an attempt to rescue his liaison, these two famous people could initially agree (while there were no children, at least) on **not** seeing each other: their careers remained paramount. Angie even unofficially went to work on Burt's behalf, introducing him to several important Hollywood contacts. His gaze had already fallen on film music composition and Angie ensured that Hollywood was to increasingly envelop his work after his mellifluous successes in 1965. In retrospect, one wonders whether this was actually a good thing.

Californication

Given the infamous hedonism (suggested by the subtitle), both musically and filmically, of America's west coast, one might argue that Bacharach's vitality was compromised by the languid lifestyles of Beverly Hills. He certainly had enough creative mileage in his tank to withstand Southern Californian unenergetic immoderation for a number of years. Yet, given his loss of muse, post-*Lost Horizon*, those somnambulant late-1970s, and even perhaps his less dynamic work up until 'God Give Me Strength', one cannot help but speculate that the cultural geography of Los Angeles was a somewhat malevolent influence (perhaps London might have been a wiser choice, artistically).

One symptom of this hidden crisis was the way that Burt began to abdicate responsibility towards his artistic practice. Firstly, via his increasingly busy concert schedule post-1970 (beginning in Lake Tahoe but often playing for the 'blue rinse brigade' in Las Vegas) he sat back with nostalgia on the art that he had previously prioritised.

Secondly, by the mid-'70s, another more serious symptom of Burt's cultural/ musical crisis appeared: the various attempts to recapture his auratic muse via large-scale offerings. These attempts manifested themselves in two somewhat contradictory pieces: the neo-expressionist *Lost Horizon* and the live Romanticist *Woman* (the latter performed with the Houston Symphony Orchestra in 1978). Both, it seems, were incongruously searching for the approval of the old-fashioned connoisseur: somebody whom Burt had shunned all of his working life! Both were unfavourably received.

In retrospect, then, perhaps the main problem with Burt's marriage to Angie Dickinson (as far as his musical genius was concerned) was less the marriage *per se* and more to do with physical relocation. Wedded bliss moved him away from the centre of his chosen universe - New York City. The couple decamped to a house in Beverly Hills, where they spent the most of the next decade. In interviews Burt usually describes his wavering relationship with Hal, not Angie:

> I moved to California [in 1966] when I married Angie. Hal would come out and we'd do some writing out there. And I had an apartment in New York – we could write there. A lot of the

work we did we'd initiate [...] in the office and at the end of the day we'd break. And Hal would continue working at home, as I would. We both worked very well independently of each other. We'd both want to get away from each other – from the collaboration – because you don't feel as much pressure. You're at home, you go to the piano, go eat dinner, come back, work a little bit [...] the system works well. The separation keeps our outlooks fresh [...] if we spent more time with each other socially, we'd have less to bounce off each other. (in Platts, 2003: 40)

Thus the work patterns had changed. Hal David remained on the east coast in Long Island and writing periods of up to three-four month blocks were established. Hal David would go to California for up to a month, Burt would reappear in New York for a month, and so on. Therefore the split was by no means permanent. However the dissonant cultural mix of New York City, the light and dark that was reflected so well in Burt's writing, the homology (or structural resonance) between the man and his cultural location was all fractured by the California sunshine. Works such as 'Hasbrook Heights', 'One Less Bell To Answer' 'Everybody's Out Of Town', and others, are certainly highly accomplished and entertaining pieces of work, but placed beside 'Alfie' or '[...] Tulsa' there is really no comparison.

Furthermore, because of Burt's relocation, he appeared (at least compositionally) to look back on certain aspects of his own immediate musical past as recyclable episodes. A succession of hits between 1967 and 1970 does suggest great productivity, yet some of these songs were actually written years before (e.g. 'This Guy's In Love With You', 'Close To You', 'To Wait For Love', 'Message To Michael') and his own albums were similarly based upon (mostly) rearrangements of his classic hits. This relative (and I emphasise **relative**!) compositional hiatus led eventually to an interesting impasse: between 1970 and 1974 his own contemporary music progressively failed to distinguish itself, while his earlier compositional searches for perfection were successfully rearticulated by others.

For example, while Richard Carpenter was rearranging the previously rather dismal 'Close To You' into a piece of vocal tiffany glass for his sister Karen, and Isaac Hayes was creating a whole new meaning to both

'Walk On By' and 'The Look Of Love', compositions such as 'Raindrops Keep Falling On My Head' appeared to be the work of a man trying to rewrite his own compositional style under the conditions of Beverly Hills 'predictability'. Occasionally we did get wonderful pieces of avant-garde strangeness such as 'Everybody's Out Of Town' (that's one that would have pleased Darius Milhaud, no doubt) but by and large there were inconsistencies.

Perhaps a life in the presence of the best of everything does not necessarily produce the best of everything, artistically. From the early 1970s–on Burt's work became increasingly predictable, moving from the inventive to the insipid at the drop of a hat. He became aesthetically bound by the historically shaped conventions (and conventionality) of Southern California. B.J. Thomas recalled Bacharach's demeanour by 1970 as being one of:

> [...] the flowing grey hair and the scarves, the ascots. He was a very Hollywood kind of guy, whereas Hal was a very downhome, unaffected person who, if you didn't know who he was you would never guess that he was involved in major music success. (Thomas to Platts, 2003:50)

Indeed, some songs were completed via long distance phone calls. There's nothing wrong with this, of course ('God Give Me Strength' is another example of writing via ansaphone!), but it does indicate detachment. As the time arrived to complete a batch of songs, Burt would jet over to New York and spend hours in the studio with Hal and Phil Ramone. Hal David informed Robin Platts:

> He moved out to L.A. but he kept his apartment in New York for many years after that [on East Sixty-First Street]. I stayed in New York and we worked out a schedule where when I came out to L.A. I checked into the Beverly Wilshire Hotel. We tended to work for about a week to ten days in New York [...] then take about a week to ten days off. And then I'd fly out to California and we'd work about a week to ten days there. It was back and forth and back and forth. That situation went on for a long, long time [...] we were working a lot. We were recording Dionne, so we always needed a lot of songs. For the most part we recorded

169

Dionne in New York. In fact, most of our records were done in New York. Phil Ramone was our recording engineer and we recorded for the most part at A&R Studios. (David ibid, 40)

From this chronological disconnection, it sounds a rather frustrating arrangement and not really conducive to bringing ideas to fruition. Despite being a highly competent production team, Burt and Hal had two different aesthetic perspectives. Phil Ramone was later to admit that he "learned incredible patience and respect for the artists and musicians" having to deal with this state of affairs and remarked strikingly "the hardest thing in the world is trying to maintain a consistency".

Profile

As with all marriages that intercede upon a male working partnership, one cannot help but feel that this high profile marriage (together with Burt's workload of (e.g.) solo albums, TV Specials, concerts, etc.) put a strain on his songwriting partnership with Hal David. Perhaps the later split with Hal was even prophesised somewhat during this busy period 1966-69 (all marriages put a strain on boys club memberships – just ask the surviving Beatles).

 From 1967 Burt and Angie were domiciled in the canyons of L.A. with their new daughter, Nikki, for whom Burt wrote an appealing tune that same year. To all intents and purposes it was a very happy time for both. Yet, there were domestic difficulties. Both before and during her pregnancy, Angie continued accepting somewhat ephemeral, inconsequential movies: the weak *Cast A Giant Shadow*, and *The Chase*, and the confusing but popular John Boorman picture *Point Blank*. Nikki was born prematurely and weighed only two pounds at birth. It was a very worrying time for the couple but the child pulled through and grew into a happy and healthy young thing. Hollywood parties were also a prominent feature of Burt's new life on the West Coast, and it was here, with the assistance of Angie, that important contacts were made into the world of film music. But when questioned these days about those Hollywood parties Burt states flatly:

I did that in another lifetime with Angie Dickinson. (Bacharach to *Independent On Sunday*, 2002)

'Another lifetime' is not simply a statement about a broken relationship: it refers, one suspects, to the inanity of the self-congratulatory syndrome of Hollywood backslappers. What was it that Bacharach fans Donald Fagen and Walter Becker of Steely Dan sang of this fraternity? "Showbiz kids making movies of themselves [...] they don't give a fuck about anybody else". It remains remarkable that any work of musical note was produced in such an enclosed environment.

Furthermore, it seems that while Angie was always very supportive, she was forced to toil away in these desultory film and TV projects while Burt reaped the benefits of her contacts. With the words of Betty Friedan on the lips of practically every enlightened woman of that age, this must have been galling to say the least. Thus, while we see Burt's music merging into film scoring and title songs transcending the films as pop hits, Angie's career remained on relative hold. Burt was somewhat baffled by this inequality:

> With the songwriting process you can stay totally in the background. But [by 1966] I'd reached a different level. I was quite a good looking guy, there was a certain photo opportunity when I was married to a high profile actress, Angie Dickinson, and still I couldn't really understand why people were paying me so much to go and play concerts in Paris or Las Vegas, just to see me conduct my music. I mean, I didn't tap dance, I sang with a very, very limited voice [...] I was sure I'd better not sing too much otherwise people would see how badly I sounded. (Bacharach to Williams, *NME*, 1996)

This retrospective analysis also tends to reflect contemporary interview material of the couple. Despite his fame and fortune Burt was somewhat ill at ease. The structural compliance but also resistance in this marriage was unconsciously stimulating and sapping its make-up (despite the pair appearing as the perfect couple - 'Mr and Mrs America' - in trendy commercials for Martini vermouth). Angie's work in filmic footnotes such as *Sam Whiskey, Some Kind Of Nut,* and *Young Billy Young* were hardly groundbreaking and barely worth the effort. Yet, like Burt, conceivably she felt she had to work or fade into obscurity: that's the way it was. But for Burt, such roles appeared a waste of time and depleting the energy of their relationship (which was already being exhausted by his own overburdening vocation).

Noted journalist Lillian Ross interviewed Bacharach during September 1968 while the musical *Promises Promises* (see on) was being worked into some kind of recognisable shape, and reported Burt bemoaning:

> I wish I could say I'm happy to be here. But I'm really sad. I had to leave my wife and little girl in Beverly Hills and I'm not ashamed to say I miss them very much. Our little girl is two and, you know, it's better for a two year old girl to be at home, running around on the grass, having the pool, backyard and everything.
>
> And besides, my wife Angie Dickinson is an actress and she's just finished a movie. I believe in dual careers. And my wife is a real actress. I can tell. I saw her in that Lee Marvin movie where she plays the girl he sends to sleep with somebody he wants to kill, and I forgot she was my wife. She had me feeling so moved. She was very sympathetic. She captured me very much. Imagine seeing your own wife up there on the screen and having her touch you that much. And with her sitting right there next to me while I'm watching her on the screen. (Bacharach to Ross [i.v.I], *New Yorker*, 1968)

Ross remarked during a second interview conducted shortly before Christmas:

> At the time, Mr Bacharach – talking nostalgically about his wife and little girl back in Beverly Hills, talking affectionately about his parents, talking about being stuck in New York and on the road for three months – had a kind of remote, permanently puzzled, and not exactly happy look, almost as though he were about to go to prison. Last week, he had a clearly happy look. He didn't look puzzled. He looked relieved and free. (Ross [i.v.II], *New Yorker*, 1968)

What do we have here? Ambition mixed with regret, mixed with homesickness, mixed with desire, mixed with love, mixed with a super ego obsessing about work. When people say that Burt had it all, they are quite correct – he most certainly did; but it was all swimming around in his head, making him an example of the typically creative male fashioned by his parents own obsessions – that's love, one supposes. The problem is, as we have discovered, the super ego also acts as a conscience:

I get into enough of a pressure cooker on my own. I'm not concerned about whether I'll be in fashion next year, or whether the bubble bursts a little. Of course I'm concerned about staying healthy. I'm a great believer in exercise. I play basketball. I swim a lot. I believe in massage. I've got this little girl, and I want to be a good father to her. And I want to be a live father. There's that.

But every time I get into a recording studio, there's that final moment of truth. The whole life leads into that one evening. It's a highly personal thing. I don't care if 32 people tell me it's great. It has to satisfy me. You preserve the success in your own mind. My gratification standard is how I personally feel. (Bacharach to Ross, *New Yorker*, 1968)

Burt wanted to work (needed to work, probably) but could only do so at the expense of everything else, including 'normal' relationships. This gradually alienated him from those around him.

Writing

Bacharach certainly entered a new phase in his writing. It took on a different character – less sombre, lighter tonally but moving, like many before and after him, inexorably towards a West Coast bland-out. Perhaps, in this way, Burt was ideal for film music. His lack of resolution, his romantic chords, together with his knowledge of Richard Wagner's *leitmotiv* – an essential part of film scoring - meant that he was able to effortlessly seam into the world of soundtracks.

For example, any classically trained musician knows that Wagnerian characterisations describing specific characters on the stage is but a small step away from film music scoring. Obviously Wagner was writing before film emerged however this idea of expressing feelings alongside a character's appearance is significant. Wagner produced layers and layers of these motifs that help us with the mental state of a character. Burt's 'Raindrops Keep Falling On My Head' from *Butch Cassidy and the Sundance Kid* (1969) works in a similar way: it goes into the 'silly' part in much the same way that Wagner textualises character (i.e. we are attempting to 'hear' what the Paul Newman and Katharine Ross couple are thinking via the music!).

But the world of movie soundtracks is also a place to hide, for it is an efficient way of reproducing and reinforcing stereotypes (and a place where the likes of Burt could fall back upon his classical training). Hollywood is that kind of place: its mood overtakes one. It takes a lot of courage to persist in presenting one's musical values as binding in a town that always places pragmatic usefulness above everything else. One should consider 'Raindrops [...]' with this in mind, perhaps. Both film and song have certainly met with as much disapproval as praise from critics over the years. For example renowned film reviewer John Simon stated of the movie:

> A mere exercise in smart-alecky device-mongering, chock full of out of place and out of period one-upmanship, a battle of wits at a freshman smoker.

James Pallot concurred and expanded:

> Too cute and overrated to high hell; a soap bubble weighed down with praise from average minds [...] nor is it helped by the flatness of Ross or the lamentable Bacharach 'Raindrops' tune, so over exposed in the annals of muzak that to even hear one measure is enough to send one running for the chainsaw. (Pallot & eds, 1994:108)

A little unfair, perhaps, but the soundtrack to *Butch Cassidy* is oddly incongruous. While (say) 'South American Getaway' is a wonderful Swingle Singers-style number and 'Raindrops [...]' is, despite the misgivings of James Pallot *et al* above, a great pop song, after all these years one is still left wondering exactly what these incredibly uplifting pieces of popular music are doing in such a film as this. Apparently 'Raindrops [...]' replaced Simon and Garfunkel's 'Feelin' Groovy' in the rough cut. While to this writer neither seem appropriate, perhaps Burt was inspired to write 'Raindrops' as a direct replacement for 'Feelin' Groovy' – one song stimulated the other, as it were.

Manic

For Burt (and Angie), this period between 1966 and 1970 was manic: creative, yes, but manic, also. Great success pre-empts failure, it announces it from afar (so far away, in fact that few people actually hear it at the time). Burt's career had always been his life, now he had a life **and** a career and something had to give – which was it to be? His creativity? His judgment? His relationship?

When people walk up to you and sing one of your songs in your face, is this a good thing or a bad thing? Does it assist or hinder one's sense of self? When you are married to an equally 'driven' individual who feels trapped by domesticity, how does it feel? Unfortunately there is no tangible history one can report on the inner self, whether one has a realistic or distorted sense of reality when important questions come to call. Bacharach revealed to Hubert Saal:

> I usually know I've got something if I can't sleep. It's a healthy sign even if I'm exhausted in the morning. What I hear is pure melody, no beat. I never write at the piano. You want to get free of your hands – they'll go to the familiar, trap you in the pretty chords. I never even orchestrate at the piano except to check. (Bacharach to Saal, *Newsweek*, 1970)

This is a painful process, not simply for the composer but for those sharing their lives with him:

> Sure I do too much. You've got to do it all, you've only one chance. How long are you going to live, stay healthy, keep your mind sharp, your body strong? I'm an impatient man. I go one month at a time. That's why Angie and I rent the house. I couldn't wait for one to get built. (ibid)

CBS presenter Richard Schlesinger asked Burt in 2002 "do you yell at people" to which Burt replied "no, never, never, never, never, never". Schlesinger then probed a little deeper: "are you self-centred?" he asked; Burt replied, "You bet, but I think that's part of my work, you know".

When interviewed in 1970 Angie philosophised about her on-going marriage to this complex individual. She informed Hubert Saal:

> He's surprised that he likes performing and the applause. It's different from the rest of us. We work for fame, to be public

personalities. He works to write great songs, not to be the one they scream for. (Dickinson to Saal, *Newsweek*, 1970)

Angie was known to help Burt with ideas for compositions. Bacharach stated that his wife was the one who came up with the phrase 'One Less Bell To Answer' in a London hotel room in 1967. Hal David turned this line into a hit song that same year. The poignant lyrics of David would certainly resonate some years later! But Hubert Saal further stated in 1970 that Angie "admits his latest venture puts a strain on their marriage". Angie revealed:

I'm a day person and so is our Nikki. I don't think I could be married to a nightclub performer. Anyway, I think that if the dent in his creative life gets any deeper he'll give everything else up. He knows what's important. I think that one proof of how good our marriage is, is that he hasn't stopped writing good songs. The reason it's good is probably separate bathrooms. (ibid)

Burt admitted (in so many words) in the same interview that his personal life was in need of reassessment. Yet he remained intransigent about his compositional and production work, evidently still heavily overloaded:

I know it's time for me not to be a public person. I just turned down both Dick Cavett and David Frost. There's writing to do. I have to record Dionne in a week and a half. I've got to get up in the morning, have a cup of coffee and write music. Or improvise, or make contact. Touch music, touch it. (Bacharach to Saal, *Newsweek*, 1970)

But what about the wife, Burt? Perhaps (like Sinatra before him) Bacharach really wanted a partner who did not work. He was in for a shock.

Police Woman – knowing when to leave?

The marriage actually lurched on after this revealing interview for another ten years, but only by virtue of the fact that Burt **did** lose his muse, **was** under pressure from Angie to cut out the work, and ultimately because **she** became a massive TV star via her role as Sgt Suzanne 'Pepper' Anderson in *Police Woman*. Angie informed David Fantle and Thomas Johnson of seniorworld.com:

Without *Police Woman* I wouldn't have had a career. The show started about the same time the women's movement was taking off. Ours was the first prime time one-hour show featuring a strong, professional woman. It paved the way for other series to follow. (Dickinson to Fantle & Johnson)

Police Woman ran for four years between 1974 and 1978 and was, as Dickinson alludes, an incredible success. Angie herself won the 1975 Golden Globe for 'Best TV Actress-Drama'. However, although the series was formative in bringing a powerful woman to the centre of the screen, it also received severe criticism towards the end of its life for doing so via Dickinson's character using entrapment (prostitution, for example) as a device. It was eventually shelved via a combination of banal plot lines and a drop in interest from the viewing public. From her promising beginnings as a liberated and independent female, 'Pepper' Anderson had degenerated into another Hollywood stereotype.

Neither Burt nor Angie could have it both ways and sadly their marriage was over as the 1970s were drawing to a close. The resumption of Angie's career undoubtedly contributed to the breakdown of their partnership. It was Burt, not Angie, who finally lost patience:

She was busy all the time. Yet I was glad to see her get that hot. When you're with somebody and care about them, you want them to do well. (Bacharach to Hunter, *Us*, 1996)

And Angie:

It was impossible, it was horrendous. I didn't balance it – he flew the coop and I don't blame him (Dickinson to *Biography Channel*, 2003).

Bacharach still holds in great esteem his relationship with Angie Dickinson. For him she was:

A terrific lady. Angie is the type of woman that would do anything for the man she loves. When I did that first movie, *What's New, Pussycat*, she would often get up in the middle of the night to change the film on my Moviola machine. In general it's often a Libran quality. (Bacharach to Wayne, *Vanity Fair*, 1996)

177

Angie was an independent woman married to a musically obsessed genius (who, as a form of relaxation, would replace obsessing about music with obsessing about horses!). She herself stated in a recent AMC biography programme about her life "I think most people would think, gee, I would have liked to have led her life". But marriage, music and the movies are about as compatible as a fish in a tree.

1966 and all that

Moving on, the hits kept coming throughout Burt's first year in the Canyons of Los Angeles but Dionne Warwick's excellent version of 'Message To Michael' aside they were mostly only minor and somewhat forgettable. Jackie DeShannon was unable to follow up 'What The World Needs Now' with anything sizeable, despite recording two Bacharach and David songs 'A Lifetime Of Loneliness' and 'Windows And Doors'.

Film was becoming the main vehicle for Bacharach and David songs: Trini Lopez recorded 'Made In Paris' (the title tune from a weak Ann-Margret movie) and Tom Jones cut 'Promise Her Anything' (the title of a Warren Beatty and Leslie Caron comedy), but neither set the world alight. Actually, both songs are curiosities in that they feature electric guitar riffs, but as a consequence of the vocals, they don't really work well. Both renditions seem uncharacteristically uncomfortable – Jones' in particular seems very affected; neither song is well suited to the movies (or indeed well-produced).

One curio also appeared that year (broadcast on December 7 1966, to be precise) when Burt and Hal wrote (rather hastily) what a few 'Burt connoisseurs' regard as the first rock opera. This was a TV special starring Ricky Nelson and Joannie Sommers entitled *On The Flip Side,* which charted the downfall of a teen idol. By 1965 Nelson's career was also hitting the skids (he had not had a hit since the British Invasion) and so the plot must have resonated with him, somewhat.

Nelson portrays Carlos O'Connor, a washed-up rock star at the age of 25. Realising that beat groups are the 'in thing', O'Connor enlists a band, The Celestials, and a Beatles sound-alike noise emerges in songs like 'Fender Mender' (complete with a name check for the 'Fab Four' and several 'yeah yeahs', to boot) and 'They're Gonna Love It'.

It is nothing like a rock opera, of course. First of all there are far too few songs and far too much script for it to count as 'opera'. Secondly, the music was hardly rock, featuring a full orchestra. The soundtrack was actually arranged and conducted by Burt's old chum Peter Matz, a graduate of the cocktail lounge if ever there was one. Bacharach does not concur with his fans in regarding it as a kind of innovative lost treasure and cares to recall very little of the show. Some might argue that it is the forerunner to the Tony winning *Promises Promises*, but Bacharach states only that he didn't "think it was very good"!

Hal David is a 'tad' more accommodating:

> I think 'They Don't Give Medals [To Yesterday's Heroes]' is a great song. That has great meaning to me [...] and it was fun working with Ricky. (in Platts, 2003:51-52)

Alfie

> I'd say the song that comes closest to expressing what I'm like is 'Alfie'. (David to Paphides, *Time Out*, 1999)

Alfie the movie was produced and directed by Lewis Gilbert and released to great critical praise in 1966. It's a British film through and through and is a surprisingly successful exercise in dramatic irony. We listen to a tawdry running commentary on the leading protagonist's sexual conquests and criminal aspirations, while the audience already instinctively and instructively knows more about him than he does himself. Screenwriter Bill Naughton had already successfully used this approach as both a play and a novel of the same title. Yet our suspension of disbelief is less to do with the screenplay and more the responsibility of Michael Caine, whose disarming naiveté as Alfie is irresistible.

Alfie is undoubtedly a time-bound film but does have a little more universality than we at first give it credit. Any longevity the film still has is carried by its non-judgemental attitude, rather than its sexual frankness. Unlike later feminist discourses that opinionatedly condemned *Alfie* as a 'crude propaganda tract for chauvinist male pigs' (Alexander Walker), it presents Michael Caine's Alfie simply as a type. Its portrayal of 'Swinging London' is persuasive however and the social realism extends far beyond that of *What's New, Pussycat* and *After The Fox*. As with the song, the film's final note is of loneliness not fulfilment. The publicity slogan that announced the film to the British public: 'Is Every Man An Alfie? Ask Any Woman' actually meant that as many women as men were attracted to the movie. 'Alfie' (the song) is timeless and arguably one of Bacharach and David's finest achievements.

It was Ed Wolpin who first suggested that the duo pen the theme song for Famous-Paramount, but the pair were less than enthusiastic and apparently declined the commission twice. Wolpin was sure that Burt and Hal could come up with something special and pitched the commission at them a third time. On this occasion Hal agreed to read the script and, discovering the pay-off line where Alfie briefly ponders 'what's it all about?' decided to position a lyric positing this question from the point of view of the women Alfie had hurt.

On this occasion he wrote the libretto before Burt had organised any music:

> [...] we've written some wonderful pieces that started with a lyric. Hal had most of 'Alfie' done before I did the music. (Bacharach to Heckman, *Los Angeles Times*, 1993)

The lyric, therefore, is almost poetic in nature: a kind of mini-libretto beginning with six significant rhetorical questions before the arrival of the bridge. Most writers would have probably chosen to enhance the hero's 'devil may care' attitude or his laddish humour, but not David:

> I've had some terrible titles thrown my way [...] I never thought 'Alfie' was going to be a great title [...] my favourite song (of mine) but [...] I didn't know which way to go. It took me a long time to figure out how to write that lyric [but] I came as close to getting it right as I've ever had, in that lyric, [...] the humanity one should have and we hope we all should have. (David to Leigh, *BBC: On The Beat*, 2001)

We don't think it's strange any more because we're used to it but when you're told 'write a song called Alfie', it sounds like an English music-hall song. You could have made it a little funny and it could have worked, but I did it very seriously. (David to Fiegal, *The Guardian*, 2000)

The fascinating point about this wonderful work of art is that instead of echoing Alfie's worldview, David places the song from the point of view of an amalgam of the Julia Foster and Jane Asher characters. By doing this he successfully expresses the feelings of the audience, and not necessarily those articulated in the movie. This is a masterstroke because, despite the connotations we now have about the 1960s, the question of a deepening crisis concerning morality was contextual of that era. It was a decidedly insensitive audience that did not walk away from the movie theatre wondering indeed what life was all about.

As far as public reception of the song was concerned, it took a variety of different pathways depending upon where one actually resided. The film was essentially a British production without any major US money and so was in a problematic position. It was only able to gain a US distributor, via United Artists, upon their insistence that an American artiste sang the theme. Consequently, a rather disinterested Cher sang on the American print. Lewis Gilbert however insisted that Cilla Black – far more popular in the UK than Cher, or even Dionne Warwick – should sing the song. So it was to be.

In typically Bacharach fashion, Burt threw his weight behind the Anglo version and went so far as to conduct Cilla in the Abbey Road Studios while George Martin produced. This session has now gone into legend as Burt pulled every last sinew from the unassuming Cilla, pushing her through one take after another in search of his particular brand of enchantment. Cilla later recalled:

> It was ever so difficult; the range in it was unbelievably hard so when I started the song in the soft voice it was awfully difficult to get all of the energy up […] from my boots to go for that high note […] I was hurting […] I certainly wouldn't have done it for a Quasimodo! Because it was Burt and he was gorgeous and so talented and I enjoyed his company. (Black to *BBC: This Is Now*, 1996)

The song was only just within Black's vocal reach and Burt spent hours attempting to get Cilla to give her all. Martin, seeing that Cilla was exhausted and past her peak, eventually turned to Burt: "Burt, what exactly are you looking for?" Burt replied "George, I'm looking for that little bit of magic." Martin retorted "well, actually, Burt, I thought we had it in take three". No reply – but we got take three on the record! Bacharach later recalled to the *Liverpool Echo*:

> I remember going into the studio when she recorded [...] 'Alfie'. It was quite an experience believe me. Cilla still talks about it. We certainly had fun [!]. It was a great moment with the legendary engineer [!] George Martin who worked with the Beatles sitting in the booth. A tremendously gifted man (Bacharach to Riley, *Liverpool Echo*, 2002)

And, perhaps with a little more contrition, to the BBC:

> I was very hard on the singer. I don't think she knew what hit her. We must have gone 28 or 29 takes with her [looking for] that little bit more [...] just some magic. (Bacharach to *BBC: This Is Now*, 1996)

Cilla was to later inform Tony Barrow:

> When I first heard Burt Bacharach's 'Alfie' I didn't like the demo disc they played me. I remember on the demo there was a fella singing. Apart from that, I mean you only call dogs 'Alfie'! Also it did remind me of Gracie Fields' song 'Walter'. Besides you only sang songs like 'Alfie' as a comic record. And I thought, couldn't it have been 'Joshua' or something like that?

> I didn't record it because I thought the film was going to be a hit or anything like that. I wasn't hoping for sales on the basis of the film's success, because the song isn't even in the film. When I recorded the song the film wasn't even out, so nobody knew whether it would be a hit or not. (Black to Barrow, 1993:38)

Cilla Black's performance of 'Alfie' is simply magnificent. If ever a vocalist reached beyond her grasp (and reinvented her career) via one performance, it was this 'take three' rendition of 'Alfie'. Judged by many up until that moment as an only average singer enjoying success on the coat tails of the Beatles, Cilla seized the moment, gave her all, and in the process rewrote her role in the history of British popular music. In fact, from this moment on Cilla's albums and singles appeared more interesting and inventive. Apart from a ruck of hit singles over the next ten years, she truly achieved greatness with her renditions of Randy Newman's 'I've Been Wrong Before', Paul McCartney's 'Step Inside Love' and Greenaway/Cook/Lordan's 'Conversations'.

'Alfie' is a difficult song, but does not challenge performance extremes as much as it at first appears (nor as much as other Bacharach compositions). Its meter is steady and its interval leaps tend to remain within the octave (the two-syllable utterance 'Alf-ie' moves up a fifth). Chordally, 'Alfie' is Bacharach's usual juxtaposing of shade with illumination. Shostakovich would have been proud of Bacharach, here. 'Alfie' displays dramatic interplay between gothic darkness and uncertain light throughout: extended majors and deep minors vie for position without either achieving superiority. It's in the key of C but Burt has Cilla singing in the key of Bb, often regarded as a key with greater tonality (Chopin used Bb minor for his more sombre pieces). The chords are classic Bacharach, beginning Cmaj9, Ebmaj9, and Abmaj9 before moving into the minor. These apparently imperceptible major 9ths are more than a little deceptive however; Michael Ancliffe:

> The first three chords are fascinating because within two of the three are contained minors – an E minor in the first and a G minor in the second. So, although we have a series of uplifting chords there is also present an element of uncertainty. This is classic Bacharach in that firstly, it presents us with a way of modulating into the minor with the suggestion of that minor already being there and secondly, that it represents note-for-word Hal's beautiful lyrics musically – symbiotically, actually. (Michael Ancliffe, personal interview, 2003)

While the voicing in 'Alfie' is gruelling, Cilla achieves great codal competency. Ancliffe:

> I often think that Cilla imagines Alfie as a Liverpudlian! But also her vocal technique is quite brilliant, given her limited range. For me Dionne's version lacks emotion and that's because, ironically, she is so unforced. But Cilla gives her all and produces that two-

vocal effect, complemented by the fullness of the arrangement. Both Dionne and Bacharach don't seem to get their arrangement right and that second version's arrangement is particularly lacking especially going into the second sequence. (ibid)

This inability to move between one type of vocality and dentality into another type is illustrative of how few singers are able to ignite this song – despite their obvious talent; the original, however, is cogent. In other words, we understand Cilla's two voicings: we know where each voice will lead us, emotionally. Therefore, although Dionne's later (US hit) version is a strong rendition (specifically her live performance on the 39th Academy Awards show in 1967), her natural vocal effortlessness actually goes against the grain of meaning in the song. One needs to hear two different vocal textures in order to fully understand the emotional turmoil of the female narrator.

The suspension at the end of 'Alfie' tells it all as it engages us musically with the same questioning that Hal David asks lyrically at the beginning. There is no conventional 'outro', as such, instead Cilla's 'light' voice plays off against the darkness of the deferment, leaving us with an utter lack of resolution and hopelessness: all human life is in this song, expressed in this performance, within this arrangement, on this 45 rpm plastic record.

Reach Out - Alpert

Burt signed a recording contract in 1967 with A&M Records. This company (Alpert and Moss) had been established in 1962 to cater principally for the work of Herb Alpert. Alpert was a trumpeter/producer/manager who via an overdubbing experiment in his own garage-based studio in 1962 had come across the commerciality of slightly out of 'synch' trumpets. He described this effect as 'Spanish flair' and proceeded to specialise in Mexican-flavoured 'Tijuana style' instrumentals incorporating the sound.

Herb Alpert's recordings fed into the US interest in 'exotica' in much the same way as Martin Denny's Hawaiian music had done, and Alpert proved very popular on both the singles and album charts up until 1967. His first single, the instrumental 'The Lonely Bull' is considered something of a minor classic and, as the 1960s progressed, like Bacharach, he tended to appeal to an older, somewhat musically disenfranchised pop audience.

Reach Out, the Bacharach album released that year by Alpert's label, was a phenomenal success. The tracks were mostly rearrangements of Bacharach and David hits, and Burt spent a great deal of time on the songs, recasting them and changing the character of the material. This was an immense job for any composer to reshape his hit material in such a way: both time-consuming and somewhat laborious. But Burt informed Skip Heller that this reworking was essential to keep his music both out of the ordinary and appealing:

> I would only sing part of a song. I was afraid to do more. Then the girls would sing the rest. Or I would have a whole instrumental. If there were key lines I'd use vocals dramatically, or maybe an English horn, which I'd try to use as judiciously as possible. Then maybe two flugelhorns. There's only so much expression you're going to get out of lead instruments, so I would try and keep it interesting. (Bacharach to Heller, *Pulse*, 1995)

It was also essential for FM radio, of course. Orchestral reworkings of his hits were perfect fodder for the stereo stations dedicated to easy listening. By 1967 these stations represented Burt's (and A&M's) chief catchment areas.

But the album also remains interesting: it sold by the lorry-load and although *Reach Out* can probably be found in car boot and garage sales around both the UK and US, Skip Heller considers it something of a masterpiece. Heller states, for him, "*Reach Out* (and the follow up *Make It Easy On Yourself*) [is] somewhat of a neglected link between the Beach Boys' *Pet Sounds* and Randy Newman's 1972 album *Sail Away*. It's the bridge between the 'teenage symphonies to God' which Brian Wilson created, and the more adult composer as auteur ethic that set Newman apart from his Southern Californian contemporaries". (ibid)

Bacharach was both charmed and bemused about the success of *Reach Out*:

> The first album I made as a recording artist, three years ago, sold thirty-five hundred copies [in the US]. My second one has been out for nine months and it's already sold over a hundred and thirty-five thousand copies. (Bacharach to Ross, *New Yorker*, 1968)

185

Burt went on to suggest that the appeal of *Reach Out* was "cross-generational", but perhaps this is incorrect. Already by 1965, cultural critics such as Susan Sontag (*On Culture and the New Sensibility*) were describing Bacharach's music (and specifically Dionne Warwick's singing) as "complex and pleasurable event[s] on a par with a Rauschenberg painting [to be experienced] without condescension" (Sontag, 1965). Sontag was suggesting that certain forms of popular music were artistically reproducing a vision of America as it might be seen through the eyes of thirty-somethings.

Bacharach also suggested in the above interview with Lillian Ross that the songs were "basically sophisticated", but Sontag was really proposing that binary definitions such as this needed re-evaluating in the light of what was occurring within popular culture. Re-evaluation of all of the arts was dismantling such high/low dichotomies: Burt was carelessly using a past language here. In actual fact, it was a level of musical disenfranchisement rather than 'sophistication' that caused labels such as A&M to prosper. *Time* was to declare about stablemates Herb Alpert's Tijuana Brass:

> The Tijuana Brass is basically just a good old-fashioned melody band that makes no pretensions towards the new. No soul-searching Thelonious Monk stuff, no revolutionary developments [...] just pleasant music that is as universal in its way as Bob Hope is in his.

Thus one could argue that Burt's association with A&M codified both his own profile (and that of the label's) as the apotheosis of disenfranchised pop. For example, his equally successful colleagues on A&M included Sergio Mendes and Brasil 66, the Sandpipers, and Julius Wechter's Baja Marimba band, in addition to the aforementioned Tijuana Brass. Soon, A&M would also include the Carpenters, Paul Williams, and Captain and Tennille on their roster. This was not a label aimed at the psychedelic or heavy rock fans of the day (although it was later to welcome left-field artists). The label concentrated on 'adult orientation', appealing to the sixties' silent majority - those who expressed a desire for classier, soothing sounds such as instrumental albums and soundtracks.

By 1968 Bacharach had taken pleasure in plenty of hit songs but was still to enjoy a US number one single. His new connections with A&M ensured that this finally came to pass in May '68 when Herb Alpert succeeded with his recording of 'This Guy's In Love With You'. Alpert's Tijuana Brass were awarded the privilege of their own US TV special that Spring and Alpert was persuaded by TV director Jack Haley Jnr to sing a song. Herb was later to document:

> I was in the habit of asking all great songwriters if there was a melody that haunted them that they had written or that had been recorded and felt should have been a hit. When I asked this question of my friend Burt Bacharach, he gave me a song entitled 'This Girl's In Love With You'. (Alpert to *Biography Channel*, 2003)

Bacharach confirmed:

> We had written the song and then we made some changes in the song for Herb. It was a pretty ideal song for him. And I was close to Herb and close to Jerry Moss, because of being signed to the label. (ibid)

And Herb Alpert continued:

> I fell in love with the melody and called Hal David to ask if he would consider doing some modifications on the lyrics, in order to suit my appearance on the television special. He graciously agreed, and I flew to New York to be with him while he made the changes in the lyric, which suited me, and the show perfectly. (ibid)

Hal David also placed his perspective on the transaction:

> We thought Herb, who's a super musician, would probably have enough range to do it and he did. [The song] is not so limited in range that we wrote it for someone whose range is minimal – we thought that Herb would have enough […]. (David to Leigh, *BBC: On The Beat*, 2001)

> He wanted to do that song on a TV special he was doing. It was a song he was going to sing to his wife and [the lyric] was not quite

appropriate for what he wanted to say. He asked us whether we could change [it] so it would fit what he needed. And I did; and he did it on the show and got a terrific reaction and recorded it. And it turned out to be a stunning hit. (David to Platts, 2003:59)

Bacharach ensured the success of the single by conducting his own arrangement on the recording date at Goldstar Studios in Los Angeles, but there was something very special about Alpert's soft and somewhat reticent voice that suited the song, irrespective of any arrangement (actually the piano is too loud).

Aided by the phenomenal success of the TV special (entitled *The Beat Of The Brass*) that May '68 – the programme reached an estimated 17 million homes - 'This Guy [...]' became one of the biggest selling records of 1968 (also reaching number 3 on the UK singles charts) and represented three significant 'firsts' for those involved. It was Alpert's first number one and first million-seller, it was the first number one for Burt as a producer, and it was the first number one for Bacharach and David as songwriters. According to a 1968 *Time* profile, Alpert grossed $30 million dollars and paid his band members $100,000 each in 1968 – both astronomical sums for the day. Both *Reach Out* and 'This Guy's In Love With You' certainly upped the ante for the entire A&M team – including our hero!

Chapter 10

(False) Promises Promises

Both Burt and Hal went crazy, because every night it was slightly
different [...]. (Phil Ramone, 2003)

It was intense [...]. (Bacharach to *Saturday Evening Post*, 1968)

By 1968 the Bacharach and David pop single, that opus of fulfilment
discovered and created through musical industrialisation, was becoming
less common. Between January 1967 and December 1969 only 20-
or-so Bacharach-related singles were issued in the States, whereas the
previous two years had witnessed at least 30 (and probably more). The
magnetism of the single played a significant role in Burt's success yet it
was now taking second place to his film work and his first (and so far only)
Broadway musical. While Herb Alpert for example, had already enjoyed a
hit single the previous year, it was as a consequence of Burt's film scoring:
the signature tune to the movie *Casino Royale*.

Casino Royale

While not in the same league as 'Alfie', the instrumental theme for *Casino
Royale* is a joyous piece of nonsense that almost (but not quite) rescues a
wretched film. Burt had revealed his hand in 1967 by stating that he wished
to work in films, preferably three per year. For the first half of 1967 he had
two scores to work on: first the Jack Lemmon and Elaine May comedy
Luv and secondly the Bond spoof *Casino Royale*. Bacharach commenced
work on both immediately, but soon realised that he could not meet the
demanding schedule and pulled out of the *Luv* project. So it was to be the
movie *Casino Royale* that dominated his work for the first six months of
1967.

Actually, dominated is hardly the word. Such was the magnitude of this
project everything else was placed on the backburner and there were no
Bacharach and David numbers on the Dionne Warwick album released that
March (although Burt did arrange one or two songs). This record was an
odd release in any case: entitled *On Stage And In The Movies,* it featured

Dionne's reworking of stage and movie themes – a bland, uneventful affair sounding rather like an afternoon gig in a Las Vegas cabaret lounge.

As a movie, *Casino Royale* is an unmitigated disaster: two hours and eleven minutes of clutter and confusion, full of witless and unfunny star-loaded vignettes. It is practically unwatchable. Critics have described it thus:

> Woeful all-star kaleidoscope, a way out spoof which generates far fewer laughs than the original [...] One of the most shameless wastes of time and talent in screen history.

> Donald Zec depicted *Casino Royale* as "the worst film I ever enjoyed".

> A mess. [...] two hours and eleven minutes of non sequitur. (Pallot *et al*, 1994:119)

Casino Royale first found life as a one-hour TV programme for CBS in 1954, starring Barry Mason. It was regarded as something of a success and the film rights were sold in 1955, eventually being acquired by Charles Feldman. One feels that every single actor playing a role in *Casino Royale* was also playing Mr Feldman for a chump – it was certainly 'money for old rope'.

Probably thinking that he walked on water after the success of his earlier film *What's New Pussycat*, the British wing of Columbia periodically lobbed inordinate amounts of cash at Feldman, but the result remained the same: a totally unfocused and clueless catastrophe! Anything with five (yes **five**) directors and screenwriters has to rank on most people's list of potential 'turkeys'.

The soundtrack however is a success. Not only does it feature two splendid pieces of music that became hits in their own right: the aforementioned 'Casino Royale Theme' (Herb Alpert) and 'The Look Of Love' (Dusty Springfield and also Sergio Mendes & Brasil 66), but pieces such as 'Dream On James, You're Winning' and 'Little French Boy' are excellent examples of *leitmotiv*, expressing and enhancing the characterisations in each respective scene.

Indeed, the music is literally the only saving grace of *Casino Royale*. As an album in its own right it can also take repeated listenings without prior knowledge of the movie – unusual for a soundtrack. In fact it is probably better to dwell on the music without any recourse to the questionable activities on screen!

Under such artistically appalling circumstances it is quite amazing that Bacharach pulled out the stops, at all. Surrounded by yes men in Hollywood, working for a producer who had obviously lost the plot in London, and with umpteen screenwriters (including Woody Allen) who wouldn't recognise a decent gag if they fell over it, Bacharach and David were dealing with a 'pup' from very early in the proceedings.

Upon arriving in London with the bulk of their soundtrack completed they came across disarray of such cosmic proportions that changes were being made on an almost hourly basis in attempts to save the picture. For example, Burt was forced to write another vocal track practically on site. Fortunately, he came up with 'The Look Of Love', based on a theme he had already written for the movie. Similarly by chance, Dusty Springfield was available to sing it. Hal David enlightened Spencer Leigh:

> We wrote it for the film, in London – as we wrote many, many things in London – She was available and perfect for the song; the film company liked her and that's how it happened. Dusty Springfield is one of the great pop singers of all time. (David to Leigh, *BBC: On The Beat*, 2001)

The entire soundtrack was recorded in London but Burt put out a call for help to Herb Alpert, in Los Angeles. Alpert recalled:

> […] Bacharach called me from London while he was doing the score […] and asked if I would play the trumpet over the track he had just recorded. He sent the tape and I put a couple of trumpets on, added some maracas and sent back a two-track stereo tape […] Burt was happy. (Alpert to *Biography Channel*, 2003)

Burt was probably more relieved than happy: relieved that anything had come together on this muddle of a film.

Fortunately for Bacharach, a couple of hit singles issued forth from *Casino Royale*, ensuring that his music was not dragged down with the film. In fact he received an Academy Award Nomination for best song in 1968 with 'The Look Of Love' but it lost out to (of all things) 'Talk To The Animals' from *Doctor Dolittle*.

Dusty Springfield was scheduled to sing the song at the Awards ceremony on 10 April. The event had been postponed from the 8 April out of respect for Dr Martin Luther King, whose funeral was to be held on the 9 April. Dusty, however, cancelled at the very last minute to promote her latest single in the UK – which never actually appeared. Looking back, this decision probably cost Bacharach and David their first US number one (Herb Alpert's 'This Guy's In Love With You' wouldn't touch the top of the charts for another month).

Having recorded 'The Look Of Love' for *Casino Royale*, Dusty Springfield re-recorded the song for her own record company, Philips. This recording was issued on the b-side of 'Give Me Time' in both the US and UK, but in the States it was flipped by a disc jockey and gathered enough pace on the radio to become a sizeable hit (no. 22). In the UK 'Give Me Time' remained the a-side and performed only moderately on the singles charts that summer of 1967. Hal David recalled that its success was due:

> […] in no small part to a Seattle deejay, Pat O'Day, who preferred the b-side and therefore decided to flip the disc. It became a hit in Seattle, and then from Seattle it spread to California; from California it worked its way over the radio back east to New York. It was a hit every step of the way. (David in Howes, 2001: 96)

Burt remains somewhat ambivalent about the re-recording stating:

> You don't write songs to be hits when you're scoring a movie, you write what's going to serve the movie [so] one was right for the movie and then they made a more commercial record after that, built around what I had done. (Platts. 2003:53 & 54)

However the first Screen Gems version (arranged by Burt and produced by Phil Ramone) is undoubtedly the best. The John Franz re-recording for

Philips is too long, for a start, and the lack of strings and non-attention to bass ruins the track, making it sound like a cocktail bar trio going through the motions. Furthermore, for this writer, saxophonist Reg Guest leans far too far towards plagiarising Stan Getz. Even Dusty's vocal rendition is a tad uninspired in places (she claims not to have liked the song).

In all, perhaps the best version of this number is Bacharach's much shorter orchestral arrangement on the *Reach Out* album. It is almost symphonic and its counterpoint interplay between one theme and another is explosive. Towards the end of the Bacharach adaptation the strings detonate in a cascade reminiscent of Mantovani at his best, while the melody is delivered via muted horns and a groovy Hammond organ – absolutely delightful.

Charts

There were a few chart successes for Burt during 1967 aside from his film-related material and this shortlist included one of Burt and Hals' finest efforts, 'The Windows Of The World'. There remains however an interesting split between the lyric writer and singer on the one hand and the composer on the other, concerning the importance of this song, suggesting that perhaps the Bacharach detachment spoken of in the previous chapter was prevalent at this time.

Both David and Warwick still regard the song as a valid and timely protest number. David initially pictured it as a lyrical thesis about his two sons having to fight in Vietnam, while Warwick acknowledged the song as "something that had to be said" (she also cites it as her favourite Bacharach and David song). Hal David was to state to the music press at the time that:

> [...] there are many message songs being written. More and more of them are violent. I tend to take a gentler approach in my protest. I have a feeling that in the final analysis, the gentler approach will reach more people.

Warwick later concurred in the interview cited above:

> Other people had been thinking it and one day he just found a way to say it. It's about the kind of world we live in, and the way we feel about it, and again he tells it simply in just the way we'd

like to say it ourselves (Warwick in Platts, *Discoveries*, 1997)

Yet Burt remains curiously obtuse about the lyric and has been quoted as discussing the track only in respect of its production values e.g. "I didn't do a good production and arrangement on that [...] I missed that record a little bit."

More than a clue, here, of the gradual social separation brought about by the inculcation of Southern Californian nonchalance – were these fascinating lyrics of **no** interest to him? He later stated in a TV interview that lyrics were (to paraphrase him) not important linguistically, but phonetically. They achieved their semiotic status through the sound of the words and their relationship to the arrangements rather than via their etymology, as such. This is fair enough, but 'Windows Of The Word' is practically poetry. Nevertheless, Burt remains predisposed towards the sound:

> [re 'Windows Of The World' and 'Paper Mache'] I made them too subtle. There wasn't enough energy in the mix. I treated them more the way I wanted to hear them, perhaps, than the way the world might have wanted them. They could have stood a little more grease in the sound. If the drums had been playing from the start on 'Windows Of The World', if the feel had been a bit harder, I think we would have had a better chance with it. (Bacharach to *Almo Productions*, 1979)

Given its stunning lines and judicious delivery, this is a superfluous postulation. Appearing as it did right in the middle of the 1967 Summer Of Love, the rest of the world found 'Windows Of The World' more than acceptable. To appear to display such lack of interest in David's piece remains an odd confession from Burt.

Neither did Burt like Dionne's follow-up: 'I Say A Little Prayer'. Yet this recording was even more successful than 'Windows Of The World', reaching number 4 in the US singles charts that same year:

> I didn't like Dionne's record [...] I didn't like the record we made. I thought the tempo was too fast. It was too rushed, too nervous. I even tried not to have the record come out. (in Platts, 2003:57)

Burt further explained his idiosyncrasy to Stuart Maconie thus:

> What does happen with me is that I tinker, I fiddle; I've never had
> a song come to me fully formed in a blinding flash of inspiration.
> If it comes too easy then I don't think it's any good. So I turn it
> upside down and look at it in the middle of the night. It's a short
> form, three-and-a-half minutes, so everything counts. You can
> get away with murder in a forty-minute piece but not in three-
> and-a-half. Some songs, you know, they beat you up: too notey,
> too wordy, too much. (Bacharach to Maconie, *Q*, 1996)

From this unambiguous comment, one can see that the significance lies
for Burt in the sound, not words. Yes, the scoring, the orchestration are
significant, but what he hears in his head has to be transcribed. If it isn't,
then the creative pain begins: hours and hours of it until something clicks.
In the case of 'I Say A Little Prayer', perhaps it never quite transferred
from head to score:

> It's a question of what you hear. What's going to fit, in the
> rhythm section, or on the second and fourth beat – not how can
> you show everybody what great orchestrations you can write. It's
> a goddam crossword puzzle and what I keep is what I think will
> help the song and free the singer. Of course if the song isn't there,
> you're not going to disguise it with beautiful strings. (Bacharach
> to Saal, *Newsweek*, 1970)

Despite the capricious perceptions of Burt Bacharach about Dionne's
version of 'I Say A little Prayer', it remains for this writer the song that
confirms Warwick as one of the very best chanteuses of her generation.

The very finest – a little analysis

Dionne didn't only rival Aretha Franklin, she surpassed her on this number
for both tone colour and versatility. Warwick could literally sing anything
that was put in front of her. Although Aretha's arrangement of 'I Say A
Little Prayer' is both inventive and articulate, this writer has always been
of the opinion that the Warwick version was probably too difficult for
Franklin to sing.

The verses and choruses in Warwick's original are set up antiphonally, separating Hal David's narrative of a dubious daily ritual from the desires of eternal love expressed in the mind of the singer. There is a tension in the Dionne version of the song, perhaps even an air of desperation expressed in this version that suggests uncertainty – particularly in the somewhat manic 'Forever and Ever […]' line in the original. Hal David:

> In 'I Say A Little Prayer', where the chorus is 'forever forever', that's where the title would ordinarily be, and yet the song for me took place in the verses, so that's where I put the title […]. (David to Fiegel, *The Guardian*, 2000)

This tension actually appears in many other Bacharach and David songs and Hal expressly used lyrics to display ambivalence between melody and language. For example, in the same interview he admitted:

> 'Do You Know The Way To San Jose' is bright and rhythmic and so most people would think it was instinctively happy – but it wasn't to me. (ibid)

The ambivalence, the internal ambiguity is undoubtedly dissipated in Aretha's version, which expresses confidence rather than distraction (and does so by flattening the chorus diatonics into pentatonics). This is rather odd when such apparent certainty comes to be undercut by the pleading 'say you'll love me too […] answer my prayer'. One tends to feel that Aretha narrates the words rather than interprets them.

In the albeit capable hands of Aretha Franklin the song effectively becomes a soul number (and of course there's nothing wrong with that), but the gospel grace-notes somehow relieve 'I Say A Little Prayer' of its original objectives. Musicologist Robin Hartwell referred to this when discussing Bacharach's exchange of ideas at the 2003 Polar Music Prize in Sweden:

> […] Bacharach spoke about positive collaborations […] with singers who would say 'But Burt I can't sing something my soul doesn't feel', and there would be note changes. I heard this in Aretha Franklin's recording of 'I Say A Little Prayer'. There was one interval that was a bit too complicated, so she simplified it, although the interval as composed is much more interesting

compositionally. But who cares? That's 'soul'. (Robin Hartwell, personal communication, 2003)

It remains worthy of note just how few of these Bacharach songs are actually 'soulful' in their original state. Chapter three of this work quotes Donald Fagen of Steely Dan stating that Burt's work was (to paraphrase him) a kind of meeting of soul and classical music. But Dionne Warwick is not (and never has been) a soul singer ("[the songs] were considered R&B because I happened to be a Black woman") and Bacharach does not write soul music. With the notable exception of 'All Kinds Of People', Bacharach does not even write with the gospel tinge that so affected the later work of his white Brill contemporaries such as Carole King. All of this suggests that the creative triad of Burt, Hal and Dionne was bound to be special.

Notation

Furthermore (and, perhaps deeply ironically, given we are working in the untheoretical, pseudo-nihilistic area of popular music), this was partially because of the importance of traditional notation. An approach that tries to put everything in the score becomes too difficult to read, but Burt's notation facilitated the process of communicating information to Dionne (a good reader), who could then interpret the text in her way (the music was written down specifically for **her**, in the first place).

Via notation, Burt was able to transmit a whole way of thinking about music but his thoughts were not 'notated' as such. A score sets up a framework that identifies certain essential properties for a singer such as Dionne Warwick but Bacharach understood that in and around his notes there lay a vast domain of interpretive possibilities and articulations. Dionne was still able to express herself in many different ways, vocally (e.g. in terms of timbre - notation says very little about this). Bacharach later stated:

I think it's important to be able to write music down. I try to encourage young people [to] learn the rules. Then you can break the rules down the line. But learn to write it down. (Bacharach to Rowland, *Musician*, 1996)

Burt became the master of the smallest link in a score. Even the smallest museme could become a style indicator – perhaps this is what begins to separate Burt's work from his contemporaries. Like a brilliantly written screenplay, everything was carefully scripted but appeared spontaneous. Perhaps, too, the pattern of 'notated nuances' (another oxymoron) not only expressed to Dionne what Burt required of her, but also suggested self-expression. This writer would suggest that this is where her version of 'I Say A Little Prayer' succeeds.

Hal David was to state later that Dionne understood the meaning of words and music together as a kind of symbiosis of sound:

> She was terrific with lyrics – a great translator - and so musicianly, with the lyrics as well as the music. (David and Bacharach to Heckman, *Los Angeles Times,* 1993)

Burt Bacharach echoed this by stating in the same interview:

> Right. The more that she could do musically, the more chances we could take – and she did it almost effortlessly. The range didn't matter; the difficulty didn't matter. I don't think there was another singer who could have listened, taken direction and then delivered the way Dionne did. (ibid)

He is on record as reiterating his 'ship in a bottle' analogy thus:

> One of the great things about Dionne [Warwick] is that she's capable of singing very softly and you know that's her voice because it's enclosed like in a glass bottle – like they put those ships in glass bottles? It's 'so cool Dionne' but she is then able to have this explosive thing. (ibid)

Burt was to state further to the *L.A.Times*:

> When Aretha recorded [the song] she changed the melody a bit, some other things, and I thought, 'hmmm', but when I got used to it – and she's incredible - I was fine with it. Those kind of things give your tune an existence beyond its original self. (ibid)

Well, sorry Burt, but I cannot agree with your 'take' on 'I Say A Little Prayer'. The tempo, delivery, and arrangement of Dionne's original far outweigh the Aretha Franklin version, which at times sounds like a 'jam session'.

Dionne completed her triumvirate of hits the following April (1968) with 'Do You Know The Way To San Jose' – a song for which she initially had little time. Apart from the 'whoa whoa whoa whoa whoa', its lyric is its strong point with the great hook 'L.A. is a great big freeway' being the one line most people remember of all Bacharach and David songs. Hal David liked San Jose as a lyrical hook. He had already used it earlier in his career and, having spent time there in the US Navy, held both place and name in affection. He told Spencer Leigh:

> 'L.A. as a great big freeway' is how I saw L.A. the first time I came out here to go to work. (David to Leigh, *BBC: On The Beat*, 2001)

Dionne Warwick found the song rather trite upon first hearing, but grew to love and understand it. It was especially satisfying for her as far as the British market was concerned, being only her second top ten hit of that decade. She informed Robin Platts:

> Time has a wonderful way of making people understand things that they don't, and I finally got the complete picture, living in Los Angeles for as long as I did. And it is a great big freeway, you know, and people are pumping gas or waiting tables while they're waiting for that opportunity. (Warwick to Platts, 2003: 57)

In spite of its Mexican feel '[...] San Jose' was not a west coast recording but the very last Warwick/Bacharach/David session at Bell Sound in New York City. All other subsequent sessions were with Phil Ramone at A&R. Yet Burt was to all intents and purposes a classic Californian. Lillian Ross even felt the need to describe his attire to her *New Yorker* readers thus:

> [...] Mr Bacharach, [...] had a Beverly Hills tan, and was wearing Italian black-rimmed sunglasses pushed up on top of his head [...] his hair was curly dark brown with a lot of grey in it.

[He] was wearing bright California clothes: a green jacket, rust-coloured slacks, a brown and yellow striped tie and a dark blue shirt. (Ross, *New Yorker*, 1968)

Dionne won the 1968 Grammy Award for Contemporary Pop Vocal with '[…] San Jose'. The song was included on her album *Valley Of The Dolls*, which featured Andre and Dory Previn's 'take' on Bacharach's compositional techniques viz 'Theme From The Valley Of The Dolls' – a massive US hit single for Warwick the previous year.

Promises Promises

"It made me crazy – it made me just crazy!" (Bacharach to *Biography Channel*, 2003)

Well, in London, one day two years ago [1966] David Merrick came over to me at a party. I was in the middle of scoring 'Casino Royale' I wasn't thinking about doing a show. I was just getting my feet wet scoring movies […] Later on Merrick asked me if I'd be interested in working on a musical version of *The Apartment*. Merrick is very astute. He told me the theatre was going to change – that it had to open-up to people to do their own thing. And he was thinking correctly. So I started working on the show last summer. (Bacharach to Saal, *Newsweek*, 1968)

Merrick was a Broadway producer of great note having produced several successes (*Hello Dolly*, *42nd Street*, *Gypsy*). But he was also a man to be watched and could be highly unpleasant at times if he did not get his own way. Both Burt and Hal were somewhat wary of Merrick's reputation as a hustler. Hal David's recollection of the Merrick approach differs greatly from that of Burt. Hal recalls being a kind of buffer between Merrick and Bacharach:

I was out in Los Angeles […] Merrick called me in my room. I didn't know he was out there. He said 'do you have a minute for me? I've got something of interest to tell you' […] I said 'that sounds fantastic' […] so we put a call in, and Burt was there. I said 'David Merrick is here and he has a wonderful idea for us. Let me have him tell you'. So I put Merrick on the phone, and

Burt reacted the same way I did. And we agreed to do the show. (in Platts, 2003:61)

So it was to be: on 23 November 1968 (the run 'officially' began on Dec 1) at New York's Shubert Theatre it was now the turn of two of the most successful pop songwriters of the mid-1960s to present a creditable (and thus far only) original contribution to Broadway with their score for *Promises Promises*. It was undoubtedly an eagerly awaited event: the US press followed Bacharach around throughout the various touring incarnations of *Promises Promises* until he and it reached New York City in September '68.

Adapted from the 1960 Neil Simon screenplay *The Apartment,* the subject matter of the musical was 'trendy' in the Broadway sense, in that it followed other recent offerings such as *How To Succeed In Business Without Really Trying* and *I Can Get It For You Wholesale* by revealing a method of getting ahead in the business world. But it lacked what one might describe as popular music 'cool'. Not only due to subject matter, but also because the musical theatre genre as a whole had become rather uncool (Mel Brooks' 1967 movie *The Producers* being an apt parody). By the late-1960s younger music lovers displayed little interest in Broadway musicals. In fact it took the likes of *Hair!* to rekindle their curiosity. One can hardly imagine the majority of American youth being turned-on by a Neil Simon story about men in suits and ties.

The plot replicated *The Apartment*: Chuck Baxter (Jerry Orbach), the faceless hero of *Promises Promises* 'gets on' by lending his apartment to various executives of Consolidated Life for their extra-marital dalliances. Among them is J.D. Sheldrake (Edward Winter) whose paramour, Fran Kubelik (Jill O'Hara) just happens to be the girl beloved by Chuck. Fran eventually reciprocates his feelings but only after he rescues her from a suicide bid after J.D. decides to return to his wife – and that's it, really.

According to some this was the musical that was supposed to bring 1960s modernity into the theatre, but it was never going to happen. Despite a good score, it was for some a disappointment. For example, Jack Kroll stated in his *Newsweek* review:

'*Promises*' is engaging [...] But Bacharach's score does not come at the ear and heart with that glittering shifting kaleidoscopic

variety that is the hallmark of the great musical [...] Jill O'Hara
[...] is not really right [...] she lacks the edge, depth and
melancholy [and] Hal David's lyrics are not quite strong enough
for the music. (Kroll, *Newsweek*, 1968)

Reviews were mixed, of course, and some were far more complimentary
than Kroll's lack of enthusiasm:

It is an absolutely marvellous musical and [...] all two hundred
million of my fellow citizens should make plans to go and see it
as quickly as possible. (Review, *New Yorker*, 1968)

Promises Promises ran for 1,281 performances, won a couple of Tonys, and
only closed in January 1972, so far be it from me to suggest that it was in
any way lacking with the public. Weekly profits were as much as $35,000
per week – a record at the time. It also produced several good songs, but
it appeared to represent a great tranche of society that was attempting to
retreat back into the early 1960s. Of course, as a consequence, the adult-
oriented silent majority, dismayed at the changing direction of US and UK
society, loved it. In October 1969 the show was also produced at the Prince
Of Wales Theatre in London's West End (running for a far shorter 560
performances).

Songs

The show did spawn at least three good, innovative compositions, the
first of which appeared as a Dionne Warwick 45 soon after the run began:
'Promises Promises'. Dionne's rendition of this incredibly complex title
tune reached number 19 on the US singles charts. Burt later stated:

'Promises Promises' is a very difficult song for a singer. They
used to hate me. Dionne can do it but Dionne could make
anything sound easy. (Bacharach to Maconie, *Q*, 1996)

He also recalled to the *L.A. Times*:

When I wrote it out, I realised that it was changing time signatures
nearly every bar. The reason it was written like that was because
of the urgency of what was happening on the stage. But when I
wrote it out it felt natural and good to me.

Renowned jazz critic Leonard Feather offered his comments on 'Promises Promises' as follows:

> More than Lennon and McCartney, more than any other writer or pair, this team had succeeded in drawing popular song away from the dreary old 32-bar format and away from the verse-and-chorus tradition. For example, 'Promises Promises' bulges around its midsection with one bar each successfully in 5/4, 3/4, 4/4, 6/4, 3/4, 4/4, 6/4, 3/8, 4/8, and 4/4. Stop already!

'Wanting Things' and 'I'll Never Fall In Love Again' were the other two gems. 'Knowing When To Leave' would be the other title vying for inclusion (although this does have its flat spots). The Broadway show even won a Grammy for 'Best Original Soundtrack Recording Of A Musical Play'. However, it must be stated that one or two of the numbers were rather weak ('She Likes Basketball', 'A Young Pretty Girl Like You') and the best song 'I'll Never Fall In Love Again' was actually written-in at the last minute after Burt was taken ill in Boston.

The musical appeared to him to be something of a disaster. Prior to the tour Burt had presumed that, having written the score, his role as songwriter was effectively over – the production would develop its own dynamic, thereafter. How wrong could he have been? His work had barely begun: during rehearsals he and Hal realised that massive changes had to be made.

For instance, one number was too difficult to choreograph; the lyrics of another song did not fit the mood. Other numbers were shortened and by the time the production reached its opening night in Boston, Burt had changed the running order of songs. Following the opening night yet another song ('Wouldn't That Be A Stroke Of Luck') was dropped and 'I'll Never Fall In Love Again' added.

By the time of its four-week run in Washington, yet another song had been dumped! It was all quite the reverse to what Burt had been used to as a studio-bound maestro. Although a great believer in trial and error, his perfectionism could not accommodate live theatre with all of its unpredictabilities and impurities.

After that three month experimental tour Burt arrived in New York in September of 1968 with the adapted score and immediately began re-working everything in rehearsals with his producer David Merrick, writer Neil Simon and of course Hal David – more revisions! Burt informed Hubert Saal of *Newsweek* in no uncertain terms that he was glad the tour was over. Not only had he been hospitalised with pneumonia shortly after the show opened in Boston, but it was evident from his guarded comments that he considered that earlier incarnation a mess:

> In the hospital I knew there was work to be done. There were new songs to be written for the show. But I felt to hell with the show. It's my life, I've just got to live and get out of here. Then, as soon as I got out, I wrote a new song for the show 'I'll Never Fall In Love Again' which just might, by the way, turn out to be the biggest hit of the show. And there I was getting the new number into the show, working with people learning it, and everything. And that is not the way to recuperate from pneumonia. (Bacharach to Saal, *Newsweek*, 1968)

In response, Saal asked about the current state of the production:

> What has happened to the show since Labor Day? (ibid)

To which Burt replied:

> It's tighter, funnier, shorter and it plays better than it did when we started. In Boston we were half an hour over what we are now. Neil really knows how to cut. He was great on the cutting. (ibid)

Bacharach's quest for perfection evidently did not match being on the road with one's first and only musical and (perhaps for the first time) Burt issued forth the language of somebody almost running on empty as far as ideas were concerned:

> One song came out and stayed out. Five songs came out and were replaced. About a third of the score, I'd say […]. (ibid)

Trial

Why was *Promise Promises* such a trial for Bacharach? Self-imposed pressure must have had something to do with it. Burt was known to quote the Jule Styne mantra that 'one had not achieved anything in popular music until a successful Broadway show had been written'. Burt had accomplished so much but seemed unduly confined by this pompous turn of phrase: after all this was 1968 not 1938.

Disorientation also had a large part to play. Bacharach's efficient and disciplined approach to work had won him the attention of impresarios such as Merrick; but the principles Burt had imbibed from his cocktail of solfege and production values was rigid, set in stone. Theatre was a real life-challenge for him for it did not match his carefully assimilated way of doing things, which in turn could not be easily transferred to an environment where flying by the seat of one's trousers frequently comes into the equation. His was a quasi-religious approach to music: the actors were expected to interiorise a text. This was simply completely antithetical to the way most of them worked!

Like Burt's move to Beverly Hills mentioned previously, *Promises Promises* was also a precursor of the musical breakdown to come. Perhaps even more than Hollywood, the US theatre business of the 1960s remained far closer to the traditional notions of Barnum mixed with high art elitism than the more flexible record industry. Thus it must have been rather like *déjà vu* for Bacharach: a system that embraced all that Burt had fought long and hard to supersede. It was also, of course, another completely different way of approaching sound. Burt had spent the previous ten years digesting how records could be turned into art. He had now moved into an erstwhile and institutionalised method of music production. If he were to continue in the theatre, he would have to start all over again.

The evidence for this discomfort appears in several sonic methods used in *Promises Promises*. One might say that Bacharach approached the musical with the idea of turning a theatre in to a recording studio. Phil Ramone came along and placed 17 microphones and four female singers in the pit and several speakers around the theatre. It was all brought together via an 11 channel mixing desk at the back of the theatre. *New Yorker's* Lillian Ross reported Burt in December '68 as avowing:

I don't think I compromised on anything [...] and we've got a
lot of electrical equipment in that pit [...] and I have to praise
Merrick for that. He spent a lot of money on the special effects
– on an echo chamber, everything. It was a gamble.

Yet in the same interview he also admitted "right now, I think I just want to
go away for a vacation" and later recalled:

Six days after it opened I couldn't listen to it without breaking
into a cold sweat at the distorted sound and the speeded up
tempos. That was a year-and-a-half out of my life.

Error

It is quite obvious that Burt felt exposed to variables that did not occur in
the studio and he felt uncomfortable with the unreliability of live music,
sound, actors, and audiences:

We're exposed, naked, like in a fishbowl. The music can be
damned difficult but you can't stop as if it were a studio. It's a
competition with one chance to win, and what you win is a live
audience. (Bacharach to Saal, *Newsweek*, 1970)

He further stated to the *Saturday Evening Post* that he had no real desire to
complete another Broadway musical:

If you do a good job in a recording studio, or if you write a movie
score, it's that way forever. But if you come back the next night
and hear what's happening in a Broadway musical, you'll rush to
the corner bar for a quick drink. It changes too much and I can't
stand it. (Bacharach to *Saturday Evening Post*, 1968)

Reading between the lines, *Promises Promises* was not a fulfilling
experience for Bacharach. It wore him out, separated him from his family,
and produced rifts that were perhaps never healed. He revealingly stated
to Mel Gussow in December 1968 that if there were to be a next time, he
would do something different:

Not in the normal format, something off centre. I would want
non-musical types in the show in terms of character. I would like

to write all kinds of things for it, songsover [sic], sung while people dance and acted in pantomime [...] if I'm going to do something that is a departure, something really really new, I'm not sure it has to be for Broadway. I may do a two-set record that tells a story, or a movie musical [...]. (Bacharach to Gussow, *Newsweek*, 1968)

Summary

Contrary to received opinion I would maintain that, although there was no perceivable decline in Burt's music after 1966, one has only to study such scores as *Promises Promises* and *Butch Cassidy And The Sundance Kid* to see that things had greatly changed for him as a composer. Burt's modification in popularity stemmed from the changing times in which his music appeared. Between 1962 and 1966 he had come to share a real dominance of the US pop scene but in the process, was gradually demarcated demographically.

Thus his music came to represent that demarcation: the areas into which his compositions moved (movies, theatre) also represented the silent majority that listened to 'musak FM'. Since Bacharach had come to trust those around him throughout his social relocation, all his later works tended to reflect this security.

By mid 1969, with filmic and musical success surrounding him, it seemed that he could do no wrong. But the forces that had brought him to this elevation were as much demographic and social (political even) as they were musical. Like every other serious popular music composer at this time Burt was probably aware of what was going on around him. But, like many great composers, he was so bound by his music that he did not embrace these social changes.

Instead, he retreated into the ASCAP-bound rituals of Hollywood. As a consequence he all but 'dissed' one of Hal David's greatest lyrics by uttering moody objections to the recording process ('Windows Of The World'), he crafted an albeit interesting soundtrack full of mainstream ambiguities (*Butch Cassidy* [...]), and placed himself in the invidious and unsatisfying position of [re]writing on the hoof almost an entire musical for the often hollow success of Broadway (*Promises Promises*).

It would be ridiculous of me to suggest that Burt might have sought musical strength elsewhere (the question remains 'where?' 'with whom?', 'how?'). But the affirmative essence of the late-1960s Cultural Revolution was that it involved vast numbers of people and one cannot exaggerate the extent of change. A great deal of it was, indeed, self-deluding and self indulgent, but many artistic elements (such as music) were brave, impressive and admirable. Many significant social practices hitherto ignored became visible. Yet, while this was reaching some kind of fruition, it appears (at least from this historical distance) that the retreats and rituals of Hollywood had decelerated Burt's muse somewhat, foredooming the musical invisibility he was later to experience.

Chapter 11

Lost Horizons – The Split

The hits kept on coming throughout 1970. The 'apple of Florence Greenberg's eye', Billy Joe Thomas, recorded 'Raindrops [...]', but only after the song had been rejected by Ray Stevens and (allegedly) Bob Dylan. The track spent a month at no. 1 as the new decade dawned and everything looked rosy for Bacharach, David, Thomas, Warwick and the team at Scepter. But changes were just around the corner for all concerned.

5th Dimension, Dionne Warwick and the Carpenters, with their marvellous re-arrangement of 'Close To You', also kept Bacharach and David in the highest profile. B.J. Thomas even had the confidence to record one of Bacharach and David's best pieces of experimental modernism. Including banjo, trombone, and tuba, 'Everybody's Out Of Town' sounded not unlike Weill and Brecht's 'Alabama Song', yet this oddity also scored reasonably well on the US singles chart, making no. 26 in April 1970.

B.J. Thomas

Billy Joe Thomas deserves more than merely a footnote here. He first came to the attention of Florence Greenberg in 1966 after his band, the Triumphs, had recorded Hank Williams' 'I'm So Lonely I Could Cry' for Huey P. Meaux's Pacemaker label. Scepter promo man Steve Tyrell had been a classmate of Thomas and when the record began breaking nationally, Scepter were large enough by this time to handle national distribution. Thomas went solo and became a mainstay for Scepter in the late 1960s, well before he had linked-up with Bacharach and David.

These days he is remembered as much for the great bubblegum hit 'Hooked On A Feeling' as for 'Raindrops [...]', but at the time he felt that his own material was dwarfed by the presence of Bacharach and David and pushed for a little Bacharach magic. He eventually came to work with Burt after a great deal of canvassing from Tyrell and Dionne's personal manager Paul Cantor. Eventually Cantor received the important phone call from Bacharach. Thomas recalled:

I got word from Paul Cantor that, when I finished that string of dates, I was going to California and that I was going to get a session with Burt Bacharach. He said 'we've got this song in this Paul Newman movie'. (Thomas to Platts, 2003:70)

Constant sales by Thomas helped to keep the Scepter label afloat in the early 1970s. The aforementioned 'Everybody's Out Of Town' was B.J.'s follow-up single to his massive hit from *Butch Cassidy*.

Notwithstanding Jamie Anders contribution to *Futures* (1977), Thomas' recording of 'Everybody's Out Of Town' is the nearest any professional vocalist came to actually replicating Burt's voice on disc and, for this writer, is an example of what was to later contribute to the break up of Burt and Hal (i.e. it was clearly a song that Burt had written for himself). Not only is it a great single, one of Burt's best compositions of the entire 1970s, but also reflects, lyrically, Hal's understanding of Burt's predicament. Like the character in the song, under changing social circumstances an internalised individual no longer felt part of any kind of community. One suspects this was David speaking directly to Bacharach, but the latter wasn't listening.

By this time, Burt's songwriting had stalled somewhat and it was his aforementioned live work that kept him going artistically. He had turned to the refuge of live performance as part of his internalisation, but in the process had become a consummate performer and was now a big draw in his own right. A series of successful TV specials also kept him in the public eye. Shows such as *The Burt Bacharach Special*, *Another Evening With Burt Bacharach*, and (later) *Burt Bacharach In Shangri-La* included performances by him and his favourite artistes. At the 1971 Emmy Awards two Bacharach programmes were nominated for the best show with *The Burt Bacharach Special* getting the award.

In May 1970 Bacharach sold-out five straight shows at the Westbury Music Fair in New York, not far from where he had grown up. The Carpenters opened for him and *Billboard's* Robert Sobel reviewed the show:

Burt Bacharach is a romantic visionary who views the world through love-colored glasses tinged with whimsy and wonderment [...] he sang and played piano with refreshing truthfulness, conducting the spirited 28-piece orchestra with fiery tenderness, and directed the four girl singers with professionalism born from instinct. (Sobel, *Billboard*, 1970)

But his lack of availability for songwriting meant that Hal David had already seen the writing on the wall and had begun moonlighting with John Barry and Johnny Mandel (further annoying Burt, one suspects). For example, 'We Have All The Time In The World' from *On Her Majesty's Secret Service* (another dreadful Bond movie!) is one of Hal David's most durable compositions from this non-Bacharach period.

That year of 1970 was actually Bacharach's most active period as a recording artist, releasing two singles and one LP. But there was little in the way of new material and those new items such as 'Paper Mache', 'Long Ago Tomorrow', and 'Freefall' made no impression on the US singles charts – by this time in the throes of bubblegum.

The following year, in the summer of 1971, Burt decided to come off the road and revert to songwriting. The 18 months touring was a release valve, but had also been exciting and rewarding. He informed the *New York Times* that:

I'd never had a more frenetic year. Concert appearances in cities clear across the country. TV shows, all-night recording sessions, travelling all the way to Japan. I just thought 'wait a minute! you're doing too much. You're not writing enough'. Principally I believe I'm supposed to write more than I perform. (Bacharach to *New York Times*, 1971)

But, in truth, there were also problems 'back at the ranch'. Dionne Warwick was suffering at the hands of this dearth of Bacharach material (her albums had progressively featured fewer Bacharach songs as the '60s moved on). Furthermore, in March 1971, a dispute had cropped up between Blue Jac Productions (Bacharach and David's company) and Scepter Records. The problem concerned the accounting of record sales as far back as 1963. Scepter allegedly owed Blue Jac all kinds of royalties. Eventually the figure settled upon was circa $339,000. Coincidentally, Warwick's contract was up for renewal with Scepter and Burt/Dionne/Hal decided to leave the company that May. Before too long, Warners had signed Dionne for allegedly the biggest advance a female artiste had ever achieved at the time.

That wasn't the end of the matter, however, for on advice from their lawyers the songwriters took further measures over the forthcoming years to track down lost royalties from another contract signed with Scepter in 1966. This regarded royalties and payments due for recordings made mainly with Dionne Warwick and (later) B.J. Thomas between 1966 and 1971. By 1975 Bacharach and David's legal team had filed enough evidence to enable them to view Scepter's accounting and sales information (like Motown, Scepter organised their books along the 'closed-collateral' accounting system).

This information was reluctantly passed over to Blue Jac and the following year the US Arbitration Association ordered Scepter to pay $430,602 in back payments and to terminate forthwith any further contractual obligations that remained between Bacharach and David and Scepter/Wand. Burt and Hal were also awarded the rights to their Scepter recordings. This last decree pushed Scepter over the edge.

By 1975 Scepter were already well past their prime as an effective record company and were basically living on their back catalogue – which in the main was propped-up by Bacharach and David recordings. Florence Greenberg retired in 1976 and sold her label and subsidiaries to Springboard International. They subsisted on a constant stream of repackagings and reissues and made few new signings. Springboard filed for bankruptcy and Scepter closed down in 1976. The final release on Scepter was Jesse Green's 'Nice And Slow' (Scepter 12424). It was a sad moment, not only for those involved, but also for all popular music people. Scepter had contributed to changing the face of American popular song and, despite their unethical dealings, deserved to stay in business. It was a rather cruel, typically 1970s, legal outcome that eliminated them.

As for Dionne, however, her first important album for Warners (*Dionne*, 1972) revealed that her Bacharach quota was very low. Two of the songs 'Close To You' and 'One Less Bell To Answer' were oldies. Warwick[e], had decided at this stage to add an 'e' to her surname for 'vibratory reasons'. This was at the suggestion of noted psychic Linda Goodman, but her fortunes were not improved. The album was not particularly well received nor favourably reviewed.

That year of 1972 really was the first lean year in Bacharach's history since 1959. Hal and Burt had not given their fullest possible attention to the *Dionne* album because they were preoccupied by what was then regarded as their most ambitious project to date, but what turned out to be their nadir – *Lost Horizon* – a movie musical remake of the 1937 Frank Capra story of a group of plane crash survivors who discover the lost city of Shangri-la in the Himalayas.

Lost Horizon

> "If you're looking for a trigger that blew everything up in the air
> [...]". (Bacharach to *Biography Channel*, 2003)

Lost Horizon was a torpid affair. It began well enough but the opening was followed by slabs of immature philosophising dialogue and an unbroken series of what turned out to be one-dimensional songs expressing the mawkish sentiments of a post-hippie US. The movie was written by Larry Kramer and directed by Charles Darrott. Darrott was the film's third director, but the large part of the blame must go to Ross Hunter who was riding high in Hollywood after the success of *Airport* in 1970. *Lost Horizon* was Hunter's first (and last) picture for Columbia Studios and no money was spared – always a dangerous sign! Big names such as Peter Finch, Liv Ullman, Sally Kellerman, Bobby Van, George Kennedy and Michael York made little or no effort to save it. It has since been labelled the worst movie remake of all time – few would argue.

Furthermore, few films have been accompanied by more media hype than *Lost Horizon* and this undoubtedly contributed to its proportionally inverse critical mauling. For instance, while Columbia were suggesting:

> The excitement of *Lost Horizon* holds all your senses nerve-taut
> [...] the escape from the rebels and the airplane crash are spell-
> binding moments of entertainment!

Reviews were actually howling the likes of:

It will never play again outside of Shangri-La: Les Keyser, *Hollywood In The Seventies*.

Only Ross Hunter would remake a 1937 movie into a 1932 one: Judith Crist.

[the set] resembles the valley of the Jolly Green Giant – a fitting showcase for a film that is so much spinach [...] It can't even be enjoyed as camp: *Newsweek*.

The narrative has no energy, and the pauses for the pedagogic songs are so awkward that you feel the director's wheelchair needs oiling: Pauline Kall.

All that is missing from this Himalayan 'wonderland' is the putting green and the Olympic-sized pool: Harry and Michael Medved.

Furthermore, while the hype for the soundtrack suggested:

The music of Lost Horizon lives and breathes [sic] fresh-ness [...] the ten new Burt Bacharach-Hal David songs will make you dance with joy!

Harry and Michael Medved have opined that while various intense reactions had indeed been reported about physical responses to the music of *Lost Horizon*, 'dancing with joy' was not one of them. The score was viewed by many as being monotonously idealistic; bouncy with an atmosphere approaching that of folksy-elevator music. Moreover, Hal David's lyrics were criticised for being "inane" in attempting to provide "philosophical profundities" to order. The Medveds found it all almost too comical for words:

This is never more true than in the meaningful 'Living Together, Growing Together' sequence, in which scores of Tibetan monks walk in slow procession with swinging teapots in front of them. The flavour of this unforgettable scene calls to mind an international yo-yo tournament convened with high solemnity in San Francisco's Chinatown. (H&M. Medved, 1980:84)

Lost Horizon was of course symbolic hippiedom for middle-aged Californians. Four years after Altamont, the west coast still gave refuge to the lingering cadaver of the counter culture and it had seeped back into the bourgeoisie from whence it had appeared. The problem was that by 1973 the world had changed dramatically and simplistic idealism espoused by the childish dialogue of the film and the equally one-dimensional lyrics of Hal David appeared backdated and superfluous to modern times. *Lost Horizon* should have been made in 1967, not 1973! Bacharach and David had never received such a lambasting – so what went wrong?

Re-evaluation?

As far as the film is concerned it would take a post-graduate thesis to go through its trials, tribulations and dreadful *mise en scene*. Save to say that such a mess does affect our reception of the music. For example, the musical sequences were very poorly steered by incredibly dull choreography and this inevitably influences our reading of the score. Perhaps, then, the songs were not as mediocre as has often been suggested? It is worth looking briefly at a couple independently to see if there are any of merit.

One gets the feeling that Burt still has sleepless nights over *Lost Horizon*, so much did it damage his credibility and his career. However Hal David was far more enthusiastic about the project, and has repeatedly come to the defence of the score:

> 'Lost Horizon' was a film that just didn't work. And the score suffered because of it, in my opinion. Many people now seem to think the score's rather good. The picture deals with hope for things wonderful and people getting along […] And there are things in that score that are very dear to me. 'Where Knowledge Ends, Faith Begins' is a song I always loved. (in Platts, *Discoveries*, 1997)

But Burt sees it differently:

> I just went down to the beach at Del Mar and sort of hid. It was such a giant bust. I didn't want to be seen walking around the community […]. (ibid)

Burt was recently (2000) asked whether *Lost Horizon* could ever be salvaged. He quickly dismissed the idea:

> […] there ain't no chance that that's gonna happen. While I was doing it, it was just an unbelievable amount of work, and it was still fun. And I thought the songs were good. But the movie […] it was a disaster. It doesn't matter if Peter Finch sings 'If I Could Go Back' which is really a damn good song. That song by itself has a lot of heart. But you saw it in the movie and you don't give a fuck if he goes back or not.
>
> The whole experience was pretty bad because I kept fighting for the way the music should sound and they wound up banning me from the dubbing stage and the mixing stage. It should've been thrilling because that's the way it was on tape. But it came out sounding compressed. After that it was just 'I wanna get away from everybody, live down on the beach' and that's what I did.
> (Bacharach to Dominic, *Phoenix New Times*, 2000)

Despite Burt's bitterness, it is tempting to re-evaluate the music taking in the broader picture. We should, for example, always consider that Bacharach was beginning a very unhappy time in his life. His marriage to Angie Dickinson was on the rocks (*Lost Horizon* would have broken the strongest of bonds, one suspects) and, of course, this apparent failure was made worse by her diametrically successful starring role in *Police Woman* the following year.

Notwithstanding, however, ultimately one can only believe the evidence of one's own ears and, despite this valid contextual information, Burt is probably more correct than Hal. There is really only one Bacharach masterpiece from the soundtrack: the theme tune, itself. Shawn Phillips made a passable job of the song - and it certainly suited his profile as a rather wet folkie - but it is Burt's own arrangement of the 'Lost Horizon Theme' that stands-out. His orchestral version on the subsequent Bacharach solo album (*Living Together*) is the one to hear.

Clocking in at almost five minutes we get the full force of the beautiful melody and arrangement without any recourse to the movie (and this is how it should be heard). We do often 'dream of a place away from it all' and Burt's own arrangement is very effective in conveying a kind of other world ambience (as is Ronnie Aldrich's version).

Full marks for the 'Lost Horizon Theme', then, but what of the rest? Well, while 'Living Together, Growing Together' is a pleasant enough song – the final Bacharach and David chart hit, in fact (for 5th Dimension) - it does have a tendency to 'stick in the craw', somewhat, after repeated listening. The lyrics are a little too sweet to bear and one can understand why Hal received so much stick. 'Question Me An Answer' sounds like a leftover from *Promises Promises* and the immediate charm of 'The World Is A Circle' is eventually replaced by irritation. 'I Might Frighten Her Away' is disagreeable kitsch.

One of the best things Burt ever did was to remake 'Reflections'. In the movie Sally Kellerman's voice was just dreadful and his version of the song is far more agreeable. He told the *NME*:

> I had to teach the singers and go through pre-records and score the whole film, which was a monstrous film to score. It was just a huge lumpen disaster. I hated the movie. I hated the embarrassment of being involved with it. And it was killed, I mean absolutely **killed**. (Bacharach to Williams, *NME*, 1996)

Burt also mentioned to *The Biography Channel* (to paraphrase him) how difficult and laborious it was for him to attempt to teach non-singers to sing his material (and how soul destroying it was to hear his material so poorly performed).

Why?

Why Bacharach's popular music became so colourless is not simply down to the movie. By 1973-75 mass tastes in popular music were experiencing several bland-outs (e.g. country rock) and self-indulgencies (e.g. *Tubular Bells*). Folkies and folk-rockers were approximating equally vapid sounds (one only has to listen to albeit decent bands such as Poco, Firefall, Orleans, Loggins and Messina, etc to hear these artists too often cross into mawkishness). If the world was indeed a circle then that circle had come full turn and the shallowness of *Lost Horizon* was surplus. It was once again the times as much as the music.

What we can say with a level of certainty is that Burt was very depressed and full of resentment about the whole experience. He described the event as "very disheartening". But this demoralization had been brewing for some considerable time, masked as it was by relative success. It seems that he was never far away from melancholy: it was just laid bare by this awful film. The period between *Promises Promises* and *Lost Horizon* was one of disappointment masked by achievement. *Promises Promises* hid the disillusionment well – it was a fair-to-middling production when all was said and done. But *Lost Horizon* had nothing to say artistically and exposed Burt's discouragement fully.

Despite one truly great moment, I would not (unlike many Bacharach and David fans) recommend the re-release of the *Lost Horizon* soundtrack. Burt's album *Living Together* actually covers the ground well enough. This later recording is also of some historical significance in carrying some of the last songs Burt penned with Hal David ('The Balance Of Nature' and 'Walk The Way You Talk') in addition to a handful of the *Lost Horizon* tunes. Needless to say it has worn far better than the film.

Wedge

The enormous pressure of this seemingly unending collaboration on *Lost Horizon*, mixed with its terrible mauling by the critics and Burt's crumbling private life, drove a wedge between Burt Bacharach and Hal David. Bacharach admits that the failure of the movie was the:

> [...] Overwhelming reason. I just kind of resented that the picture did so badly. I resented that I had to keep working with singers and the voices that we would use for Liv Ullman and Peter Finch. I just broke my ass on that, with the score. I felt like I put in a year, maybe longer, than Hal did. And it didn't feel equal to me. That's wrong. I mean that's the role I assume as a composer. The musician takes it further. There are certain areas that Hal couldn't have done [...]. (Bacharach to Platts, 2003:87-88)

Hal David suggests that he did not really pick up on these vibes but he probably would have been less aware of a deteriorating relationship and more wary of Burt's gradual isolation. By 1973 Burt was not in a position to partner anybody at anything.

If we look at music creativity, what do we see? Few permanent partners, that's what! There are the occasional species that 'mate' for life but on the whole we watch the exercise of power, dominance and convenience. The composer and the lyricist interpret life differently. The lyricist looks to express organised sound, the composer looks for ways to organise sound. But popular music can only be sustained in such a partnership as a critical practice if a self-conscious synthesis between the two is achieved.

Songwriting partnerships can only be defined in relationship with one another. The relational character of the partnership then permits the interpretive generalisation of the public. But it cannot last forever. Personalities are dynamic – they change, they flux - and so once the equilibrium within the creative partnership becomes imbalanced, the creativity is effectively at an end.

Hal David did not even see *Lost Horizon* as a catalyst for the split appearing 'on the horizon', so to speak. But he wouldn't, would he? Not when the internal power relationships were imbalanced:

> I certainly didn't feel that way. Burt may have. I was dreadfully disappointed in the movie [but] That was the culmination [...] It was that we were suddenly not writing songs, except for that which was a very big undertaking. [...] Burt's part in it was very burdensome. And we were not recording Dionne. We were not writing songs for Dionne and she was very unhappy [...] when Burt went in to record, he was recording for himself as opposed to recording with Dionne and me. That was where his interest was going and where his career was going [...] that led up to *Lost Horizon* – where all the tensions were kind of high. (David to Platts, 2003:88)

Wilderness

By 1974 Bacharach was 'happy' making demos for a new publishing outlet 'Blue Seas And Hidden Valley' and preparing to play Las Vegas. He was most certainly taking the easy option, suggesting to Ron Baron of *Cash Box* that performing was easier than writing: "Performing is easy since it's the enactment of your own songs". According to Baron, Burt apparently did not want to think that the *Lost Horizon* songs would be the last ones that they wrote together, but the tone of the interview suggested otherwise: solo projects came first.

Burt could not reconcile himself to relativity: the relative failure of *Lost Horizon*, the relativity of his own place in the popular music canon, the relative blandness of some of his work, the recoding of his material into music for the shopping mall. So he flew the coop, leaving each respective partner with only ideas of why it had occurred. Those outside of the immediate relationships, such as Dionne, were never quite sure why Burt had done this – and it continues to be so, even to this day. Burt had been involved in popular music for such a long period of time that it had become an individual ideology involving not simply acts of music practice but also acts of theorization. The activity of thinking and writing about musical possibilities informed the writer to such an extent that he felt alone, isolated – a voice crying in the wilderness. Furthermore via the advent of several significant popular music and technological 'events', it appeared that he might just be right.

Take, for instance, the mainstream use of the Moog Synthesiser: Burt has never and probably will never fully embrace this form of technology. He is still on record as stating that buttonpushing is simply not music as he knows it. While the advent of such a device in the early 1970s probably interested him, he seldom if ever used it. Sonically, however, Robert Moog placed Bacharach's organic way of making music on the back burner.

Consider, too, the dawning of disco by 1975, which placed the majority of musical structure on a four-to-the-floor beat and emphasised the bass as a frequency rather than a melody. Not only did disco versions of Burt's music sound utterly ridiculous (for example, Stephanie Mills' 'This Empty Place'), it also dated Burt's time signature irregularities in an instant as 'pre-disco'.

Bear in mind, too, the advent of punk by 1976. This ensured that Burt's music further receded in public consciousness – at least until the end of the decade (and also placed Hal's later post-hippy lyrics in a different context). Punk was about a lot of things, but musically it was primarily concerned with simplicity: three chord tricks. While Burt was extending chords, searching for complexity and Hal was writing some of the most mawkish lyrics of his career, the times were also against the pair: as the 1970s progressed, a split was inevitable.

The end?

In February 1973, the month before *Lost Horizon* was released (or escaped) *Variety* reported that the pair were "clearing the decks" for another venture with David Merrick. But this was paper talk. Burt had no desires to work with either Merrick or Hal David at this stage – and certainly did not wish to return to the theatre. Following the release of *Lost Horizon* Burt and Hal brought their songwriting partnership to a somewhat acrimonious end. The split baffled the ever-patient Dionne Warwick:

> I had heard the scuttlebutt but I thought if anybody would know, I would know - famous last words. I found out in the paper like everybody else that they weren't going to do the album, they weren't writing together, they weren't even talking to each other. What hurt me the most was that I thought I was their friend. But I was wrong. They did not care about Dionne Warwick. It was devastating. (Warwick to Holden, *Rolling Stone*, 1979)

and:

> [...] All I know is that they split and left me kind of in the lurch.

She had (perhaps unwisely) come to depend upon the team for the bulk of her material:

> The last Bacharach/David/Warwick collaboration was the 1972 album 'Dionne', the first record of Dionne's new deal with Warner Bros Records. The album had plenty of strong moments, but Bacharach was disappointed with it. (Platts, 2003:88)

Bacharach was now disappointed with everything about the popular music process. The context of the 1970s may well have reminded him of what he had been fighting against in the 1950s. No wonder he spoke of "defeat" after *Lost Horizon*. The last thing he wanted to do was create something indifferent – but that's what he had done with Dionne's album. The worst thing one can say about something emanating from Burt Bacharach is that is it ordinary. He stated:

I don't think we delivered. I really don't think we delivered well
on that. I don't think I ever felt right about that album. It was the
first with Joe Smith and Mo Ostin at Warners […] I felt that we
didn't give them an album like we'd been delivering at Scepter.
(in Platts, 2003:89)

The Bacharach/David/Warwick era had ended and it left Dionne unable
to fulfil her contractual obligations to Warner Bros., the record company
with whom she had signed the previous year in order to specifically record
Bacharach and David material! Warwick sued Bacharach and David and
eventually won an out-of-court settlement. Hal David:

We were obligated to Warner Bros. and to Dionne […] and we
had let her down […] were not fulfilling […], so she sued us.
(David to Leigh, *BBC: On The Beat*, 2001)

Therefore, concurrent with the other on-going legalities against Scepter
Records came this further lawsuit – this time incoming. In August 1975
Warwick's lawyers filed a suit against Burt and Hal. *Variety* covered the
case and gave the following account:

Warwick, who claims she had an agreement with defendants for
them to produce and deliver an album to Warners, which she
said they did not do, asks $5,000,000 exemplary damages for
breach of fiduciary duties, and $1,000,000 for alleged breach of
contract. (*Variety*, 1975)

Dionne places a slightly different perspective on the matter, however. She
was under intense pressure from Warners in her own right to persuade
Burt to work again with her. Warners even went so far as to fly Dionne
to a west coast meeting with Burt in an attempt to lure him back into the
studio, but he was a discouraged man by this stage and not interested in
collaborations of any sort. Dionne was thus presented with little choice
– Mo Ostin of Warners spelt it out: if she did not get out of her management
and production contract with Bacharach and David and restart her career
with Warners with a clean slate then Warners would sue her as part of that
production team.

Obviously, the great problem was that Dionne was still contractually
tied to Bacharach and David and could not simply walk away. She had

to dissolve the contract with her (by now former) producers. In order to release her from these unenviable shackles, lawyers had to be brought in to broker a deal at her own instigation. Bacharach stated that he would not willingly let her walk. Burt later (1993) stated that it was "a very messy situation [...] and a very unfortunate time". Dionne:

> [...] I was obliged to give Warners a certain amount of albums **and** produced by Bacharach and David. There became a conflict – basically two people that weren't speaking to each other, so you couldn't expect them to write with each other – that's logic. Because of this problem, I would have been sued by Warners [...] had I not sued Bacharach and David – and that's the story folks! (Warwick to *BBC This Is Now*, 1996)

By 1975 Burt was involved in a three-way legal process with his former collaborators while also effectively closing down Scepter. This was a terrible indictment on the collapse of a series of very creative relationships. Donald Heckman of the *Los Angeles Times* stated in 1993 when Burt and Hal were brought together for the ASCAP Founders Awards:

> Looking back on the 10-year hiatus during which he only talked "through attorneys" with Hal David and Dionne Warwick [...] Bacharach's primary desire was to put the past to rest.

Burt replied:

> Look, there's no point in going over all the gory details. It's all over now. I had a falling out with Dionne, then Hal got involved. And if I had to do it over again [...] I never, never would do it the same way. (Bacharach to Heckman, *Los Angeles Times*, 1993)

Interesting comment, this: there is just a suggestion that it might have been a quarrel over the lack of product for Dionne that led to the subsequent rift between Burt and Hal. If David was less involved with *Lost Horizon* than his writing partner then perhaps he was ready to work with Dionne; Burt's isolation and intransigence – he quite clearly did not wish to collaborate with anyone by 1974 – split them. Hal and Dionne were both negatively affected by a level of bloody mindedness.

Perhaps they were effectively standing fast, shoulder-to-shoulder, in one corner, even though legally they appeared unconnected. Burt did later suggest to *Mojo* (1996) that "part of me wanted to go all the way to court but it wasn't a big enough part. So I pushed myself to settle it, because it was draining my energy. By moving to settle it, I would end up paying considerably more than Mr David – he would have gone all the way to court." These do not sound like the words of a man utterly reconciled (as appeared to be the case in 1993).

Burt later stated to the *Los Angeles Times*:

> For whatever reason, it happened. But we finally made our settlement, Dionne and I are touring again, and Hal and I found a touch of the old spark when we wrote 'Sunny Weather Lover' for Dionne's new album. It was the first song we'd written together for 17 years. (Bacharach to Heckman, *Los Angeles Times*, 1993)

Warwick's suit against Bacharach (and David) was eventually settled out of court in 1979. A reported $5.5 million passed between each set of lawyers. Whether Dionne received anything like that amount is debatable. Perhaps her greatest victory was that she also received a share of rights to her recordings. What a great pity that all of this creativity, all of this magic was brought down by one of the worst movies in cinematic history. Dionne remains unequivocal that *Lost Horizon* was to blame:

> It **was** *Lost Horizon*. That was the straw that kind of broke everybody's back. During the time when they were writing their songs for the film was apparently when they were having their differences.

But *Lost Horizon* was not guilty of **creating** the rift, rather it acted more as a catalyst. It was an artistic disaster of vast proportions and Burt's insecurity – something that goes all the way back to playing the piano for his mum – was cruelly exposed by such a terrible waste of time. And wasting time is a criminal offence for somebody as active and obsessive as Burt.

Bacharach had already been wondering about his direction, commitment, performance and recording throughout the first three years of the 1970s and presumed that through his work with this neo-hippie bullshit he could re-codify his future direction: but there was never a chance of this happening. Whereas the Brill Building before had been a kind of vehicle for Burt's muse, this dog of a movie undermined his already dwindling self-confidence so much that it became a catalyst of encumbrance and a forewarning of doom.

Stephanie Mills

Bacharach and David actually worked together in 1975 but it was a strange, unfulfilling affair with 15-year-old Stephanie Mills. Mills was signed to Motown – by that time also on the west coast of the US and also losing their way, somewhat - and Berry Gordy arranged that the teenager's first album should be with a reunited Burt and Hal. Anything with Berry Gordy at the helm during the 1970s was bound to be touch and go and although an album ensued, entitled *For The First Time*, it was a tiresome affair. Phil Ramone recollects it was "more David that Bacharach", and despite eight 'new' Bacharach and David songs (and, as mentioned, a dreadful disco version of 'This Empty Place') not one of them sounded at all like they had emanated from that team.

The finished album was so undistinguished that one could propose it lurches from one mediocre moment to another. This was not simply because of any Bacharach loss of inspiration: Mills' vocal talents were not exactly out of the ordinary. The Mills long player soon became another of the many quasi-disco deletion-bin items that came to clog-up record shops in the late-1970s. As a consequence of its poor sales, it is now rather difficult to find and is regarded by Bacharach completists as a rarity. Burt was honest enough about the reformed collaboration stating "[...] the Stephanie Mills album [...] We were running out of gas [...] I took a year off [...] feeling defeated by the *Lost Horizon* situation".

Possible *Futures?*

Burt commenced work with a few other writers after the "defeat" of *Lost Horizon*. Aside from the rather mundane effort quoted above, he wrote a couple of songs with Bobby Russell, most notably 'Us', which was recorded by Tom Jones. Burt also wrote with Neil Simon for a shelved movie version of *Promises Promises*. This generated one lovely song 'Seconds', recorded by Gladys Knight, which has more than a touch of Bacharach magic to it – and contains exquisite wordplay, to boot. But Burt was less than fascinated by the writing procedure. Robin Platts records an interview with *Billboard* in 1974. Burt was basically bellyaching to the journal that he felt the very process of popular music writing to be a "trap [...], writ[ing] an arrangement [...], talked into producing [the] album and get[ting] stuck six months in the studio".

225

Both commercially and internally he was at a very important stage in his life, having been effectively overrun by circumstances. As per usual Burt disappeared into live work – his 'retreat', as it were. However, as a consequence of performing a series of shows throughout the US with British songwriter/actor Anthony Newley, he regained a little enthusiasm and began stopping off, in 1976 and 1977, in New York City to record what was to be his seventh A&M album (his first studio album in four years), the more-than-interesting *Futures*.

Bacharach had also experimentally written a couple of songs with Norman Gimbel (he of 'Killing Me Softly' fame) and poet and ex priest James Kavanaugh and they duly turned up on this ensuing album. Together with the Gimbel ('When You Bring Your Sweet Love To Me' and 'Where Are You') and Kavanaugh ('The Young Grow Younger Every Day', 'We Should Have Met Sooner' and 'Night') songs, the album featured two Bacharach and David tracks 'I Took My Strength From You' and 'No One Remembers My Name', in addition to the excellent 'Seconds' that Burt wrote with Neil Simon. Also included was the aforementioned 'Us', the song co-written with Bobby Russell, which although somewhat incongruously delivered by singer Joshie Armstead, appeared lyrically and musically biographical in its display of great sadness, sensitivity and reflection upon (Burt's?) marital failure.

Futures is a very pleasing album in several respects – particularly instrumentally - but illustrates perfectly that Burt's muse with Hal was well and truly buried. The two Bacharach and David songs are actually the weakest on the album. The singing parts (rather glutinous here and there) are handled by a variety of guests: some of whom are reasonably well-used (Peter Yarrow, Melissa Mackay, Sally Stevens, Marti McCall), but others who don't really gell (Joshie Armstead, Jamie Anders). However, there is a terrific instrumental album waiting to escape, here.

The title track is by far the most interesting and dynamic cut on the album and suggests great possibilities for a suite with piano and orchestra. The piece breaks in and out of several fascinating strategic moments with horn players David Sanborn and Marvin Stamm sympathetically playing what could only be described as 'total Bacharach'. Burt ties it all together with inventive legato and exciting keyboard bridges and (perhaps unconsciously) almost perfectly segues into the following track 'Us'.

The two songs work so well together and are so interesting and at times so moving, speaking as they do with one emphasis on a hopeful urbane groove ('Futures'), but the other concerning disintegration ('Us'), that while listening one cannot imagine a better piece of Bacharach. Bobby Russell's beautiful lyrics on this latter piece speak volumes as they exclaim with pain 'shame on we, what have we done to us?'

Furthermore, the striking electric piano jazz phrasing on the following track - 'Where Are You' - is so Lyle Mays-oriented that one can envisage a whole musical vista mapping out before Burt, here – sod Las Vegas, get a deal with ECM! The tune is such a lovely *canzonetta* there is no need for a vocal track (although some Joni Mitchell style singing - circa *Hejira* - would not have gone amiss). One could even imagine a little Pat Metheny guitar or Jaco Pastorius bass creeping-in towards the 'outro' (Burt can't quite envisage where to go with it next).

It's by no means a great album but there are undoubtedly **great** pieces of music here. This writer remains perplexed therefore about Burt's next move: the neo-Romanticist backward step that was *Woman*.

Perhaps it was something to do with the luke-warm reception to *Futures* – it barely received one review. But, let's face it, how could Burt attract any attention at all in 1977 the year of the first Sex Pistols album, the year the Eagles, Fleetwood Mac, Kiss and disco were cleaning-up, commercially. Had the album dropped a couple of its vocal tracks (e.g. 'We Should Have Met Sooner') and been marketed at a jazz audience, it would surely have fared better than it did.

Woman

It seems that Burt was performing a volte- face with *Woman*, entering into the domain of the classical while also attempting to comprehend where he stood in relationship to the opposite sex. He appeared to be expressing musically his own bewilderment as to why things tend to fall apart, why people cannot stay together, what it was between a man and a woman that prevented them from embracing the difficulties of rivalry. Why people **needed**, rather than **wanted** to do things was always close to his heart, of course!

Woman was recorded live at Houston's Jones Hall November 2, 1978 and released in July 1979. It was his first symphonic suite but sadly did

227

not follow the direction of *Futures'* better moments. Recorded with the Houston Symphony Orchestra, it did have majestic orchestral parts and jazzy noodles but an odd underscoring that seemed often at odds with the sometimes typically ingenious Bacharach melodies.

 Burt invited Carly Simon and Libby Titus to each write small *librettos* and sing a section. Anthony Newley and Sally Stevens also contributed, but the album was primarily an instrumental showcase. The Newley track ('The Dancing Fool') had been scheduled for a Broadway musical based on the life of Charlie Chaplin, but this never materialised. So in some respects it was a mish-mash of ideas, cross-fertilisations and existing parts that, in the long run, really didn't hang together at all well.

 Burt claimed he was attempting to make an album dedicated to femininity. He stated on a 1979 press release:

> One of the reactions I get to this record is that it's a very feminine album that would appeal to a wide range of women's feelings. I don't know about labels. I just try to write. I don't try to make things difficult. I don't try to write complexly. But the most success I've had has been with women singers and towards female emotions. Whether that came from lyrics or musical expression, I don't know. (Bacharach to Kit Buckler, *A&M*, 1979)

While Bacharach rehearsed the rhythm section prior to recording, he held only one trial concert before the actual session in Houston. Working within the strict demands of musician union regulations caused a degree of strain for Burt. The truly daft idea was for it all to be 'organically' recorded in four hours (!). But when Bacharach arrived in Houston for the recording, he found he could not use the Jones Hall for rehearsing and had to keep one eye on the clock so that the orchestra did not walk out, having played for their union-allocated time. Memories of producing Dionne in London's Marble Arch studios in 1965 must have come flooding back:

> I couldn't even hear what I had written. There wasn't any real perspective until we got onstage. For all of us it was a pressure cooker. There was a clock onstage. You knew what you had to do. You knew how much time you had – and you knew you couldn't come back a third day. It was as intense as it could be. But also I

like the aspect that it makes everybody challenged. (ibid)

Burt also informed *Billboard* that same month:

> [...] the results are hard to peg. It isn't classical, although it leans that way. It covers a wide range of feelings [...] it represents a free, different type of music people don't associate with me. (Bacharach to *Billboard*, 1979)

In a revealing addendum to the whole experiment, Burt admitted, while being interviewed by the BBC in 1996, that the process was perhaps somewhat ambitious and ultimately:

> [...] wasn't necessarily successful. It wasn't successful at all [...] an expensive failure. All live – if there was a mistake then that was it, we were saddled with it. I dreamt about that whole process for two months afterwards [...] every night the same dream. I never had anything like that [...] once about a lady every night for two whole weeks - but an album? It was always the same: always the panic, always the fear I wasn't going to get it done – interesting! (Bacharach to *BBC: This Is Now*, 1996)

Not a dismal failure by any means but a direction, perhaps he should not have taken.

At least Burt could see out the 1970s with a little moderate single success. In 1979 he collaborated with old friend Paul Anka on the soundtrack for the film *Together*. The title song 'I Don't Need You Anymore' featured vocals by Michael McDonald, Libby Titus and another 'blast from the past' Jackie DeShannon and later became a minor hit single.

Upon being asked by trade mag *Billboard* in 1979 about the somewhat modest success of this project, Burt stated that his chances of major appeal were being hampered by the fact that very little contemporary Bacharach material was making its way onto the radio (most of the American public have still never heard either *Futures* or *Woman* – which, in the case of the former is a great pity). He realised that the previous association of his music to the 'Beautiful Radio' FM demographic was now working against him. According to certain deejays, Bacharach stood for 'easy listening', 'muzak', 'pipe and slippers' music. He acerbically informed *Billboard*:

> The world tends to link me to the Henry Mancini 'school' of

music. As a result I get pigeon holed by radio stations and my records don't usually stand much of a chance for airplay. (Bacharach to *Billboard*, 1979)

Of course these stereotypes were ridiculous. Songs like 'Where Are You' were adventurous pieces of work but while he was being associated with the likes of Mancini, Ray Conniff or Andy Williams, Burt was never going to receive much coverage for his recent material. Some of his more experimental tracks were also too long for radio. Thus the generic demarcations that so successfully codified his appeal in the 1960s, worked against him by 1979.

The commonly held idea that Bacharach had totally lost his musical lustre by 1979 is, however, incorrect. He was indeed struggling for both motivation and recognition but, despite his patchy try-out with *Woman*, his musical genius had actually returned. It was just that nobody paid attention to it. Future wife and songwriting partner Carole Bayer Sager was to declare:

We'd go somewhere and people would say 'Hey Burt don't you write any more?' 'How come we don't hear songs of yours any more?' and to me the absurdity of it was here was this man whose contribution to music was phenomenal. (Sager to BBC: *This Is Now*, 1996)

But, live concerts aside, he wasn't being heard. The best parts of *Futures* (and bits and pieces of *Woman*) are without doubt the finest recordings he made between the mid-1970s and his late-1990s work with Elvis Costello. Yet he seldom ever performs them live.

In between playing oldies in Las Vegas, Burt still occasionally appeared on the TV – mostly chat shows. On one such occasion, co-hosting the Mike Douglas Show for a week, he met the next love of his life. After an appearance by singer/songwriter Carole Bayer Sager on the show, Burt invited her to write a song with him (and also to join him for dinner); in 1982 they married. Carole is now known to sit and ponder inquisitively on exactly which invitation came first! She has not thus far entirely recalled the sequence of events, but perhaps in stronger moments (!) her instinct informs her that it was probably as written above.

Chapter 12

Carole, Kitsch, Costello

"I never mix the two. I only did it one time, and that was with Carole". (Burt Bacharach, 1996)

"He said he thought he was done – my response was 'where did it go?' I think I inspired him to […] find his way back to the radio a little bit". (Sager, 2003)

Carole

Carole Bayer Sager was born March 8 1946 in New York City and began to write songs lyrics while attending, in the early 1960s, New York High School of Music and Art. She was yet another Don Kirshner prodigy and worked for Screen Gems Publishing. In 1966 she penned the hit 'A Groovy Kind Of Love' (a US recording for Pattie LaBelle and a hit for the Mindbenders). She collaborated on several songs for the Monkees and wrote the lyrics for the 1970 off-Broadway hit *Georgy*. In 1975 she co-wrote Melissa Manchester's smash hit 'Midnight Blue' and then two years later enjoyed her own British top ten record with 'You're Moving Out Today' (a hit for Bette Midler in the US). She also achieved a UK number one as a lyricist with Leo Sayer's version of 'When I Need You'.

Sager was, by the mid-'70s, married to composer Marvin Hamlisch and joined forces with him to write the popular Broadway musical *They're Playing Our Song*, a semi-autobiographical work that explored the romantic entanglements of a hit songwriting team. The pair also received an Oscar Nomination in 1978 for their work on the James Bond movie *The Spy Who Loved Me* – yet another example of a weak Bond film with excellent music. Hamlisch wrote the score and the theme 'Nobody Does It Better' for which Carole wrote the lyrics – a worldwide success for Carly Simon.

Like Burt, Carole's marriage was all-but over as the decade ended and their new relationship initially developed around their respective songwriting skills. Sager was very independent, very successful; Bacharach:

Carole's got a real alert nose for the business – I was out in leftfield then. (Bacharach to *Biography Channel*, 2003)

Sager enjoyed her biggest Stateside hit in 1981 with 'Stronger Than Ever' from her third solo LP, co-written with Burt, entitled *Sometimes Late At Night*. This album gave the game away somewhat about their relationship for it was basically a loosely-tied concept work concerning their love affair. In fact, so well did the album sell that Neil Bogert, president of Carole's label (Boardwalk Records), candidly remarked that he hoped there would be further successful albums detailing this interesting relationship! But Sager divorced Hamlisch that same year.

During 1981 Carole and Burt also received the Academy Award for 'Arthur's Theme (Best That You Can Do)' co-written with Christopher Cross and Peter Allen. Unlike a great deal of previous movie work for Burt, *Arthur* was in point of fact a good film starring the multi-talented Dudley Moore (and of course, the majestic Sir John Gielgud), which elevated the song into public consciousness somewhat. It's a pretty good song, well sung by the ghostly talent of Christopher Cross (whose first album remains an American pop landmark), but it would take a talented musicologist to spot the Bacharach parts.

Within twelve months of her divorce, Carole and Burt were married. After the success of *Sometimes Late At Night,* Bacharach and Sager entered into a very fruitful, but also very commercial, songwriting relationship. Carole insisted that in order to rediscover his talents (which he probably had not lost) Burt had to appease the disc jockeys, write less experimental material, and at least attempt to change his musical priorities.

Burt was to later announce at the 1986 Academy Awards ceremony that he thought that his late-1970s work was not accessible enough, and that Carole had inspired him to become commercial once again. Hence, perhaps the rather standardised approach to 'Arthur's Theme'. Sager's creative influence on Bacharach was probably at its most comprehensive during the first three years or so of their relationship.

Perhaps the most prominent Bacharach and Sager song remains 'That's What Friends Are For', originally written in 1982 for the Ron Howard-directed film *Night Shift*. This is a tasteful little film starring Henry Winkler (ex 'The Fonz') whose life changes as a morgue attendant when he is assigned to the night shift with bizarre colleague Michael Keaton. Winkler undoubtedly turns in the best performance of his career here, and Burt's score is very sensitive in dealing with Winkler's mundane life yet pleasing humanity. Actually, the combination of Howard, Winkler, Keaton and Bacharach is something of a 'gentle revelation' and it's a pity that this formula was never again attempted.

The song closes the film and, incongruously sung as it is by Rod Stewart, sounds like a bit of a nonentity. In the hands of Rod it plods and the now terribly dated sound of the 'state of the art' 1980s keyboards is crass, to say the least. Burt states, however that such songs as these from the 1980s were for him just as hard work as his earlier periods:

> Everything I have written I can honestly say has never come off the back of a truck. Everything has come from what has moved me. I have enjoyed writing songs as well as musicals and scoring for the films. (Bacharach to Riley, *Liverpool Echo*, 2002)

Carole, with some degree of frustration, agrees:

> In the beginning of 'That's What Friends Are For' […] he [Burt] goes 'no, that's da-dum'. [I said] 'What's the difference, just get rid of the 'da-dum' and go into […]'. I got so pissed-off, it's just a 16th note – what does it matter? […] He was so precise about it, it was so important to him and he sits in the music room and spends an hour on whether he wanted the 16th note. If you are the lyricist [it] could be rather maddening. But, he was right, and I finally wrote 'and I'. (Sager to *BBC: This Is Now*, 1996)

One gets the feeling that Burt's hour-long meditations were spent attempting to follow Carole's directive, avoiding the temptation of putting too much music into the song.

There **is** something about this song, but the magic lies less within the melody as in the days of old, and more in the lyrics. The resonance of the simple, but affective, words were strong enough for the song to be revisited in 1985 when re-recorded by Dionne Warwick and friends (Elton John, Stevie Wonder, Gladys Knight). It certainly became a very cogent fund-raiser for AIDS awareness (The American Foundation For AIDS Research), earning over $1 million in the US alone. It was Dionne Warwick herself who spotted 'That's What Friends Are For' while watching *Night Shift* on TV one evening, and she decided to record it herself. The final session was a typically 1980s all-star affair - after Live Aid it seems that these kind of fund-raisers were occurring every week – but, held together by Elton John's fine keyboard and Stevie Wonder's distinctive harmonica playing, it became the first ever Bacharach and Warwick number one hit single.

Other hit recordings from the partnership in 1982 were 'Making Love' for Roberta Flack and 'Heartlight' for Neil Diamond. The latter of these is the most remembered. It was inspired by (of all things) the movie *E.T.* and was co-written with the song's vocalist, Neil Diamond. It ranks as one of Bacharach and Sager's biggest-selling hits but it has not aged well, is very 1980s in its sound, and somewhat unremarkable.

It is worthy of note just how dated this synthesized stuff now sounds in comparison with the timelessness of Burt's previous undubbed material. The everlasting durability of an orchestra playing 'Don't Make Me Over', for example, certainly outlives the squeaky clean, shrill sounds of a 1980s Yamaha, Roland or Korg keyboard. One could literally date 'Heartlight' within 12 months of its release simply via the sound pads used on the keyboard.

Spelling

In September 1984 it was made public that Bacharach and Dionne Warwick would be reunited. Carole and Burt were recruited by Aaron Spelling to write the theme tune to his *Finder Of Lost Loves* TV show and Spelling insisted that Burt call Dionne to invite her to sing the theme. The ever-forceful mogul was adamant that it should be Dionne and nobody else singing the signature tune, and so Burt was effectively required to phone her. Dionne stated to Robin Platts:

> I hadn't spoken to him in almost a dozen years. We were in two different worlds at that time. And he called me and said he had a song he wanted to come over and play for me [...] and I told him to come on over.

> It was an amazing sort of reunion [...] based on the fact that I've always said that friendships prevail, regardless of what goes up

or down – that's what makes a true friendship. And after all that time had gone by, it was as if no time had passed at all. (Warwick to Platts, 2003:100)

Dionne has further suggested in various interviews that the initial 'hello' on the telephone was very strained, very difficult; but once she had agreed to hear the song, and Burt had gingerly made his way over to her residence, the ice melted. Burt stated that there were tears, particularly when Dionne sang the song; it was as if they had fleetingly caught up with time.

But time had passed and the studio and keyboard technology mentioned above turned out to be cold and soulless for somebody such as Dionne (used to more organic methods). Burt had embraced technologically-driven recording methods by the 1980s – he had no choice – but Dionne later suggested that, by doing so, this was when his songs lacked the elemental dynamism, the creative edge, of his earlier work:

> Burt was still basically the producer but it was a different kind of feeling […] I did not really work with Carole that much, In fact it was basically with Burt that I worked [but] I truly miss[ed] live recording. There was something very special about recording with people in the studio, playing music with real instruments – not synthesizers and almost-strings, you know. It was quite different. (ibid)

Another era, another sound: Burt's commerciality during the first half of the 1980s was undoubtedly a result of his collaboration both artistically and emotionally with Carole Bayer Sager. She brought him out of himself and transformed the man who, by his own admittance, was making (apparently) inaccessible music. Now he was not only scoring movies once again, but also writing chart successes. Yet, listening now, perhaps it was all a bit laboured, a little lethargic; maybe, even, a little desperate.

It was without doubt rather conventional, structurally. No three bar phrases anymore, no 3/8 or 6/8 time signatures. Standard AABA forms were *de rigeur*. Perhaps Carole was right, Burt had been too leftfield by the late 1970s – after all they were now having hits. But back in the 1950s Burt was writing hits such as 'The Story Of My Life' with three vanilla chords (C, F, G7), an AABA structure and he **hated** it (he has repeatedly stated to interviewers about the above song "that was not **my** music!").

I stated earlier in this work that Burt in 1960 was not quite at the peak of his art, that songs such as 'Tower Of Strength' were 'rhythm and blues for people who did not like rhythm and blues'. Because he was attempting to consciously shape popular music reception according to certain definitions, he was writing parodies. Bacharach eventually pleased himself and in doing so learned that one could not determine what people hear: magic ensued. But by the 1980s that deterministic approach had returned: he had slipped back into this mode of thought.

One of Burt's better moments of the 1980s came with the Pattie LaBelle and Michael McDonald soul ballad 'On My Own', another worldwide hit in 1986. This perhaps more than any other 1980s Bacharach melody reflected at least something of his muse. The duettists who apparently, were not even in the same city when they recorded their parts, sing it beautifully. The intense sadness of the lyric and the melody matches practically anything written by Bacharach and David. Barney Hoskyns of *Mojo* has the same opinion:

> It is customary to write-off Bacharach's work of the late '70s and '80s. The Patti LaBelle and Michael McDonald hit 'On My Own' is routinely dismissed as glutinous L.A. soul, whereas it is actually a peerless duet that more than redeems the slush of 'Arthur's Theme' and 'That's What Friends Are For'. (Hoskyns, *Mojo,* 1997)

Chordally it moves as a Bacharach song ought to move, it reaches levels of intensity that few other Bacharach songs of that era reach. It is a song that transcends all barriers. It can be sung solo by men or women: the lyrics are interchangeable and, perhaps like the aforementioned song 'Us', probably reflect an emotional distress signal from home.

Sager and Bacharach continued to collaborate musically as the 1980s progressed, but their work was less prevalent after 1986. That year they had a child (a boy – Christopher) and music industry life slowed down, somewhat. Burt's visits to the track and stud increased. His obsession for racing ownership and punting have been a constant feature in his adult life ("when I got involved with racing it was the only thing that took my mind off the writing, the recording"), and things began to slowly untangle for the couple. In 1988 they worked together on *Arthur 2 On The Rocks* – a flat sequel barely worthy of a mention, filmically or musically - and also on a number of rather anonymous tracks on an insipid Barbra Streisand LP.

Platts (2003) records that Bacharach had stated to *Billboard* towards the end of the 1980s that he felt the need to make another solo album but considered that neither his vocal technique nor personal style were suited to the current music scene. Burt was later prompted about this false start by Serene Dominic of the *Phoenix New Times* in 2000 when she reminded him that a Bacharach solo project had not appeared since 1979's *Woman*. Burt self-consciously admitted:

> I know, I know. I've been approached by a couple of people. But for me to go in and make an album and put six or seven months into it and then they can't sell it, can't get it played on the right radio format at the right level, or the company is suddenly acquired, taken over by somebody who doesn't give a shit about it [...] I'd rather just keep writing for other people. (Bacharach to Dominic, *Phoenix New Times*, 2000)

It was only a matter of time before he and Carole split. Inevitably by 1991 they had gone their separate ways. The two speak well of each other and there only remains a little understandable frustration, rather than bitterness, from Carole. Burt claimed in a later (1996) interview that he was "no expert on marriage" – or that after four such adventures, "perhaps I am"! He evidently continued to be philosophical about what little 'private life' he had, but also stated honestly that, for him, a dual work-and-home relationship could not function for long:

> Any time you work with somebody [...] you're married to, it [brings] a severe degree of difficulty. Recording studio all day and then you come home! I think it's very tough without having that kind of strain. (Bacharach to *BBC: This Is Now*, 1996)

And his by then ex-wife Carole agreed:

> It could be 2 or 3 o'clock in the morning [...] maybe that Bb7 is wrong, maybe I should have brought up the bass [...] Burt just never [...] he always felt he could make something better. (Sager to *Biography Channel*, 2003)

Burt revealed:

> If I was making love to a woman [...] you should leave that stuff

alone, the current song you're working on [...] you should not
have to go and write it down on a piece of paper what you're
hearing [and say] 'be right back honey!'(Bacharach to *Biography
Channel*, 2003)

Reunited

At the age of 63 Burt was back to flying solo, but he was working: concert
performances and songwriting (although still with vanilla chords). Burt
had co-written two songs for smooth soul singer James Ingram ('This Is
The Night' and 'Sing For The Children'). Produced by legendary Philly
Soul man Thom Bell, the latter received considerable airplay. That same
year he wrote 'Two Hearts' with Philip Bailey for Earth Wind And Fire's
album *Millennium*.

He also co-wrote 'Don't Say Goodbye Girl' for Tevin Campbell and
worked with British lyricist B.A. Robertson on an unfortunate modern
musical retelling of *Snow White*. However, the news that received the most
interest from fans was his reunification with his erstwhile songwriting
partner, Hal David. It was announced in 1993 that they were to be honoured
by ASCAP (Hal became president of the organisation in 1980).

According to the grapevine all past ill feelings were long since forgotten
as the two men accepted the ASCAP Founder's Award on May 24, 1993 in
Los Angeles. Don Heckman of the *L.A. Times* reported:

> The reconciliation is an appropriate lead-in for tonight's ninth
> annual ASCAP Pop Awards Dinner at the Beverly Hilton Hotel,
> at which composer Bacharach, 65, and lyricist David, 72, will
> receive the song licensing organization's prestigious Founder's
> Award, and Warwick will sing many of their best known songs.

> 'We use this award' explained Morton Gould, ASCAP's
> president, 'to celebrate the founders of the society by honouring
> our most gifted contemporary songwriters. And I can't think of
> any team that deserves the honor more than Burt and Hal' [...].

> Now that they've broken the ice with 'Sunny Weather Lover' for
> Warwick, will the duo produce more tunes together? 'It's always

possible', said Bacharach. 'Yeah we'll probably write more songs', continued David 'why not?'

Then came Burt's rider:

'But there has to be a real purpose – a reason to sit down for a specific project, like the title song for a film, or maybe even another Broadway show. That would really interest me' said Bacharach. 'How about you, Hal?'

'It sure would' David replied.

'But you never know if you can do it again', said Bacharach, who prides himself in not living on past glories. 'All you can do is try. Can you get the same magic you had before? Who knows? I guess we're a pretty tough act to follow'.

They did eventually work together but lightning did not strike twice. A couple of years later, while Burt was camping it up in his (and his music's) cameo in the Mike Myers movie *Austin Powers International Man Of Mystery,* Hal philosophised:

Things happen with every group. Through it all, the fact that we – at a certain point – stopped writing together is just really a blip in our relationship. We really remained good friends all the way through as we are today. I think time erodes […] You're together x number of years. Your mind goes one way and the other guy's mind goes the other way. I didn't think there was anything abnormal about it, in retrospect. Everybody changes and you just go where your life takes you. (David to Platts, *Discoveries,* 1997)

The pair wrote the aforementioned 'Sunny Weather Lover' for Dionne Warwick, and it was heralded as a major event. But by now these two elder statesmen of popular music were unable to reproduce the magic of their bygone partnership. It has frequently been stated that the problem with most 1960s musicians is that they are not so much sonically stuck in the sixties, but, rather, in the eighties. And so it proved to be with 'Sunny Weather Lover'. Hal David admitted that:

We thought it was good, but it just didn't work. I didn't think it was one of our great songs. I think under certain circumstances it could have happened. (ibid)

Or perhaps not: despite a more than competent delivery from the timeless Dionne, 'Sunny Weather Lover' was, with its anodyne chord progressions and rather faceless lyrics, a refugee from the 1980s, to be sure.

Burt has always lived in and for the present and in order for him to regain his enthusiasm he had to know that his work was feted by younger generations. He had to feel relevant, he had to know that his earlier pieces were timeless, that the leftfield work of the 1960s and 1970 was not too radio unfriendly. Oddly enough, via one of the most interesting musical revivals of the post 1960s era - the mid-1990s easy listening phenomenon - this information got through.

Kitsch

The twin polarities of grunge and dance music had, by 1995, alienated many young people. In the UK, for instance, digital dance music had been popular for almost ten years, yet it was faceless, driven by bass frequencies rather than melodies and modulations, and anti-melody. The absurd hyped battles between Britpop bands Blur and Oasis only heightened the sense of hyper-reality surrounding contemporary releases and so, from car boot sales and Oxfam shops all over the country, emerged vinyl record collectors purchasing the albums rock-oriented collectors had previously left behind.

In the US a similar movement concerning 'incredibly strange music' arose. Collectors were interested in listening to anything that did not fit the already over-scrutinized genres of rock, jazz and soul. 1950s and 1960s sound effects albums, uncensored sex albums, living stereo albums for the bachelor pad all became desirable and highly collectable.

Literally anything would do, for it was about sound, about weirdness, about 'grooviness': from the Hammond organ of Alan Haven to the cod-Hawaiian sounds of the Waikiki Beach Boys; from Top Of The Pops covers albums to Mrs Mills Plays Party Pops, collectors were looking at all vinyl product in search of unique cultural differences.

Together with the revival of interest in such TV programmes as *The Avengers, The Prisoner, Bewitched, I Love Genie*, etc. collectors began to realise that the 1960s was not all about rock music. Rock, in fact, had been a major villain in eradicating artistic divergence. Arrangers and orchestra leaders such as Alan Caddy, Laurie Johnson, Les Reed, and Mark Wirtz became collectable.

'Loungecore' club nights (such as the famous 'Boutique' in Liverpool and Manchester) were established, fanzines appeared, and CD compilation albums fed this curious but refreshing change - from London to Tokyo. Groups such as Air in France or the Pizzicato Five in Japan were interested in playing but also ironizing melodic easy listening. This irony was problematic, for it was a hollow discourse inviting people to 'like' or like something as the fancy took them, but there was a healthy anti-canonic postmodern discourse going on, here: all genres were relative, tenets were false, all music was up for grabs. At the centre of all of this activity lay a fascination with Burt Bacharach's music.

Categories

By the end of the decade Serene Dominic of the *Phoenix New Times* was able to place Bacharach fans into three distinct categories; all problematic, of course, but all worthy of our attention. For example, she stated that type A acolytes were long time fans able to appreciate Burt and Hal's music the first time around, but also unfortunate enough to have lived through the "clackety eighties tracks".

Type B, she identified were "newly minted adults" who made their childhood memories connect in the mid-1990s, supported by several CD re-releases and the ability to "assign the correct adult emotional response" to the music.

Type C were the fanatics who keep looking for the obscurities and checking upon countless undiscovered songs, frantically downloading stuff from Napster and trading tapes and CDRs on various Bacharach internet sites.

However, none of this behaviour would have been possible without the record collector and the youthful loungecore enthusiast investing time and money digging out vinyl copies of *Reach Out* from the charity shops. It all came together for Burt via this curious, yet refreshing (but at times rather childish and some might say foolish) movement. Simon Williams of the *NME* stated in 1996:

> So you think easy listening was all about irony-laden cheesiness for people with a taste bypass who like their musak to be of the wallpaper variety? Well think again. It's just not that easy. To begin your re-education we give you Burt Bacharach [...] sartorially–pissed clubs have sprung up in the past few years eulogizing Burt's way with a tune and teeth-quavering perfection. (Williams, *NME*, 1996)

In the same article, Bacharach stated with some bemusement:

> My attitude is: call it what you want, but keep playing it, keep liking it! You wanna put a name on it? Put a name on it! I mean [...] it doesn't matter what the tag is. Does it affect you? Great! (Bacharach to Williams, *NME*, 1996)

From the above comments Burt was erudite enough to realise that these kind of movements, as useful as they are in recodifying popular music without R&B fetishists, and po-faced dance music deejays, cannot last for too long – just long enough in fact to make an impact, to make people think, to make people regret giving away all of that lovely music on vinyl first time around. Music writer Stuart Maconie understood the 'easy' revival in the following terms:

> What this amounts to is one freak, amusing hit single [Mike Flowers Pops version of Oasis' 'Wonderwall'] and a handful of fashion students dressing up [...] what really galls about it is that term 'easy listening': whilst it might just about apply to 'A Walk In The Black Forest', it offers no purchase on Burt Bacharach. (Maconie, *Q*, 1996)

Maconie was both right and wrong, here. Loungecore was far more significant than merely revolving around a "handful of students". The record industry alone understood both the reasons and directions of this fetish and supplied it with a continual stream of CD reissues (that sold well until its demise in 1999). Yet he was correct in suggesting that despite being regarded as some kind of "Lounge Wizard" (*NME*) Burt's music could not have been further from the 'easy' signifier. As Maconie, himself, went on to state:

> Ever heard a busker playing 'Promises Promises', a song whose melody is reminiscent of climbing the stairs in the dark and finding extra stairs that aren't there? (ibid)

While Burt's music became a camp signifier at least a new generation of people were able to discover that compositional complexity and quality pop music were not mutually exclusive. It mattered not that vodka gimlets were all the rage, for eventually kitsch gave way to genuine appreciation.

It was this revival of interest in vodka martinis and pink fluffy cushions that directly led to Burts' involvement with the spy spoof *Austin Powers International Man Of Mystery*. Encouraged by this 1990s interest in the 'other' 1960s, comedy actor Mike Myers created the idea of an imperfect British spy from the 1960s who, despite a pot belly and bad teeth, was considered sexy simply because he was from the 1960s: but which 1960s exactly? The one represented in films such as *In Like Flint* or *A Hard Day's Night*? or the corny L.A. version of 'Swinging London'?

Our fascination with that period of time was being increasingly blurred by the postmodern 1990s, the sixties were regarded almost as a kind of hyper real geographic place, rather than a place in time. In order to ironize our perceptions of the 1960s, Myers recruited Burt and his music to aurally express the differences between the 1960s and the 1990s. It was a great success.

Charles Taylor of the *Boston Phoenix* perfectly summarized this glorious period of rampant kitsch when he wrote in 1998 re the resurgence of interest in Bacharach:

> It's unlikely any of this would be happening if Bacharach weren't part of the subterranean influences that are causing all sorts of unexpected things to bubble to the surface in popular music right now. There's no denying that much of the craze for lounge music and exotica is nothing more than a sort of camp superiority. But in the hands of people who genuinely care for them, soundtrack music, French pop, ambient music, space-age instrumentals, and all of the other things that have been incorporated into pop and

dance music can function as the opposite of cool disengagement. (Taylor, *Boston Phoenix*, 1998)

Grace Of My Heart

Burt's renaissance then was both surprising and inevitable. Despite not having written a new top 40 song in over a decade, his name (and his music) lived again. By 1997 *Promises Promises* was being performed at the City Center, New York. The previous year Warwick's recording of 'Wives And Lovers' featured in the hit movie *The First Wives Club*, and Harry Connick Jnr sang 'This Guy's In Love With You' on the soundtrack of *One Fine Day*. But perhaps the greatest moment for Burt in this mid-late 1990s revival of interest in his music came when he was asked to write a song for a movie set largely in the Brill Building world of the early-mid 1960s – Allison Anders' *Grace Of My Heart*.

Grace Of My Heart is a kind of glorious failure. I remember going to see the movie upon its release in 1996 in Liverpool with my BBC colleague Spencer Leigh. We both agreed that, while the music was superb, the movie was rather one-dimensional in its attempts to trace the 1960s via a kind of Carole King pastiche. Apparently, the film was intended to be about King but she did not agree to the characterisation and so the Illeana Douglas character became a kind of montage of songwriters.

Matt Dillon, Eric Stolz and John Turturro all featured as concoctions of various Brill stereotypes. All look uncomfortable, not only with the rather prosaic script, but also in the ridiculous wigs. Yet the movie does try hard to overcome its own limitations and should be congratulated for that. Popular music history is notoriously difficult to represent on the silver screen. Ultimately, *Grace Of My Heart* only reinforces this dilemma.

In an attempt to recapture the atmosphere of that era, Burt, like other former Brill writers Lesley Gore, Carole Bayer Sager, and Gerry Goffin, was asked to write a song that reflected his muse at the Brill. Each of these writers, however, was also asked to share their task with a contemporary songwriter – a stroke of genius (and luck, as it turned out).

The soundtrack is most certainly a success. A few of the songs do suffer from weak vocal deliveries such as 'Take A Run At The Sun' by J Mascis, but others are glorious: of particular interest is the Carole Bayer Sager and David A. Stewart song 'I Do' and the marvellous 'Man From Mars' sung by Kristen Vigard and written by Joni Mitchell (but where did Joni fit into this narrative/experiment?). The entire music production was left in the capable hands of Larry Klein with the exception of Bacharach's contribution, which was co-written over the ansaphone and fax with Elvis Costello (this combination also produced their own track).

Burt and Elvis co-wrote the song 'God Give Me Strength' for the Carole King 'type' so it was sung in the movie by Kristen Vigard; but on the soundtrack album duties were performed by Costello and Bacharach: it turned into an opus running at over six minutes. Burt was to state:

> It was in that 6/8, 12/8 thing I used to write in, that I hadn't done in years. Musically I can't go back and say, I want to write something like 'Don't Make Me Over'. I just don't think that way. But this was for a movie about the Brill Building, so I thought, great! [...] I suggested a couple of new chords and changes, wrote the bridge and did the orchestration. To me the song has a certain timelessness. It works as a period piece, but it also works for the time the movie's being released in. (Bacharach to *Vanity Fair*, 1997)

Burt underrates himself here for 'God Give Me Strength' was masterful and perhaps one of the greatest songs of the entire decade.

Costello

Nothing could be further removed from 'Sunny Weather Lover' than the sublime 'God Give Me Strength'. Elvis Costello was evidently able to offer Burt something that Hal David could not. Costello was a child of the 1960s (he is the same age as this writer) and grew up listening and rearticulating Bacharach's music from an early age. He was a younger version of the British receptive community of musicians who rearticulated American music through the recording process.

Everything Elvis learned he learned from listening to records. He was beginning to make music with Liverpool legend Alan Mays at about the same time that Bacharach was struggling against all odds via *Lost Horizon*. Elvis was fully aware of the popular music schism of the mid-1970s. In fact, he was soon part of it by 1976, recording for legendary British independent label Stiff. Unlike many of his counterparts, however, Costello was writing music that was obviously looped-back into the melodies of the 1960s.

Like Bacharach, Costello did not fully embrace technology and throughout the time that Burt was writing his aural candy with Carole Bayer Sager, Costello was turning-out interesting songs based upon a traditional 1960s combo format. The British indie rock press feted his most accomplished works but he was also very different from the average indie rocker. Not only were his tastes locked into the popular music of a previous era, but he also understood many aspects of the American songbook, recording a beautiful version of 'My Funny Valentine', Burt's 'I Just Don't Know What To Do With Myself' and a very successful country music album *Almost Blue*, which sported a sticker on the cover declaring "warning! this album […] may produce radical reaction in narrow minded people".

However, Costello's music always lacked melodic syncopation. By the 1990s he had also grown tired of repeating himself, and began experimenting with collaborations: first with Paul McCartney then with the Brodsky Quartet (both were relatively unsuccessful). Similarly, Bacharach's music was derailed in the vanilla plantations of Beverly Hills. One might argue that it was fate that brought them together.

Burt's alliance with Elvis Costello was just the critical stance that both required. No Hollywood 'yes' men, no L.A soul merchants, no 'belle époque' or L.A. hyper reality, but a British fan and musician who understood Burt's music from the perspective of sound and reception, sending ideas and lyrics over the telephone. It beggars belief what kind of track might have emanated from this project had Burt not been thrown together with Costello.

Eternal perfectibility

The creative input for this piece of musical perfection was codified by the eternal perfectionism of the American who admired the English, mixed with the sublime defeatist nature of the Englishman who guardedly admired the American. It was this combination of factors that created a piece of music that shone via its innovation and ability to stir up memories. Burt understood that something was happening the moment the lyrics appeared on his fax:

I just think Elvis is one of the great, great lyric writers of all time – a very unique voice. Most of our discussions did not deal with words because that was a given. There was some beautiful stuff coming in. (Bacharach to Di Martino, *Mojo* 1998)

The Anglo/American axis also worked immediately for Costello:

[…] you know what I learned was that I think we were very good at criticising, in a creative way, each other's suggestions. But to never jump to conclusions. The real clue is to listen. (Costello, ibid)

What? To an L.A. A&R man the very idea of actually criticising the great man would be anathema. It took an Englishman to offer critical comment, and this was exactly what Burt needed. We have already spoken of the songwriting partnership and its internal dynamics. It has to thrive on some kind of balance. In the case of Bacharach and Costello this was to do with mutual critique. It's no good telling Burt he's wonderful. That's what he's wanted to hear all of his life and he'll just believe you and leave it at that. Costello was (perhaps like Hal David) Burt's sparring partner. Carole Bayer Sager wasn't – as we have seen, it "pissed [her] off".

Painted From Memory

Some have described the album that emerged from their collaboration as rather patchy, but not this writer. *Painted from Memory* was two years in the making and was finally released in 1998. It was the Burt Bacharach album that some of us had been waiting for since 1977's *Futures*. The music within this recording was both soothing and disturbing. It most certainly evoked another era, but at the same time was resonating in the post-'Boutique' 1990s. As such it replicated nothing that had come before it. It was in many respects **the** great Bacharach record, and we have Elvis Costello to thank for that. Costello had rarely sung better than on that record:

Unlike the latter-day squad of Bacharach singers, Elvis' voice oozes with character, passion and subtlety, as did that of so many of the earlier, better vocal interpreters like Springfield, Shaw and Warwick. There is drama in these songs, and Costello focuses on it more grippingly that James Ingram – a perfectly fine singer, mind you – might ever be able. (DiMartino, *Mojo*, 1998)

The American can offer the Brit a great deal. The constant striving towards perfection is an admirable American trait. The great thing about the Yank is he never loses heart, he always feels that he can reach some kind of perfection, always feels that he can come again, return restored. But the Brit can also offer his cousin a great deal, too. The critical faculty of an Elvis Costello (consider this stage moniker for a second!), the sobering relativism, the pragmatic underachieving, all acts as a perfect artistic foil. To know that we are object as well as subject is the knowledge of defeat. The Brit embraces this knowledge for it is a knowledge fit for pragmatists of communication. 'Painted From Memory' (the song) illustrates this perfectly. Costello's greatest downbeat lyric is married to possibly Burt's most sublime motif.

What Elvis Costello could see is that the return to ones origins is both inevitable and admirable. The critic, the deejay, the popular music academic (indeed Burt himself) is often wary of origins, or likes to consign them disdainfully to the waste bin ('where's the bass?'), but the artist needs to get in touch with himself. Burt had no means of correcting the discoloration of his compositional muse because he would not willingly go back into the past. It took a 'forty-something' from Birkenhead to convince him of the wisdom of that move. *Painted From Memory* is the perfect 'fin de siecle' recording. Unlike many works of art that appeared at the end of the 1990s it is not culturally pessimistic. It looks back over its shoulder towards a different time while moving on towards the next century. It offers realism: both hope and despair in equal quantities and it is an album for 'everyman'.

Summary

Burt and Elvis went on a mini tour after the success of *Painted From Memory*. The dates were well received and in February 1999 they deservedly won a Grammy in the Pop Collaboration With Vocals category for 'I Still Have The Same Girl' from the album. The pair also joined forces on a rendition of 'I'll Never Fall In Love Again' for the soundtrack to the

Austin Powers sequel *The Spy Who Shagged Me* (and both made cameo appearances, too).

Bacharach continued to team-up with others after *Painted From Memory* but, thus far, has not come up with anything on a par to his work with Costello. He's been back working with the likes of Neil Simon and Hal David on safer projects such as the revival of *Promises Promises* ("it's so different when it's not a marketplace kind of thing") and the 1999 Bette Midler film *Isn't She Great*. Burt scored the film and wrote two rather ordinary songs with Hal David.

To this day he continues to tour, playing over 30 dates per year, and is now happily married to ski instructor Janet, a native of Cleveland and a graduate of Ohio State University (finally he twigged: nothing to do with music); they have two children together.

In recent times, rap artist and producer Dr Dre has sent Burt a few tape loops in the hope that he will produce something melodic with him – a great compliment, especially as Burt is known to hate rap:

> I am not a fan of hip-hop or rap music, although I am going to be working with Dr Dre very soon […] I listened to his recent album with Eminem and I can't say I got into that lyrically. But while it may not be to my taste I do understand it. It is real. (Bacharach to Cowan, *The Times,* 2002)

And:

> [it] was Dre's idea. He gave me about seven drum loops to work with. It's very different from writing a pop hit. I can go back to my jazz or classical roots without having to worry about putting a lyric to it. (Bacharach to *Morning Call,* 2002)

Perhaps we shall witness a piece of minimalist rap emerge soon!

Burt is also still in search of perfection. His brief Academy Awards appearance in 2000 took him:

> a couple of months to arrange, to make it as seamless as possible.(Bacharach to *Dayton Daily News*, 2001)

But despite his attention to detail he never treats musicians as 'note carriers' and professionals still love to work with him.

Very sensibly he eschews the Simon Cowell *Pop Star/American Idol* backdoor into the business:

> That show is like last week's newspaper. The voters have short-term memories. They don't remember what you did last week. Kelly [Clarkson – the winner] had a no. 1 hit right away. This kid's now out on the road. I'm not sure she can fill an arena. (Bacharach to *Morning Call*, 2002)

Further collaborations are probably occurring as I write. Further concert performances will also continue to take place as long as Burt's health remains sound. This live work no longer represents the escape, the internalised sadness that once haunted him. His horses keep winning – and losing - at the track, and his young family continues to live together and grow together.

Something 'gave Burt strength' again to rediscover himself musically but it wasn't 'God'. No spiritual decoding could offer this to Burt Bacharach. The eternal perfectionist was able to rediscover his muse by virtue of a lad who grew up **listening** to Merseybeat and Dionne Warwick in England. That's how significant popular music reception is; that's how 'Presbyterian' pop can be. Despite all of Burt's adherence to the solfege, despite all of his musical education and knowledge, he was eventually to write some of the finest music of his career with an instinctive self-taught musician.

We must never underestimate the power of popular music to rescue itself from the anodyne; and we must never underestimate the power of the non-musician to change the life of the formally trained. Burt has often spoken about trusting one's own instincts (in the men's room, mostly!) – he eventually took his own advice. Our closing words should come from the man himself:

> The biggest thrill for me is being able to make a dent, even a small one, in somebody's life. The reward is when someone tells you one of your songs means something special to them.

It might be the memory of a good time, or a love affair, or when their baby is born. (Bacharach to *Billboard*, 1965)

References

Adorno, T.W. (1941), 'On Popular Music' in Frith, S, & Andrew Goodwin (1990), *On Record*, London: Routledge.

Ancliffe, Michael, B.A. (hons), M.Mus, personal interview 23 April, 6 June 2003.

Auslander, Philip (2001), 'Looking At Records', *The Drama Review 45:1*, New York: University Press & Massachusetts Institute of Technology.

Baron, Ron (1974), 'Burt Bacharach: The Balance Of His Nature', *Cash Box*, 16 February.

BBC TV documentary: *Burt Bacharach: This Is Now,* 1996.

Biography Channel TV: *Burt Bacharach*, 2003.

Black, Cilla (1993), *Through the Years: My Life In Pictures* [ed. Tony Barrow], London: Headline.

Bowden, Marshall (2001), 'History of Jazz 4: The Bebop Revolution', *Jazzitude*, www.jazzitude.com/histbop.htm

Brett, Bernard & Nicholas Ingman (1972), *The Story of Music*, London: Ward Lock Limited.

Britt, Stan (1972), 'Burt Bacharach Part 2: Sinatra Was Disappointing', *Record Collector* (version i), June.

Buckler, Kit (1979), *A & M Records Press Release.*

Calcutt, Andrew. (1998), *Arrested Development: Pop Culture and the Erosion of Adulthood*, London: Cassell.

Callaghan Mike & David Edwards (1999), *The Scepter/Wand Story*, www.bsnpubs.com

Clarke, Donald [ed.] (1990), *The Penguin Encyclopedia of Popular Music*, Harmondsworth: Penguin.

Cohn, Nik (1970), *Awopbopaloobopalopbamboom*, London: Paladin.

Cowan, Amber (2002), 'My Cultural Life: Burt Bacharach', *The Times*, 27 July.

Cumming, Alec (2001), 'There's Always Something There To Remind Me: The Burt Bacharach Story', *The Look Of Love, The Burt Bacharach Collection*, Warner Music 94583 96745 7.

Cunningham, M. (1998), *Good Vibrations: A History of Record Production*, London: Sanctuary.

Davis, Francis (1997), 'The Man From Heaven', *Atlantic Monthly*, June.

'Angie Dickinson' www.swingingchicks.com/angie_dickinson

Dietrich, Marlene (1965), 'liner notes to *Hitmaker! Burt Bacharach'*, London HAR 8233 UK.

DiMartino, D. (1998), 'Gentlemen Prefer Diminished Sevenths', *Mojo* 59, October 1998.

Dominic, Serene (2000), 'Burt's Still The Word', *Phoenix New Times*, 5 October.

Evans, (1995), Dusty 'Scissors and Paste', London: Britannia Press.

Fantle, David and Thomas Johnson, 'Interview with Angie Dickinson', www.seniorworld.com

Fagen, Donald (1993), interview with *Melody Maker*.

Fiegal, Eddie (2000), 'Love's Lexicon', *The Guardian*, 30 June.

Gendron, Bernard. (1986), 'Theodor Adorno Meets the Cadillacs', *Studies in Entertainment – Critical Approaches to Mass Culture*, [ed. Tania

Modleski], Bloomington & Indianapolis: Indiana University Press.

Gilmour, Alan M. (1988), *Erik Satie*, Boston [USA]: Twayne.

Gregory, Hugh (1998), *The Real Rhythm And Blues*, London: Blandford

Gussow Mel (1968), 'Promissory Notes', *Newsweek*, 16 December.

Robin Hartwell, Music Department, Liverpool Hope University College, personal correspondence.

Hardy, Phil & Dave Laing (1992) [eds.], *The Faber Companion To 20th Century Popular Music*, London: Faber & Faber.

Heckman, Don (1993), 'Bacharach and David: Reconciled and Honored', *Los Angeles Times*, 24 May.

Heller, Skip (1995), 'Props for Burt Bacharach', *Pulse*, October.

Hildreth, Peter (1970), *Name Dropper. Profiles of the Top Names of Our Times*, Trowbridge & London: Redwood Press Limited.

Holden, Stephen (1979), 'Interview with Dionne Warwick', *Rolling Stone,* 15 November.

Hoskyns, Barney (1997), 'Review: Burt Bacharach: The Look Of Love', *Mojo*, December.

Howes, Paul (2001), *The Complete Dusty Springfield*, London: Reynold & Hearn.

Hunter, James (1996), 'Burt Bacharach', *Us*, October.

Kroll, Jack (1968), 'Review: Promises Promises', *Newsweek*, 16 December.

Laing, Dave (1991), 'A Voice Without a Face: Popular Music and the Phonograph in the 1890s', *Popular Music 10, 1.*

Lanza, Joseph. (1995), *Elevator Music. A Surreal History of Muzak, Easy Listening and Other Moodsong*, London: Quartet Books.

Leeson, Edward (2001), *Dusty Springfield A Life In Music*, London: Robson.

Leigh, Spencer (1991), *Speaking Words Of Wisdom: Reflections On The Beatles,* Liverpool: Cavern City Tours.

Leigh, Spencer. (2000), *Brother, Can You Spare a Rhyme? 100 Years of Songwriting*, Southport: Spencer Leigh Limited.

Leigh, Spencer (2001), 'interview with Hal David', *On The Beat*, BBC Radio Merseyside, 2, 3 January.

Leigh, Spencer and John Firminger (2001), *Baby That Is Rock and Roll: American Pop, 1954-1963*, Folkestone: Finbarr.

Lohof, Bruce A. (1972), 'The Bacharach Phenomenon: A Study In Popular Heroism', *Popular Music And Society*, Winter 1972

Longhurst, B. (1995), *Popular Music & Society*, Cambridge: Polity Press.

Maconie, Stuart (1996), 'See You Later, Elevator!', *Q*, July.

Marwick, Arthur (1998), *The Sixties*, Oxford: University Press.

McAleer, Dave (1994), *Beatboom! Pop Goes The Sixties*, London: Hamlyn.

Medved, H. & M. (1980), *The Golden Turkey Awards*, London: Angus & Robertson.

Meeke, Kieran (2002), 'The 60 Second Interview: Dionne Warwick', *This Is London,* 26 July.

Middleton, Richard (1990), *Understanding Popular Music*, Buckingham: Open University Press.

Millard, Andre (1995), *America On Record, A History Of Recorded Sound*,

Cambridge: Cambridge University Press.

Millar, B. (1974), *The Coasters*, London: Star Books.

Miller, S. [ed] (1993), *The Last Poet: Music After Modernism*, Manchester: Manchester University Press.

Negus, Keith (1996), *Popular Music In Theory*, London: Polity Press.

Nikolic, Djordje (1998), 'The Genius of Burt Bacharach', *Arcade*, 20 February.

O'Brien, Lucy (1995), *She Bop. The Definitive History of Women in Rock, Pop and Soul*, Harmondsworth: Penguin.

O'Brien, Lucy (1999), *Dusty*, London: Sidgewick & Jackson.

Pallot, James [ed. *et al*] (1994), *The Third Virgin Film Guide*, London: Virgin Books.

Paphides, Peter (1999), 'Hal's Bells', *Time Out*, 4-11 August.

Parsons, Tony (1995, 1999), 'Burt Bacharach', Daily Telegraph, 16 December, 1995, in *Big Mouth Strikes Again*, London: Trafalgar Square.

Patrick & Baumgart, www.spectropop.com

Pead, Debbie (1983), 'Dionne Warwick', *Record Collector* version ii 41, January.

Peterson, Richard A. (1990), 'Why 1955? Explaining the Advent of Rock Music', *Popular Music 9, 1*.

Platts, Robin (1997), 'Anyone Who Had A Heart: The Songs Of Burt Bacharach and Hal David', *Discoveries 115*, December.

Platts, Robin (2003), *Burt Bacharach & Hal David. What The World Needs Now*, Ontario: Collector's Guide Publishing.

Riley, Joe (2002), '[...] Joe Riley Meets Hit-Maker Burt Bacharach [...]', *Liverpool Echo*, 5 July.

Ross, Lillian (1968), 'Hits', *New Yorker*, 14 September.

Ross, Lillian (1968), 'Composer In Tartan Cap', *New Yorker*, 21 December.

Rowland, Mark (1996), 'This Year's Models: Burt Bacharach's Strange Communion With Elvis Costello', *Musician*, December.

Saal, Hubert (1970), 'Burt Bacharach: The Music Man 1970', *Newsweek,* 22 June.

Sanjek, Russell (1983), *From Print To Plastic: Publishing and Promoting America's Popular Music (1900-1980)*, Institute for Studies in American Music, Conservatory of Music, Brooklyn College of the City University of New York: I.S.A.M. Monographs, 20.

Schlesinger, Richard (2002), 'Coming Of Age: Mr Burt Bacharach', interview: *Sunday Morning On CBS TV,* 10 February.

Sheppard Skaerved, Malene (2003), *Dietrich*, London: Haus Publishing.

Shuker, Roy (1998), *Key Concepts In Popular Music*, London: Routledge.

Smith, Mary (1968, 1983, 1995), *Ebony*.

Sobel, Robert (1970), 'Review: Burt Bacharach in Concert', *Billboard.*

Sporto, Donald (1988), *Dietrich,* London: Bantam.

Staff Writers (1966), 'Interview with Burt Bacharach', *Newsweek*, 10 October.

Staff Writer (1966), 'Interview with Dionne Warwick', *Newsweek.*

Staff Writer (2001), 'Burt Bacharach Venerable Composer Still Coaxing Sweet Music From His Keyboard', *Dayton Daily News*, 22 June.

Staff Writer (2002), 'Burt Bacharach, Songwriter: I Guess I'm Not The Glastonbury Type', *Independent On Sunday*, 14 July.

Staff Writer (2002), 'Burt Bacharach's Pop Star Has Never Really Dimmed', *Morning Call* (Allentown, PA), 18 October.
Taylor, Charles (1998), 'The Beauty Of Bacharach, 1998: The Year Burt Broke', *Boston Phoenix,* 16 February.

Taylor, Derek. (1967), liner notes to *Burt Bacharach: Reach Out*, A&M Records AMLS 908 UK.

Toop, David. (1996), *Ocean of Sound: Aether Talk, Ambient Sound and Imaginary Worlds*, London: Serpent's Tail.

Unaccredited writer (1978), 'Bacharach and David', Library of Congress: Catalogue Card Number 77-18455.

Unaccredited article (1964), 'Bacharach interview with *Billboard'*, 1964.

Unaccredited article (1965), *Billboard.*

Unaccredited review (1968), *New Yorker.*

Unaccredited interview (1968), 'Burt Bacharach', *Saturday Evening Post.*

Unaccredited interview (1971), 'Burt Bacharach', *New York Times.*

Unaccredited article (1979), 'Burt Bacharach', *Billboard.*

Unaccredited article containing quote attributed to Barry Mann, www.nostalgiacentral.com/music/brill.htm

Unaccredited interview with Angie Dickinson (2000)*, People Magazine.*

Unaccredited interview (2002), with Dionne Warwick *Observer.*

Valentine, Penny & Vicki Wickham (2000), *Dancing With Demons, The Authorised Biography Of Dusty Springfield*, London: Coronet Books.

Visser, Joop (1996), 'liner notes to *The Magic of Burt Bacharach*', Charly CPCD 8227 UK.

Ward, Bruce (2001), 'What's It All About, Burt? […]', *Ottowa Citizen,* 11 October.
Warwick, Dionne (2001), 'liner notes to *Love Songs*', Rhino Records.

Watson, Ben (1995), *Frank Zappa The Negative Dialectics of Poodle Play*, London: Quartet.

Wayne, George (1996), 'What's New Bacharach? Burt's Back and Better Than Ever', *Vanity Fair*, July.

Williams, Simon (1996), 'Lounge Wizard', *New Musical Express,* 13 April.

Williamson, John (2002), 'When Life's Still Full Of Promises, Promises […]', *Glasgow Herald*, 27 July.

Wright, Steve (2000), 'Steve Wright In The Afternoon' interview with Burt Bacharach, www.bbc.co.uk/radio2

Burt Bacharach Versions

The following information is by no means complete but simply a gathering together of versions considered to be of significance by this writer. Please feel free to add, disagree or otherwise quibble with the list.

All US and UK chart versions of Burt Bacharach compositions are listed below, along with other key versions of those and non-chart songs.

US chart placings are from *Billboard* Hot 100 and their Country and R&B charts.

UK chart placings are taken from *British Hit Singles* (Guinness Publishing).

With grateful thanks to Spencer Leigh.

ACCEPT IT (Bacharach - David)
Tony Orlando (1964)

ACROSS THE RIVER, ROUND THE BEND (Bacharach – David)
John Ashley (1960)

A FELICDADE (Bacharach)
Burt And The Backbeats (1963)

AFTER THE FOX (Bacharach - David)
Film: *After The Fox*
Peter Sellers with the Hollies (1966)
Pied Pipers (1966)
Ferrante & Teicher (1966)
The Magistrates (1968)

A HIGHER PLACE (Bacharach - Sager)
James Ingram (1991)
ALFIE (Bacharach - David)
Cher sings on soundtrack in US, but song is not in UK version.
Cher (1966) (US 32 pop)
Cilla Black (1966) (US 95 pop: UK 9)
Dionne Warwick (1967) (US 15 pop, 5 R&B)
Dee Dee Warwick (1965)
Burt Bacharach (1967); (1998)
Sheila Southern (1969)
Anita Kerr (1969)
Johnny Mathis (1971)
Elaine Paige (1984)
Bill Evans (1972)
Stevie Wonder/Eivets Rednow (1968)
Vanessa Williams
Delfonics (1973)
Everything But The Girl
McCoy Tyner (1997)
Suzanne Hoffs ('Austin') (2001)

ALL KINDS OF PEOPLE (Bacharach - David)
Burt Bacharach (1971) (US 116)
Fifth Dimension (1973)
Jerry Butler (1973)
John Rowles (1973)
Dionne Warwick (1998)

ALL THE WAY TO PARADISE (AND BACK AGAIN) (Bacharach – David)
Stephanie Mills (1975)

ALWAYS SOMETHING THERE TO REMIND ME
See (There's) Always Something There To Remind Me

AND SO GOODBYE MY LOVE (Bacharach - David)
Burt Bacharach (1963)

AND THE PEOPLE WERE WITH HER (SUITE FOR ORCHESTRA)
(Bacharach)
Burt Bacharach (1971)

AND THIS IS MINE (Bacharach - David)
Connie Stevens (1961)
Ginny Arnell (1963)

ANONYMOUS PHONE CALL (Bacharach - David)
Bobby Vee (1962)
Or:
An Anonymous Phone Call: Frank Ifield (1963)

ANOTHER NIGHT (Bacharach - David)
Dionne Warwick (1966)
Dusty Springfield (1967)

ANOTHER SPRING WILL RISE (Bacharach)
Burt Bacharach (1976)

ANOTHER TEAR FALLS (Bacharach - David)
Film: *Ring-A-Ding Rhythm* a.k.a. *It's Trad, Dad!*
Gene McDaniels (1962)
Walker Brothers (1966) (UK 12)
Mark Wynter (1966)

ANOTHER TIME, ANOTHER PLACE (Bacharach – Unknown Collaborator)
Patti Page (1956)

ANSWER TO EVERYTHING, THE (Bacharach - Hilliard)
Del Shannon (1964)
David Alexander (1977)

ANY DAY NOW (MY WILD BEAUTIFUL BIRD) (Bacharach - Hilliard)
Chuck Jackson (1962) (US 23 pop, 2 R&B)
Mitch Ryder and the Detroit Wheels (1966)
Ian and the Zodiacs (1966)
Peter & Gordon (1966)
Oscar Tony Jnr.
Percy Sledge (1969)
Elvis Presley (1969)
Burt Bacharach (1970)
Don Gibson (1979) (US 26 country)
Ronnie Milsap (1982) (US 14 pop, 1 country)
B J Thomas (1984)

ANYONE WHO HAD A HEART (Bacharach - David)
Dionne Warwick (1963) (US 8 pop: UK 42)
Cilla Black (1964) (UK 1)
Mary May (1964) (UK 49)
Dusty Springfield (1964)
Four Seasons (1965)
Burt Bacharach (1965)
Cal Tjader (1967, 1998)
Vikki Carr (1968)
Anita Kerr (1969)
Linda Ronstadt (1993)
Luther Vandross
Wynonna (1998)
Maureen McGovern (1992)

ANY OLD TIME OF DAY (Bacharach – David)
Dionne Warwick (1964)

APRIL FOOLS, THE (Bacharach - David)
Film: *The April Fools*
Dionne Warwick (1969) (US 37 pop)
Burt Bacharach (1973)
Marvin Hamlisch
The Cozy Corners (1994)

ARE YOU THERE (WITH ANOTHER GIRL) (Bacharach - David)
Dionne Warwick (1966) (US 39 pop)
The Buckinghams (1968)
Burt Bacharach (1968)
Maureen McGovern (1992)
Carnation (1994)

ARTHUR'S THEME (BEST THAT YOU CAN DO) (Bacharach - Sager -Cross
- Allen)
Film: *Arthur*
Christopher Cross (1981) (US 1 pop: UK 7)
Roger Webb (1981)
John Gregory Orchestra (1981)

AS LONG AS THERE'S AN APPLE TREE (Bacharach - David)
Dionne Warwick (1969)

BABY IT'S YOU (Bacharach - Mack David - Williams)
Shirelles (US 8 pop, 3 R&B)
Beatles (1963)
Dave Berry (1964) (UK 24)
Cilla Black (1964)
Smith (1969) (US 5 pop)
Pia Zadora (1980) (US 55 country)
Elvis Costello and Nick Lowe (1984)
Beatles (1995) (First release of 1963 BBC recording) (UK 7)
Michael Shelley (1998)

BABY IT'S YOU / A MESSAGE TO MICHAEL (medley)
Chrissie Hynde (1998)

BALANCE OF NATURE, THE (Bacharach - David)
Burt Bacharach (1973)
Dionne Warwick (1972)

BEAUTY ISN'T EVERYTHING (Bacharach – Heyman)
June Valli (1956)

BEGINNING OF LONELINESS, THE (Bacharach - David)
Dionne Warwick (1967)

BELL THAT COULDN'T JINGLE, THE (Bacharach - Kusik)
Sometimes recorded as The Bell That Wouldn't Jingle
Bobby Helms (1957)
Burt Bacharach (1968)
Herb Alpert (1980)

BEST OF TIMES, THE (Bacharach)
Burt Bacharach

BEST THAT YOU CAN DO
See Arthur's Theme (Best That You Can Do)

BE TRUE TO YOURSELF (Bacharach - David)
Bobby Vee (1963) (US 34 pop)

BLAME IT ON ME (Bacharach – Sager)
Peabo Bryson & Roberta Flack (1983)

BLOB, THE (Bacharach - Mack David)
Film: *The Blob*
Five Blobs (1957) (US 33 pop)
The Zannies

BLUE GUITAR (Bacharach - David)
Richard Chamberlain (1963)

BLUE ON BLUE (Bacharach - David)
Bobby Vinton (1963) (US 3 pop)
Paul Anka (1963)
Burt Bacharach (1965)
Bobby Engerman (1969)

BOND STREET (Bacharach)
Film: *Casino Royale*
Burt Bacharach (1967)
Les 5-4-3-2-1 with K-taro Takanami (1994)

BOTTOMLESS CUP, A (Bacharach – David – Melamed)

BOYS WERE MADE FOR GIRLS (Bacharach – David)
Everit Herter (1960)

BREAKING POINT, THE (Bacharach - David)
Chuck Jackson (1962)

CALL OFF THE WEDDING (Bacharach - David)
Babs Tino (1963)

CAPTIVES OF THE HEART (Bacharach – Bettis)
Dionne Warwick (1994)

CASINO ROYALE (Bacharach - David)
Film: *Casino Royale*
Herb Alpert And The Tijuana Brass (1967) (US 24 pop: UK 27)
Arthur Greenslade & his Orchestra (1969)

CHANCE FOR HEAVEN, A (Bacharach – Sager – Cross)
Christopher Cross (1984)

CHARLIE (Bacharach – Russell)
Bobby Vinton (1975)

CHECK OUT TIME (Bacharach – David)
Dionne Warwick (1971)

CHRISTMAS DAY (Bacharach - David)
Also used in Promises Promises.
Johnny Mathis (1958)

CLEAN-UP TIME (Bacharach - David)
Dionne Warwick (1970)

CLOSE (Bacharach - Shaw)
Gals And Pals (1967)

(THEY LONG TO BE) CLOSE TO YOU (Bacharach - David)
Richard Chamberlain (1963) (as 'They Long To Be Close To You')
Dionne Warwick (1964)
Dusty Springfield (1967)
Carpenters (1970) (US 1 pop: UK 6 and on 1990 re-entry, 25)
Matt Monro (1970)
Johnny Mathis (1971)
Barbra Streisand & Burt Bacharach (1971)
Jerry Butler and Brenda Lee Edgar (1972) (US 91 pop)
B T Express (1976) (US 82 pop)
Gwen Guthrie (1986) (UK 25 pop)
Ethyl Meatplow (1993)
Cranberries (1994)
McCoy Tyner (1998)
Barenaked Ladies (1998)
Hannah Cranna (1998)

COME AND GET ME (Bacharach - David)
Jackie DeShannon (1966) (US 83 pop)

COME COMPLETELY TO ME (Bacharach – Hampton)
Steve Rossi (1961)

COME TOUCH THE SUN (Bacharach)
Film: *Butch Cassidy And The Sundance Kid*
Burt Bacharach (1969)

COUNTRY MUSIC HOLIDAY (Bacharach - David)
Bernie Knee (1958)
Adam Faith (1961)

CRAZY TIMES (Bacharach - Hampton)
Gene Vincent (1959)

CROSS TOWN BUS (Bacharach - David)
Gals And Pals (1960)

DANCING FOOL, THE (Bacharach - Newley)
Burt Bacharach (1978)

DANCE MAMMA DANCE PAPPA (Bacharach – David)
Joanne & the Streamliners
Karin Kent (Germany)

DESPERATE HOURS (Bacharach – Stone)
Mel Torme (1955)

DON'T COUNT THE DAYS (Bacharach - David)
Marylin Michaels (1968)
Sandi & Salli (1968)

DON'T ENVY ME (Bacharach - David)
George Hamilton (1963)
Joey Powers (1962)

DON'T GO BREAKING MY HEART (Bacharach - David)
Burt Bacharach (1965)
Dionne Warwick (1966)
Johnny Mathis (1971)
Aretha Franklin (1974)
Wondermints (1998)

DON'T MAKE ME OVER (Bacharach - David)
Dionne Warwick (1962) (US 21 pop, 5 R&B)
Tommy Hunt (1963)
Burt Bacharach (1965)
Swinging Blue Jeans (1966) (UK 31)
Cal Tjader (1967, 1998)
Brenda and the Tabulations (1970) (US 77 pop)
Petula Clark (1976)
Sybil (1989) (US 20 pop)
Jennifer Warnes (1989) (US 67 pop)
Neil Diamond (1993)

DON'T SAY GOODBYE GIRL (Bacharach – Walden - Dakota)
Tevin Campbell (1993)

DON'T SAY I DIDN'T TELL YOU SO (Bacharach - David)
Dionne Warwick (1965)
Petula Clark (1971)

DON'T YOU BELIEVE IT (Bacharach - Hilliard)
Andy Williams (1962) (US 39)

DO NOT SPEAK TO ME OF LOVE (Bacharach – David)
Sylvaine Clair (1970)

DO YOU KNOW THE WAY TO SAN JOSE (Bacharach - David)
Dionne Warwick (1968) (US 10 pop: UK 8)
Connie Francis (1968)
Jack Nathan Orchestra (1968)
Sheila Southern (1969)
Robert Goulet
Ramsay Lewis
Jane McDonald (1998)

DREAM BIG (Bacharach - Hampton)
Sonny James (1959)

DREAMIN' ALL THE TIME (Bacharach – Hilliard)
Jack Jones (1962)

DREAM SWEET DREAMER (Bacharach – David)
Dionne Warwick (1969)

ERRAND OF MERCY, AN (Bacharach – David)
George Hamilton

EVERYBODY'S OUT OF TOWN (Bacharach - David)
B J Thomas (1970)
Robert Goulet (1971)

EVERCHANGING TIMES (Bacharach – Sager – Conti Jnr)
Siedah Garrett (1987)
Aretha Franklin and Michael McDonald (1991)

EVERYONE NEEDS SOMEONE TO LOVE (Bacharach - David)
Cliff Richard (1964)
Nick Palmer (1968)

EXTRAVAGANT GESTURES (Bacharach – Sager)
Dionne Warwick (1985)

EYE OF THE NEEDLE, THE (Bacharach – David)
Cliff Richard (1965)

FACT CAN BE A BEAUTIFUL THING, A (Bacharach - David)
From *Promises Promises*
Jerry Orbach and Marian Mercer

FAITHFULLY (Bacharach - Shaw)
Johnny Mathis (1959)

FAKER FAKER (Bacharach - David)
Eligibles (1959)

FENDER MENDER (Bacharach – David)
Joannie Summers (1965)

FIND LOVE (Bacharach – Anka)
Jackie DeShannon (1979)

FINDER OF LOST LOVES (Bacharach - Sager)
Dionne Warwick with Glenn Jones (1985)

FOOL KILLER, (THE) (Bacharach - David)
Gene Pitney (1967)

FOOL ME AGAIN (Bacharach - Anka)
Film: *Together*
Nicolette Larson (1981)

FOR ALL TIME (Bacharach – David)
Russells (1962)

FOREVER MY LOVE (Bacharach - David)
Dionne Warwick (1965)
Jane Morgan

FOREVER YOURS I REMAIN (Bacharach - David)
Bobby Vinton (1964)

FORGIVE ME (FOR GIVING YOU SUCH A BAD TIME) Bacharach - David)
Babs Tino (1962)

FREEFALL (Bacharach)
Burt Bacharach (1971)

FROM ROCKING HORSE TO ROCKING CHAIR (Bacharach - David)
Paul Anka (1964)

FRONT PAGE STORY (Bacharach - Sager - Diamond)
Neil Diamond (1982)

FUTURES (Bacharach)
Burt Bacharach (1977)

GIRL LIKE YOU, A (Bacharach - Croswell)
Adam Faith (1960)

GIRLS KNOW HOW (Bacharach – Sager – Foster)
Al Jarreau (1982)

GOD GIVE ME STRENGTH (Bacharach - Costello)
Film: *Grace Of My Heart*
Burt Bacharach and Elvis Costello (1997)
Kristen Vigard (1997)
Elvis Costello (1998)

GOTTA GET A GIRL (Bacharach – David)
Frankie Avalon (1961)

GO WITH LOVE (Bacharach - David)
Dionne Warwick (1967)

GRAPES OF ROTH (Bacharach)
Instrumental from *Promises Promises*

GREEN GRASS STARTS TO GROW, THE (Bacharach - David)
Dionne Warwick (1970)

HALF AS BIG AS LIFE (Bacharach - David)
From *Promises Promises*
Jerry Orbach

HANG YOUR TEARDROPS UP TO DRY (Bacharach)
Stylistics (1991)

HANGMAN, THE (Bacharach – David)
Written for the Jack Lord movie of the same name
John Ashley (1959)

HASBROOK HEIGHTS (Bacharach)
Burt Bacharach (1970)
Dionne Warwick (1972)

HEARTBREAK OF LOVE (Bacharach - Sager - Warren)
Dionne Warwick and June Pointer (1987)

HEARTLIGHT (Bacharach – Sager - Diamond)
Inspired by film, *E.T.*
Neil Diamond (1982) (US 5 pop: UK 47)
HEAVENLY (Bacharach - Shaw)
Johnny Mathis (1958)

HERE I AM (Bacharach - David)
Film: *What's New Pussycat*
Dionne Warwick (1965)
Sheila Southern (1969)
Gals and Pals (Sweden) (1967)

(HERE I GO AGAIN) LOOKIN' WITH MY EYES (Bacharach - David)
Dionne Warwick (1966)

HERE WHERE THERE IS LOVE (Bacharach - David)
Dionne Warwick (1967)

HIDEAWAY HEART (Bacharach – David)

HE WHO LOVES (Bacharach – David)
Jerry Vale
Lenny Welch (1968)
Perry Como (1967)

HIGHER PLACE, A (Bacharach)
James Ingram (1991)

HOT FOOD (Bacharach – David)
*Written for Promises Promises but **cut***

HOT SPELL (Bacharach - Mack David)
Margaret Whiting (1958)

HOW ABOUT (Bacharach – Wolf)
Della Reese (1957)

HOW LONG? (Bacharach – Sager)
Dionne Warwick (1985)

HOUSE IS NOT A HOME, A (Bacharach - David)
Film: *A House Is Not A Home*
Brook Benton (1964) (US 75 pop)
Dionne Warwick (1964)
Ronnie Carroll (1964)
Shirley Bassey (1968)
Sheila Southern (1969)
Burt Bacharach (1970)
Della Reese
McCoy Tyner (1997)

HOW CAN I HURT YOU (Bacharach – David)
Dionne Warwick (1966)

HOW DOES A MAN BECOME A PUPPET (Bacharach – David)
Malcolm Roberts (1971)
Ed Ames (1971)

HOW MANY DAYS OF SADNESS (Bacharach - David)
Dionne Warwick (1965)

HUMBLE PIE (Bacharach – David)

HURRICANE (Bacharach - Sager - Diamond)
Neil Diamond (1982)

I COME TO YOU (Bacharach - David)
Film: *Lost Horizon*
Jerry Hutman & Diana Lee (1972)
Burt Bacharach (vocals, Cissy Houston and Tony Middleton) (1973)

I COULD KICK MYSELF (Bacharach – David)

I COULD MAKE YOU MINE (Bacharach - David)
The Wanderers (1960)
Dionne Warwick (1963)

I CRY ALONE (Bacharach - David)
Dionne Warwick (1963)
Maxine Brown (1964)
Ruby And The Romantics (1964)
Jackie Lee
Vicki Carr
Betty Carter
Jack Jones

I CRY MORE (Bacharach – David)
Film: *Don't Knock The Rock*
Alan Dale (1957)

I DON'T NEED YOU ANYMORE (Bacharach - Anka)
Jackie DeShannon (1979)

I FELL IN LOVE WITH YOUR PICTURE (Bacharach - David)
Freddie and the Dreamers (1965)

IF I COULD GO BACK (Bacharach – David)
Film: *Lost Horizon*
Jerry Hutman (1972)
Andy Williams

IF I EVER MAKE YOU CRY (Bacharach - David)
Dionne Warwick (1966)

IF I NEVER GET TO LOVE YOU (Bacharach - David)
Lou Johnson (1963)
Timi Yuro (1963)
Gene Pitney (1965)
Marianne Faithfull

IF I WANT TO (Bacharach)
Sandi Patti (1994)

IF YOU CAN LEARN HOW TO CRY (Bacharach – David)
Stephanie Mills (1975)

IF YOU NEVER SAY GOODBYE (Bacharach – David)
Dionne Warwick (1972)

I FORGOT WHAT IT WAS LIKE (Bacharach - David)
Ray Peterson
Frank Ifield
John Denver

I JUST DON'T KNOW WHAT TO DO WITH MYSELF (Bacharach - David)
Tommy Hunt (1962)
Dusty Springfield (1964) (UK 3)
Big Maybelle (1964)
Chuck Jackson (1965)
Dionne Warwick (1966) (US 26 pop, 20 R&B)
Smokey Robinson and the Miracles (1966)
Sheila Southern (1969)
Gary Puckett (1970) (US 61 pop)
Elvis Costello (1978)
Linda Ronstadt (1993)
White Stripes (2003)

I JUST HAVE TO BREATHE (Bacharach - David)
Dionne Warwick (1972)

I LIVE IN THE WOODS (Bacharach)
Burt Bacharach (1978)

I'LL BRING ALONG MY BANJO (Bacharach - Gimbel)
Johnnie Ray (1961)

I'LL NEVER FALL IN LOVE AGAIN (Bacharach - David)
From *Promises Promises*
Burt Bacharach (1969) (US 93 pop)
Dionne Warwick (1969) (US 6 pop, 17 R&B)
Bobbie Gentry (1969) (UK 1)
Johnny Mathis (1971)
Anne Murray (1971)
Sacha Distel
Matt Monro (1995, new duet Matt Monro Jnr with Matt Monro)
Liz Anderson (1972) (US 56 country)
Bing Crosby (1975)
Pattie Page
5th Garden (1994)
Deacon Blue (1994)
Splitsville (1998)
Burt Bacharach and Elvis Costello (2002)

I'LL SEE YOU ON THE RADIO (LAURA) (Bacharach – Sager – Diamond)
Neil Diamond (1982)

I LOOKED FOR YOU (Bacharach – David)
Charlie Gracie (1960)

I'M A BETTER MAN (FOR HAVING LOVED YOU) (Bacharach - David)
Engelbert Humperdinck (1969) (US 38, UK 15)
Arthur Greenslade & his Orchestra (1970)
David McAlmont (1997)

I'M GUILTY (Bacharach - Sager - Diamond)
Neil Diamond (1982)

I MIGHT FRIGHTEN HER AWAY (Bacharach - David)
Film: *Lost Horizon*
Jerry Hutman & Diana Lee (1972)
Burt Bacharach (1973)
Herb Alpert (1974)

IN A WORLD SUCH AS THIS (Bacharach - Sager - Roberts)
Dionne Warwick (1987)

IN BETWEEN THE HEARTACHES (Bacharach - David)
Dionne Warwick (1966)

INDOOR SPORT (Bacharach – Tobias)
Petula Clark (1960)

IN ENSENADA (Bacharach - Sager - Diamond)
Neil Diamond (1982)

IN MY REALITY (Bacharach – Sager)
Natalie Cole (1987)

IN THE DARKEST PLACE (Bacharach - Costello)
Elvis Costello and Burt Bacharach (1998)

IN THE LAND OF MAKE BELIEVE (Bacharach - David)
Drifters (1964)
Dionne Warwick (1964)
Dusty Springfield (1969)

IN TIMES LIKE THESE (Bacharach - David)
Gene McDaniels

IN TUNE (Bacharach – Titus)
Libby Titus & Burt Bacharach (1979)

I SAY A LITTLE PRAYER (Bacharach - David)
Dionne Warwick (1967) (US 4 pop)
Aretha Franklin (1968) (US 10 pop, 3 R&B: UK 4)
Johnny Mathis (1971)
Sergio Mendes (1968) (US 106 pop)
Cal Tjader (1967, 1998)
The Anita Kerr Singers (reissued 1999)
Glen Campbell and Anne Murray (medley with By The Time I Get To Phoenix) (1971) (US 40 pop)
Connie Francis (medley with This Girl's In Love With You)
Isaac Hayes and Dionne Warwick (1977)
Bomb The Bass (1988)
Mary Black (1989)
Mitchell Rasor (1998)

I SEE YOU FOR THE FIRST TIME (Bacharach – David)
Stephanie Mills (1975)

I SMILED YESTERDAY (Bacharach - David)
Dionne Warwick (1963)

I STILL HAVE THAT OTHER GIRL (Bacharach – Costello)
Burt Bacharach & Elvis Costello (1998)

IS THERE ANOTHER WAY TO LOVE YOU (Bacharach - David)
Dionne Warwick (1965)
Tony Blackburn (1967)

IS THERE ANYBODY OUT THERE? (Bacharach)
Mai Iijima (1995)

I STILL HAVE THAT OTHER GIRL (Bacharach - Costello)
Elvis Costello and Burt Bacharach (1998)

IT DOESN'T MATTER ANYMORE (Bacharach - David)
TV movie: *On The Flipside*
Rick Nelson (1966)
Cyrkle (1966)
BMX Bandits (1998)

IT SEEMED SO RIGHT LAST NIGHT (Bacharach – David)
Mary Mayo (1958)

I TOOK MY STRENGTH FROM YOU (I HAD NONE) (Bacharach - David)
Burt Bacharach (vocal, Joshie Armstead) (1976)

IT'S LOVE THAT REALLY COUNTS (Bacharach - David)
Shirelles (1962)
Dionne Warwick (1963)
The Exciters (1963)
Merseybeats (1963) (UK 24)
Barely Pink (1998)

IT'S ONLY LOVE (Bacharach – Sager – Bishop)
Stephen Bishop (1981)

IT'S WONDERFUL TO BE YOUNG (Bacharach - David)
Cliff Richard (1962)

I WAKE UP CRYIN' (Bacharach - David)
Chuck Jackson (1961) (US 59 pop, 13 R&B)

Jimmy Justice (1962)
Ray Charles (1964)
Tom Jones
Gene Chandler

I'VE GOT MY MIND MADE UP (Bacharach – Anka)
Michael McDonald (1979)

JUANITA'S PLACE (Bacharach - David)
Celestials (1965)
Burt Bacharach (1966)

JUST FRIENDS (Bacharach - Sager)
Carole Bayer Sager (1981)

KEEP AWAY FROM OTHER GIRLS (Bacharach - Hilliard)
Helen Shapiro (1962) (UK 40)
Babs Tino (1963)

KEEP ME IN MIND (Bacharach - Wolf)
Patti Page (1954)
Alma Cogan (1955)

KENTUCKY BLUEBIRD (SEND A MESSAGE TO MARTHA)
See Message To Martha

KNOWING WHEN TO LEAVE (Bacharach - David)
From *Promises Promises*
Dionne Warwick (1970)
Burt Bacharach (1973)
The Carpenters
Hugo Montenegro
Liz Callaway (1995)

LAST ONE TO BE LOVED, THE (Bacharach - David)
Lou Johnson (1964)
Dionne Warwick (1964)
Burt Bacharach (1965)
Billie Davis (1965)

LAST TIME I SAW MY HEART (Bacharach – David)
Marty Robbins (1958)

LET ME BE LONELY (Bacharach - David)
Dionne Warwick (1968) (US 71)
5th Dimension (1973)

LET ME BE THE ONE (Bacharach – Sager – Sevelle)
Gladys Knight and the Pips (1987)

LET ME GO TO HIM (Bacharach - David)
Dionne Warwick (1970) (US 32 pop)

LET THE MUSIC PLAY
See Make The Music Play

LET YOUR LOVE COME THROUGH (Bacharach – David)
Roland Shaw Orchestra
Shani Wallis (1967)

LIFETIME OF LONELINESS, A (Bacharach - David)
Steve Alaimo (1963)
Jackie DeShannon (1965) (US 66 pop)

LIKE NO ONE IN THE WORLD (Bacharach – Bettis)
Johnny Mathis (1996)

LIQUIDATOR, THE (Bacharach - David)
Film: *The Liquidator*
Shirley Bassey
P.J. Proby (unissued)

LISA (Bacharach - David)
Burt Bacharach (1967)

LITTLE BETTY FALLING STAR (Bacharach - Hilliard)
Gene Pitney (1963)
The Cascades (1963)
George Hamilton (1964)

LIVE AGAIN (Bacharach - David)
Irma Thomas (1965) (unissued – 1995 Polygram)

LIVING ON PLASTIC (Bacharach – David)
Stephanie Mills (1975)

LIVING TOGETHER, GROWING TOGETHER (Bacharach - David)
Film: *Lost Horizon*
James Sigheta & Chorus (1972)
Fifth Dimension (1973) (US 32 pop)
Burt Bacharach (1973)
Ferrante & Teicher (1973)
Tony Bennett (1972)
Ed Ames (1973)
Reunion (1975)

LIVING WITHOUT LOVE (Bacharach - David)
Vince Hill

LONDON LIFE (Bacharach - David)
Anita Harris (1965)

LONELINESS OR HAPPINESS (Bacharach - David)
Drifters (1961)

LONELINESS REMEMBERS (WHAT HAPPINESS FORGETS) (Bacharach
- David)
Dionne Warwick (1970)
Stephane Mills (1975)

LONG AFTER TONIGHT IS ALL OVER (Bacharach - David)
Irma Thomas (1964)
Jimmy Radcliffe (1964)
Dusty Springfield (1965)

LONG AGO LAST SUMMER (Bacharach – David)
Diana Trask (1963)

LONG AGO TOMORROW (Bacharach - David)
Film: *Long Ago Tomorrow* a.k.a. *The Raging Moon*
B J Thomas (1971)
Burt Bacharach (1973)

LONG DAY, SHORT NIGHT (Bacharach - David)
Dionne Warwick (1966)
Shirelles (1966, unissued until 1987)

LONG DIVISION, THE (Bacharach - Costello)
Elvis Costello and Burt Bacharach (1998)

LOOK IN MY EYES, MARIA (Bacharach - David)
Jay And The Americans (1963)
Cliff Richard (1965)

LOOK OF LOVE, THE (Bacharach - David)
Film: *Casino Royale*
Dusty Springfield (1967) (US 22 pop)
Burt Bacharach (1967)
Jack Jones (1967)
Zombies (1967)
Sergio Mendes and Brazil '66 (1968) (US 4 pop)
Sheila Southern (1969)
Isaac Hayes (1971) (US 79 pop)
Johnny Mathis (1971)
Four Tops
Gladys Knight And The Pips (1973) (UK 21)
T-Empo (1990) (UK 71)
Buddy Greco (1976)
Soul Bossa Trio (1994)
Bill Tarmey (1996)
Susanna Hoffs (1997) (Film*, Austin Powers*)
McCoy Tyner (1997)
Diane Krall (2001)

LOOKING WITH MY EYES, SEEING WITH MY HEART (Bacharach –David)
Dionne Warwick (1965)

LORNA DOONE (Bacharach – David)
Marty Gold Orchestra & Chorus (1959)

LOST AMONG THE STARS (Bacharach - Sager - Diamond)
Neil Diamond (1982)

'LOST HORIZON' (Bacharach - David)
Film: *Lost Horizon*
Ed Ames (1972)
Shawn Phillips (1973)
Burt Bacharach (1973)
[…] Theme (Bacharach)
Ronnie Aldrich (1972)
Guy Chandler (1973)

LOST LITTLE GIRL (Bacharach – David)
Light Brothers (1964)

LOVE ALWAYS (Bacharach - Sager)
El DeBarge (1986) (US 43 pop, 7 R&B)

LOVE IN A GOLDFISH BOWL (Bacharach - David)
Film: *Love In A Goldfish Bowl*
Tommy Sands (1961)

LOVE IS FIRE (LOVE IS ICE) (Bacharach - Sager)
Gladys Knight and the Pips (1987)

LOVE IS HERE BEFORE THE STARS (Bacharach – Unknown Collaborator)
Brian Foley (1964)

LOVE IS MY DECISION (THEME FROM ARTHUR 2 – ON THE ROCKS)
(Bacharach – Sager – De Burgh)
Chris De Burgh (1988)

LOVE LESSONS (Bacharach – David)
Sam Butera (1961)

LOVE LIGHT (Bacharach - Sager)
Barbra Streisand (1988)

LOVE OF A BOY, THE (Bacharach - David)
Timi Yuro (1962)
Dionne Warwick (1963)
Julie Rogers (1964)
Francoise Hardy ('L'amour d'un Garcon')(1964)

LOVE POWER (Bacharach - Sager)
Dionne Warwick and Jeffrey Osborne (1987) (US 12 pop: UK 63)

LOVE WAS HERE BEFORE THE STARS (Bacharach - David)
Engelbert Humperdinck (1969)
Brian Foley
Doc Severinson

LOVING IS A WAY OF GIVING (Bacharach - David)
Jose Werner
Steve Lawrence (1959)

MADE IN PARIS (Bacharach - David)
Film: *Made In Paris*
Trini Lopez (1966)

MAGDELENA (Bacharach)
Burt Bacharach (1978)

MAGIC MOMENTS (Bacharach - David)
Perry Como (1958) (US 4 pop, while A-side was No.1: UK 1)
Ronnie Hilton (1958) (UK 22)
Erasure (1995) (Film: *Lord Of Illusions*)

MAGIC POTION (Bacharach - David)
Lou Johnson (1963)
Johnny Sandon and the Remo Four (1963)
The Searchers (1965)
The Kubas (1965)

MAKE IT EASY ON YOURSELF (Bacharach - David)
Jerry Butler (1962) (US 20 pop)
Dionne Warwick (1963)
Cilla Black (1964)
Walker Brothers (1965) (US 16 pop: UK 1)
Ian and the Zodiacs (1965)
Four Seasons (1965)
Burt Bacharach (1969)
Steve Lawrence
Dionne Warwick (1970) (live recording) (US 37 pop)
Tommy Jennings (1975) (US 96 country)
Kyoto Jazz Massive (1994)
Idle (1998)

MAKE ROOM FOR THE JOY (Bacharach – David)
Film: *Juke Box Rhythm*
Jack Jones (1959)

MAKE THE MUSIC PLAY (Bacharach - David)
Drifters (1963) (Let The Music Play)
Lena Martell (1963) (Let The Music Play)
Dionne Warwick (1963)

MAKING LOVE (Bacharach - Sager - Allen)
Film: *Making Love*
Roberta Flack (1982) (US 13 pop, 29 R&B)

MAN WHO SHOT LIBERTY VALANCE, THE (Bacharach - David)
Gene Pitney (1962) (US 4 pop)
The Fairmount Singers

MAYBE (Bacharach – Sager - Hamlisch)
Peabo Bryson & Roberta Flack (1983)

ME BESIDE YOU (Bacharach – Sager – Diamond)
Neil Diamond (1986)

ME JAPANESE BOY I LOVE YOU (Bacharach – David)
Bobby Goldsboro (1964)
Harper's Bizarre (1968)
Pizzicato Five (1994)

MESSAGE TO MARTHA (Bacharach - David)
Jerry Butler (1963)
Lou Johnson (1964) (as Kentucky Bluebird (Send A Message To Martha) in US,
Message To Martha in UK) (UK 36)
Adam Faith (1964) (UK 12)
Ian and the Zodiacs (1964)
Dionne Warwick (1966) (as Message To Michael) (US 8 pop, 5 R&B)
Cal Tjader (1967, 1998)
Burt Bacharach (1968) (as Message To Michael)
Deacon Blue (1990)(as Message To Michael)

MESSAGE TO MICHAEL
See Message To Martha

MEXICAN DIVORCE (Bacharach - Hilliard)
Drifters (1962)
Ry Cooder (1974)

MIRACLE OF St. MARIE (Bacharach – Hilliard)
Four Coins (1961)

MONEYPENNY GOES FOR BROKE (Bacharach)
Film: *Casino Royale*
Cal Tjader (1967, 1998)

MONTEREY PENINSULA (Bacharach)
Burt Bacharach (1973)

MOON GUITAR (Bacharach - David)
Rangoons
Billy Vaughn
Tommy Garrett

MOON MAN (Bacharach – David)
Gloria Lambert (1959)

MORNING MAIL, THE (Bacharach – David)
The Gallahads (1956)

MOVE IT ON THE BACKBEAT (Bacharach)
Burt And The Backbeats (1963)

MULINO BIANCO (Bacharach)
Burt Bacharach (1994)

MY HEART IS A BALL OF STRING (Bacharach - David)
Rangoons (1961)

MY LITTLE RED BOOK (all I do is talk about you) (Bacharach - David)
Film: *What's New Pussycat*
Manfred Mann (1965)
Love (1966)
Mel Torme
Burt Bacharach (1965)
The Standells (1966)
Cal Tjader (1967, 1998)
Toni Basil (1981)
Greg Kihn (1979)

MY ROCK AND FOUNDATION (Bacharach – David)
Peggy Lee (1971)

MY THIEF (Bacharach - Costello)
Elvis Costello and Burt Bacharach (1998)

NEED A LITTLE FAITH (Bacharach - Sager)
Patti Labelle (1989)

NET, THE (Bacharach – David)
John Ashley (1959)

NEW YORK LADY (Bacharach)
Burt Bacharach (1978)

NIGHT SHIFT (Bacharach – Sager – Ross)
Quaterflash (1982)

NIGHT THAT HEAVEN FELL, THE (Bacharach – David)
Tony Bennett (1978)

NIKKI (Bacharach - David)
Burt Bacharach (1966)

NO ONE REMEMBERS MY NAME (Bacharach - David)
Stephane Mills (1975)
Burt Bacharach (vocals, Melissa Mackay, Sally Stevens, Marti McCall) (1977)

NOT GOIN' HOME ANYMORE (Bacharach)
Film: *Butch Cassidy And The Sundance Kid*
Burt Bacharach (1969)

OBSESSION (Bacharach – Child)
Desmond Child (1991)

ODDS AND ENDS (Bacharach - David)
Dionne Warwick (1969)
Johnny Mathis (1971)

OLD FUN CITY, THE (N.Y.SEQUENCE) (Bacharach)
Film: *Butch Cassidy And The Sundance Kid*
Burt Bacharach (1969)

ON A BICYCLE BUILT FOR JOY (Bacharach)
Film: *Butch Cassidy And The Sundance Kid*
Burt Bacharach (1969)

ON MY WAY (Bacharach – David)
Film: *Isn't She Great*
Dionne Warwick (1999)

ON THE FLIP SIDE (Bacharach – David)
TV movie of the same name
Ricky Nelson (1965)

ONCE BEFORE YOU GO (Bacharach – Sager - Irby)
Klymaxx (1993)

ONE LESS BELL TO ANSWER (Bacharach - David)
Keely Smith (1967)
Fifth Dimension (1970) (US 2 pop)
Burt Bacharach (1971)
Dionne Warwick (1972)
McCoy Tyner (1997)
Sheryl Crow (1998)

ONE MORE TIME AROUND (Bacharach - Sager)
Barbra Streisand (1988)

ONE PART DOG, NINE PARTS CAT (Bacharach - Hilliard)
Dick Van Dyke (1961)

ONLY LOVE CAN BREAK A HEART (Bacharach - David)
Gene Pitney (1962) (US 2)
Timi Yuro (1975)
Margaret Whiting (1967) (US 96)
Bobby Vinton (1977) (US 99)

ONLY THE STRONG, ONLY THE BRAVE (Bacharach - David)
Dionne Warwick (1965)

ON MY OWN (Bacharach - Sager)
Dionne Warwick (1986)
Patti LaBelle and Michael McDonald (1986) (US 1 pop: UK 2)
Reba McEntire

OOOOH, MY LOVE (Bacharach - David)
Vic Damone (1958)

OPEN YOUR HEART (Bacharach – David)
Vanessa Williams (1999)

OUR LITTLE SECRET (Bacharach - David)
From *Promises Promises*

OUT OF MY CONTINENTAL MIND (Bacharach – Shaw)
Lena Horne (1961)

OVERNIGHT SUCCESS (Bacharach - Sager)
Gladys Knight and the Pips (1987)

PACIFIC COAST HIGHWAY (Bacharach)
Burt Bacharach (1969)

PAINTED FROM MEMORY (Bacharach - Costello)
Elvis Costello and Burt Bacharach (1998)

PAPER MACHE (Bacharach - David)
Dionne Warwick (1970)
David Whitaker & his Orchestra (1971)

PARADISE ISLAND (Bacharach – David – Hampton)
Four Aces (1959)

PEGGY'S IN THE PANTRY (Bacharach – David)
Sherry Parsons (1957)

PERFECT LOVERS (Bacharach – Sager – East)
Ray Parker Jnr. (1987)

PICK UP THE PIECES (Bacharach – Hilliard)
Jack Jones (1962)

PLEASE LET GO (Bacharach – David)
Stephanie Mills (1975)

PLEASE MAKE HIM LOVE ME (Bacharach - David)
Dionne Warwick (1963)
Ray Lynn (1966) 'Please Make Her Love Me'

(Don't Go) PLEASE STAY (Bacharach - Hilliard)
Drifters (1961) (US 14 pop, 13 R&B)
Zoot Money and the Big Roll Band (1965)
Cryin' Shames (1966) (UK 26)
Cryan' Shames (1966)
David Garrick (1967)
Elvis Costello (1995)

POOR RICH BOY (Bacharach – Pack - Puerta)
Film: *Arthur*
Ambrosia (1981)

POWER OF YOUR LOVE (Bacharach – Sager – Sevelle)
Taja Sevelle (1991)

PRESENTS FROM THE PAST (Bacharach – David)
Cathy Carr (1957)

PROMISE HER ANYTHING (Bacharach - David)
Film: *Promise Her Anything*
Tom Jones (1966)
Gladhands (1998)

PROMISES PROMISES (Bacharach - David)
From *Promises Promises*
Dionne Warwick (1968) (US 19 pop)
Liz Callaway (1995)
Connie Francis (1968)
Percy Faith
Gary Puckett & the Union Gap (1969)
Peter Paul and Mary
Herb Alpert

QUESTION MARK (Bacharach)
From *23rd Olympics*
Burt Bacharach (1984)

QUESTION ME AN ANSWER (Bacharach –David)
Film: *Lost Horizon*
Ed Ames (1972)
Bobby Van (1972)

RAINDROPS KEEP FALLIN' ON MY HEAD (Bacharach - David)
Film: *Butch Cassidy And The Sundance Kid*
B J Thomas (1969) (US 1 pop: US 38)
Burt Bacharach (1969)
Dionne Warwick (1970)
Bobbie Gentry (UK 40)
Sacha Distel (1970) (UK 14)
Manic Street Preachers (1995)
Andy Williams (1981)
Ben Fold Five (1998)
Shonen Knife (1998)

REACH OUT FOR ME (Bacharach - David)
Lou Johnson (1963) (US 74)
Dionne Warwick (1964) (US 20 pop: UK 23)
Nancy Wilson (1968)
Burt Bacharach (1967)
Olivia Newton John (1975)

REFLECTIONS (Bacharach - David)
Film: *Lost Horizon*
Sally Kellerman (1972)
Burt Bacharach (1973)

RIVERBOAT (Bacharach)
Burt Bacharach (1978)

ROME WILL NEVER LEAVE YOU (Bacharach - David)
Richard Chamberlain (1964)

SAD SACK (Bacharach - David)
Film: *Sad Sack*
Jerry Lewis (1957)

SAIL ALONG SILV'RY MOON (Bacharach – Unknown Collaborator)
Burt Bacharach (1966)

SATURDAY NIGHT IN TIA JUANA (Bacharach – David)
The Five Blobs (1959)

SATURDAY SUNSHINE (Bacharach - David)
Burt Bacharach (1963) (US 93 pop)
Burt Bacharach inst. (1965)
Johnny Mathis
Petula Clark

SAY GOODBYE (Bacharach – David)
Pat Boone (1965)
John Rowles (1969)

SECONDS (Bacharach - Simon)
Burt Bacharach (vocal, Joshie Armstead) (1977)
Gladys Knight (1974)

SEND ME NO FLOWERS (Bacharach - David)
Film: *Send Me No Flowers*
Doris Day (1964))

SEND MY PICTURE TO SCRANTON, PA (Bacharach - David)
B J Thomas (1970)

SHARE THE JOY (Bacharach –David)
Film: *Lost Horizon*
Andrea Willis (1972)

SHE'S GONE AWAY (Bacharach)
Burt Bacharach (1969)

SHE LIKES BASKETBALL (Bacharach - David)
From Broadway musical, *Promises, Promises*

SING FOR THE CHILDREN (Bacharach - Bettis)
James Ingram (1993)

SINNER'S DEVOTION (Bacharach - Hilliard)
Tammi Terrell (1967)

SITTIN' IN A TREE HOUSE (Bacharach - David)
Marty Robbins (1958)
Craig Douglas (1958)

SLEEP WITH ME TONIGHT (Bacharach – Sager -Diamond)
Neil Diamond (1984)
Pattie Labelle (1986)

SO LONG JOHNNY (Bacharach - David)
Jackie DeShannon (1966)

SOMEBODY'S BEEN LYING (Bacharach – Sager)
The Carpenters (1981)

SOMEONE ELSE'S EYES (Bacharach – Sager - Roberts)
Aretha Franklin & Michael McDonald (1991)

SOMEONE ELSE'S SWEETHEART (Bacharach - David)
Wanderers (1961)

SOMETHING BIG (Bacharach - David)
Film: *Something Big*
Mark Lindsay (1971))
Burt Bacharach (1973)

SOMETIMES LATE AT NIGHT (Bacharach – Sager)
Carole Bayer Sager (1981)

SOUTH AMERICAN GETAWAY (Bacharach)
Film: *Butch Cassidy And The Sundance Kid*
Burt Bacharach (1969)

SPLIT DECISION (Bacharach – Sager)
Natalie Cole (1987)

STAY DEVOTED (Bacharach – Sager)
Dionne Warwick (1985)

STORY BEHIND MY TEARS, THE (Bacharach - David)
Kenny Lynch (1961)
Gary Miller (1961)
Vic Dana (1961)

STORY OF MY LIFE, THE (Bacharach - David)
Marty Robbins (1957) (US 15 pop, 1 country)
Michael Holliday (1958) (UK 1)
Gary Miller (1958) (UK 14)
Dave King (1958) (UK 20)
Alma Cogan (1958) (UK 25)
Bobby Vee
Don Williams (1983)
Neil Diamond

STRONGER THAN BEFORE (Bacharach – Sager - Roberts)
Carole Bayer Sager (1981) (US 30 pop)
Chaka Khan

SUCH UNLIKELY LOVERS (Bacharach - Costello)
Elvis Costello and Burt Bacharach (1998)

SUMMER OF '77 (Bacharach)
Burt Bacharach (1978)

SUNDANCE KID, THE (Bacharach)
Film: *Butch Cassidy And The Sundance Kid*)
Burt Bacharach (1969)

SUNNY WEATHER LOVER (Bacharach - David)
Dionne Warwick (1993)

SWEETEST PUNCH (Bacharach – Costello)
Elvis Costello & Burt Bacharach (1998)

TAKE A BROKEN HEART (Bacharach – David)
Rick Nelson (1966)

TAKE GOOD CARE OF YOU AND ME (Bacharach – Sager - Goffin)
Dionne Warwick & Jeffrey Osborne (1989)

TEARS AT THE BIRTHDAY PARTY (Bacharach - Costello)
Elvis Costello and Burt Bacharach (1998)

TELL HER (Bacharach – Sager – Allen)
Carole Bayer Sager (1981)

TELL IT TO YOUR HEART (Bacharach – Tonio K)
Randy Crawford (2000)

TELL THE TRUTH AND SHAME THE DEVIL (Bacharach – David - Wolpin)
Harry Carter Singers (1956)

TEN TIMES FOREVER MORE (Bacharach - David)
Johnny Mathis (1971)

THAT KIND OF WOMAN (Bacharach - David)
Movie theme
Joe Williams & the Count Basie Orchestra (1958)

THAT'S NOT THE ANSWER (Bacharach - David)
Dionne Warwick (1965)

THAT'S THE WAY I'LL COME TO YOU (Bacharach – David)
Jack Jones (1963)
Bobby Vee

THAT'S WHAT FRIENDS ARE FOR (Bacharach - Sager)
Film: *Night Shift*
Rod Stewart (1982)
Dionne Warwick and Friends (Elton John, Stevie Wonder and Gladys Knight) (1985) (US 1 pop, 1 R&B: UK 16)
Cilla Black and Cliff Richard (1993)
Perry Como (1985)
Helen Reddy (1998)

(THERE GOES) THE FORGOTTEN MAN (Bacharach - David)
Jimmy Radcliffe (1964)
Gene McDaniels (1964)
Frankie Vaughan

THERE IS TIME (Bacharach)
Burt Bacharach (1978)

(THERE'S) ALWAYS SOMETHING THERE TO REMIND ME (Bacharach - David)
Lou Johnson (1964) (US 49 pop)
Sandie Shaw (1964) (US 51 pop: UK 1)
Four Seasons (1965)
Burt Bacharach (1965)
Wayne Fontana (1966)
Dionne Warwick (1968)
Lou Christie (1966)
R.B. Greaves (1970) (US 27 pop)
Jose Feliciano (1968)
Tin Tin Out featuring Espiritu
Naked Eyes (1983) ('Always Something There To Remind Me') (US 8 pop)
McCoy Tyner (1997)
All Saints (1998)
Absolute Zeros (1998)

THE LAST TIME I SAW MY HEART (Bacharach – David)

THE THINGS I WILL NOT MISS (Bacharach – David)
Film: *Lost Horizon*
Sally Kellerman & Andrea Willis (1972)

THEY DON'T GIVE MEDALS (TO YESTERDAY'S HEROES) (Bacharach - David)
Chuck Jackson (1963)
Ben E. King (1966)

Rick Nelson (1966) (TV movie, *On The Flipside*)
Lainie Kazan (1968)
Dionne Warwick (1970)

THEY DON'T MAKE THEM LIKE THEY USED TO (Bacharach - Sager)
Film: *Tough Guys*
Kenny Rogers (1986)) (US 53 country)

THEY LONG TO BE CLOSE TO YOU
See Close To You

THINGS I WILL NOT MISS (Bacharach - David)
Lost Horizon
Diana Ross & Marvin Gaye (1973 not released until 2001)

THIS DOESN'T FEEL LIKE LOVE ANYMORE (Bacharach – Sager - Irby)
Klymaxx (1993)

THIS EMPTY PLACE (Bacharach - David)
Searchers (1964)
Ian and the Zodiacs (1964)
Fortunes (1965)
Cissy Houston (1970)
Stephanie Mills (1976)
Cilla Black (1965)
Tangeers (1969)
Stephanie Mills (1975)

THIS GIRL'S IN LOVE WITH YOU
See This Guy's In Love With You

THIS GUY'S IN LOVE WITH YOU (Bacharach - David)
Herb Alpert (1968) (US 1 pop: UK 3)
Dionne Warwick (1969) (This Girl's In Love With You) (US 7 pop, 7 R&B)
Dusty Springfield (1968) (This Girl's In Love With You)
Connie Francis (1969) (This Girl's In Love With You: medley with I Say A Little Prayer)
Brenda Lee (1970) (This Girl's In Love With You)
Salena Jones (This Girl's In Love With You)
Petula Clark (1970)
Sheila Southern (This Girl's In Love With You) (1969)
Johnny Mathis (1971)
Sacha Distel (1971)
Jerry Vale (1969)

Des O'Connor
The Spiral Staircase
The Dells (1972)
Ian McShane (1992)
Grenadine (1994) (This Girl's In Love With You)
Les Reed Orchestra
Stanley Turrentine (1999)

THIS HOUSE IS EMPTY NOW (Bacharach - Costello)
Elvis Costello & Burt Bacharach (1998)

THIS IS THE NIGHT (Bacharach)
James Ingram (1993)

THREE FRIENDS, TWO LOVERS (Bacharach - David)
Turbans (1961)

THREE WHEELS ON MY WAGON (Bacharach – Hilliard)
Dick Van Dyke (1961)
New Christie Minstrels (1963)

THROUGH THE EYE OF A NEEDLE (Bacharach - David)
Cliff Richard (1964)

TICK TOCK GOES THE CLOCK (Bacharach - David)
Cut from Promises Promises
Judy Malloy and Debbie Pavelka (1968)
Lisa Mayer, Judy Malloy, Debbie Pavelka (2001)

TIME AND TENDERNESS (Bacharach)
Burt Bacharach (1977)

TIMELESS TIDE (Bacharach – David)
Joe Arthur (1959)

TOLEDO (Bacharach - Costello)
Elvis Costello and Burt Bacharach (1998)

TOO LATE TO WORRY (Bacharach - David)
Richard Anthony (1963)
Babs Tino (1961)

TO WAIT FOR LOVE (Bacharach - David)
Jay And The Americans (1964)
Paul Anka (1965)
Jackie De Shannon (1966)
Tony Orlando (1964)
Tom Jones (1965)
Herb Alpert (1968) (US 51 pop)

TOWER OF STRENGTH (Bacharach - Hilliard)
Gloria Lynne (1961) (US 100)
Gene McDaniels (1961) (US 5 pop, 5 R&B: UK 49)
Frankie Vaughan (1961) (UK 1)
Paul Raven (1961)

TRAINS AND BOATS AND PLANES (Bacharach - David)
Burt Bacharach (1965) (UK 4)
Billy J Kramer with the Dakotas (1965) (UK 12)
Wally Stott Chorale (1968)
Dionne Warwick (1966) (US 22 pop)
Anita Harris (1965)
Jacqui Brookes (1984)
Dan Kibler (1998)

TRUE LOVE NEVER RUNS SMOOTH (Bacharach - David)
Gene Pitney (1963) (US 21 pop)
Petula Clark (1964)
Don & Juan (1963)

TRUTH AND HONESTY (Bacharach – Sager)
Aretha Franklin (1981)

TRY TO SEE IT MY WAY (Bacharach - David)
TV movie: *On The Flipside*
Rick Nelson (1966)
Peggy March (1969)

TURKEY LURKEY TIME (Bacharach - David)
From Broadway musical, *Promises, Promises*
Debbie Shapiro-Gravitte (1970)

TWENTY-FOUR HOURS FROM TULSA (Bacharach - David)
Gene Pitney (1963) (US 17 pop: UK 5)
Dusty Springfield (1964)

Burt Bacharach (1965)
Jay & the Americans

TWO HEARTS (Bacharach – Bailey - White)
Earth, Wind And Fire (1993)
UNDERNEATH THE OVERPASS (Bacharach – David)
Jo Safford (1957)

UNINVITED DREAM (Bacharach – Gallop)
Peggy Lee (1957)

UPSTAIRS (Bacharach - David)
From Broadway musical, *Promises, Promises*
Sung by Jerry Orbach

US (Bacharach - Russell)
Tom Jones (1975)
Burt Bacharach (vocals, Joshie Armstead) (1976)

WAITING FOR CHARLIE TO COME HOME (Bacharach - Hilliard)
Etta James (1962)
Dionne Warwick

WALK BACKWARDS DOWN THE ROAD (Bacharach - David)
Dionne Warwick (1968)

WALKING TALL (Bacharach – Rice)
Lyle Lovett (1999)

WALK LITTLE DOLLY (Bacharach - David)
Dionne Warwick (1967)
Terry Baxter (1971)

WALK ON BY (Bacharach - David)
Dionne Warwick (1964) (US 6 pop: UK 9)
Burt Bacharach (1965)
Four Seasons (1965)
Cal Tjader (1967, 1998)
Isaac Hayes (1969) (US 30 pop)
Sheila Southern (1969)
Johnny Mathis (1971) ·
Gloria Gaynor (1975) (US 98 pop)
Stranglers (1978) (UK 21)

Timi Yuro
Average White Band (1979) (US 92 pop: UK 46)
D Train (1982) (UK 44)
Melissa Manchester (1989)
Sybil (1990) (US 74 pop: UK 6)
Gabrielle (1997) (UK 7)
Helen Shapiro (1964)
Mel Torme
Ron Goodwin Orchestra
Cockeyed Ghost (1998)

WALK THE WAY YOU TALK (Bacharach - David)
Dionne Warwick (1970)
Sergio Mendes & Brasil 66
Burt Bacharach (1973)

WANTING THINGS (Bacharach - David)
From: *Promises, Promises*
Edward Winter
Dionne Warwick (1968)
Connie Francis (1970)
Astrud Gilberto
Pointer Sisters

WARM AND TENDER (Bacharach - David)
Film: *Lizzie*
Johnny Mathis (1957)
Bobby Vinton

WASTIN' AWAY FOR YOU (Bacharach - David)
Russells (1962)

WAY I FEEL ABOUT YOU, THE (Bacharach – David)
Stephanine Mills (1975)

WENDY WENDY (Bacharach – David)
Four Coins (1958)

WE SHOULD HAVE MET SOONER (Bacharach - Kavanaugh)
Burt Bacharach (vocal, Jamie Anders) (1977)

WHAT AM I DOING HERE (Bacharach - David)
Liz Callaway (2001)

WHAT'S HER NAME TODAY? (Bacharach – Costello)
Elvis Costello & Burt Bacharach (1998)

WHAT'S NEW PUSSYCAT (Bacharach - David)
Film: *What's New Pussycat*
Tom Jones (1965)) (US 3 pop: UK 11)
Four Seasons (1965)
Burt Bacharach v. Joel Gray
Bobby Brooks (1965)
Cryan' Shames (1966)
k.d. lang (1998)
Mike Myers (1998)

WHAT THE WORLD NEEDS NOW IS LOVE (Bacharach - David)
Jackie DeShannon (1965) (US 7 pop)
Four Seasons (1965)
Dionne Warwick (1967)
Burt Bacharach (1968)
Madeline Bell (1965)
Jack Jones (1966)
Cal Tjader (1967, 1998)
Sheila Southern (1969)
Tom Clay (1971) (Medley with Abraham, Martin And John) (US 8 pop)
Ron Shaw (1979) (US 90 country)
Billie Jo Spears (1981) (US 58 country)
Sarah Vaughan (1995)
Burt Bacharach & the Posies (1997) (Film, *Austin Powers*)
McCoy Tyner (1997)

WHEN YOU BRING YOUR SWEET LOVE TO ME (Bacharach - Gimbel)
Burt Bacharach (vocal, Jamie Anders) (1977)

WHERE ARE YOU (Bacharach - Gimbel)
Burt Bacharach (vocal, Joshie Armstead) (1977)

WHERE CAN YOU TAKE A GIRL (Bacharach - David)
From *Promises, Promises*

WHERE DID THE TIME GO? (Bacharach – Sager)
Pointer Sisters (1980)

WHERE KNOWLEDGE ENDS (FAITH BEGINS) (Bacharach –David)
Film: *Lost Horizon*

Also known as 'Where Knowledge Ends (Trust Me)
Diana Lee (1972)

WHERE THERE'S A HEARTACHE (Bacharach – David)
This is a vocal version of a main theme from 'Butch Cassidy and the Sundance
Kid' score used in 'Not Goin' Home Anymore' and 'Come Touch The Sun'.
Pat Boone (1971)
The Sandpipers (1971)
Oliver
Astrud Gilberto
Van McCoy

WHERE WOULD I GO (Bacharach - David)
Dionne Warwick (1968)

WHOEVER YOU ARE (Bacharach - David)
From *Promises, Promises*
Jill O'Hara
Dionne Warwick (1968)
Tony Bennett
Bobby Short
Anita Kerr

WHO GETS THE GUY (Bacharach – David)
Dionne Warwick

WHO IS GONNA LOVE ME (Bacharach - David)
Dionne Warwick (1968) (US 33 pop)
Peter Nero

WHO'S BEEN SLEEPING IN MY BED (Bacharach - David)
Linda Scott (1963)
Carol Deene (1964)
WHO'S GOT THE ACTION? (Bacharach – Hilliard)
Phil Colbert (1965)

WILD AGAIN (Bacharach – Sager)
Carole Bayer Sager (1981)

WILD HONEY (Bacharach – David)
Cathy Carr (1957)

WINDOWS AND DOORS (Bacharach – David)
Jackie DeShannon (1966) (US 108 pop)
Truly Smith

WINDOWS OF HEAVEN (Bacharach – David)
Four Coins (1962)

WINDOWS OF THE WORLD, THE (Bacharach - David)
Dionne Warwick (1967) (US 32 pop)
Isaac Hayes (1973)
Scott Walker (1970)
David Whitaker & his Orchestra (1971)
Burt Bacharach (1973)
The Pretenders (1988)
McCoy Tyner (1997)

WINDOWS OF THE WORLD, THE / WHAT THE WORLD NEEDS NOW
– medley (Bacharach – David)
Luther Vandross (1998)

WINDOW WISHING (Bacharach - David)
Dionne Warwick (1966)

WINTER WARM (Bacharach – David)
Gale Storm (1959)

WINE IS YOUNG, THE (Bacharach - David)
Dionne Warwick (1970)

WISHIN' AND HOPIN' (Bacharach - David)
Dionne Warwick (1963)
Dusty Springfield (1964) (US 6 pop)
Merseybeats (1964) (UK 13); (1986)
Vandalias (1998)
WITH A SMILE (Bacharach)
Burt Bacharach, vocal Jane Miller (1994)

WITH OPEN ARMS (Bacharach - David)
Jane Morgan (1959) (US 39 pop)
Adam Faith

WIVES AND LOVERS (Bacharach - David)
Inspired by film, *Wives And Lovers*
Jack Jones (1963) (US 14 pop)
Dionne Warwick (1965)
Burt Bacharach (1965)
Sheila Southern (1969)
Andy Williams
Julie London
David Sanborn & George Duke (1998)

WOMAN (Bacharach)
Burt Bacharach (1979)

WORLD IS A CIRCLE, THE (Bacharach – David)
Film: *Lost Horizon* Ed Ames (1973)
Diana Lee & Bobby Vann (1972)

WOULDN'T THAT BE A STROKE OF LUCK (Bacharach – David)
Written for *Promises Promises*, but **cut** during the Boston run and replaced by
'I'll Never Fall In Love Again'.

YOU AND ME FOR ALWAYS (Bacharach – Sager)
Barbra Streisand (1988)

YOU BELONG IN SOMEONE ELSE'S ARMS (Bacharach – Hampton)
David Whitfield (1963)

YOU DON'T KNOW ME (Bacharach – Sager)
Carole Bayer Sager (1981)

YOU'LL NEVER GET TO HEAVEN (IF YOU BREAK MY HEART)
(Bacharach - David)
Dionne Warwick (1964) (US 34 pop: UK 20)
Cal Tjader (1967, 1998)
Sheila Southern (1969)
Stylistics (1973) (US 23 pop, 8 R&B: UK 24)
McCoy Tyner (1997)

YOU'LL THINK OF SOMEONE (Bacharach - David)
From *Promises Promises*

YOUNG AND WILD (Bacharach – David)
The Five Blobs (1960)

YOUNG GROW YOUNGER EVERY DAY (Bacharach - Kavanaugh)
Burt Bacharach (vocal, Peter Yarrow) (1977)

YOUNG PRETTY GIRL LIKE YOU, A (Bacharach - David)
From *Promises Promises*
Jerry Orbach and A. Larry Haines.

YOU'RE FOLLOWING ME (Bacharach - Hilliard)
Jimmy Breedlove
Perry Como (1963)
Peter Gordeno (1961)

YOUR LIPS ARE WARMER THAN YOUR HEART (Bacharach – David)
Rose Marie Jun ('Rosemary June') (1956)

YOU'RE TELLING OUR SECRETS (Bacharach –David)
Dee Clark (1961)

YOU'RE THE DREAM (Bacharach – David)
Marvellos (1956)

Index

Note About The Author

Dr. Michael Brocken teaches popular music and media studies at Liverpool's John Moores University where he specialises in the history of the popular music and broadcasting industries, communications and cultural history and archive resource gathering.

After experiencing the highs and lows of performing country rock covers in the aftermath of Merseybeat, he eventually became one of the very first to receive both an M.A (with distinction) and a Doctorate in Popular Music Studies at the Institute of Popular Music, University of Liverpool. It was while at the IPM that he organised the highly successful Dylan-related Robert Shelton conferences. He is also a well-known presenter and contributor for BBC Radio Merseyside. His own series, 'The Brock'n'Roll Files' - dealing with popular music history - has now entered its third year.

He has been published on such diverse subjects as The Beatles, Sexuality and Merseybeat, The British Folk Revival, and The Folk Industry and Media. 'The British Folk Revival' is also due for publication by Ashgate in 2003.

He is an accomplished acoustic guitarist who specialises in country blues and has recently started his own reissues label 'Mayfield', which has thus far released two albums and two singles (see website mayfield-records.co.uk). Mike hopes to turn Mayfield into an archive resource of significance over the forthcoming years.

Michael Brocken lives in Chester with his wife Chris and his 'rock chick' daughter Steph and, aside from his obsession with Burt Bacharach and Boulevard label record collecting, enjoys non-league soccer and the occasional visit to the races!

319

Picture Credits

Front cover: courtesy of

REDFERNS

Back cover: courtesy of

REX

Inside photos: courtesy of

REDFERNS, REX, LFI